MW01055818

John W. Rollins. (*Bachrach Photo*)

Hanging the Moon

CULTURAL STUDIES OF DELAWARE AND THE EASTERN SHORE

Hanging the Moon

The Rollins Rise to Riches

Drury Pifer

Newark: University of Delaware Press
London: Associated University Presses

Associated University Presses
2010 Eastpark Blvd.
Cranbury, NJ 08512

The paper used in this publication meets the requirements of the American National Standard for Permanence of Paper for Printed Library Materials Z39.48-1984.

Library of Congress Cataloging-in-Publication Data

Pifer, Drury L.
  Hanging the moon: The Rollins rise to riches / Drury Pifer.
    p. cm. — (Cultural studies of Delaware and the Eastern Shore)
  Includes index.
  ISBN 0-87413-744-6 (alk. paper)
    1. Rollins, John W. 2. Businessmen—United States—Biography. 3. Entrepreneurship—Biography. I. Title. II. Series.

HC102.5.R564 P54 2001
388.3'243—dc21
[B]   00-034386

SECOND PRINTING 2007
PRINTED IN THE UNITED STATES OF AMERICA

My dad thought my mother hung the moon.

—John W. Rollins

Contents

Preface

In March of 1995, I was invited to meet John W. Rollins Sr., one of America's prominent entrepreneurs. The nature of big business has always intrigued me, especially the power it has to make over the world in its own image. Meeting John Rollins, I thought, would afford me a glimpse of this force in action.

I was ushered into John's office by his son, John Rollins Jr., an affable man who had read my memoir, *Innocents in Africa*, and thus knew me better than I knew him. His father, John Sr., is tall, humorous, and shrewd, with preternaturally blue eyes. Our interview convinced me that his story was well worth telling, his life a supreme example of the (much maligned) American Dream. His family had no money and little land. In his Georgia childhood, the Rollins family had to preserve their food by burying it underground. Despite a rudimentary schooling and having to support his parents (his father had a damaged heart), John made the most of what he had to work with: an iron will, intelligence, and a society eager to reward those with a talent for commerce. In the thirties, John labored for ten cents an hour on Georgia's highways; in the fifties, he was elected lieutenant governor of Delaware.

John is a storyteller, mixing down-home humor and anecdote. He also has a creative approach to high finance. With his brother Wayne and their associate, Henry Tippie, he was a major player in setting up the first leveraged corporate buyout in history.

The best way to approach any creative individual is through his work, and that's the path I've taken. What writers from Dickens to Tom Wolfe hold against the businessman is a lack of inner life. But to succeed, the entrepreneur must develop not his inner life but his relations with the practical world. Like Alice in Wonderland trying to play croquet with hedgehogs and flamingoes, the entrepreneur must control dozens of elements that forever threaten to wander away. Materials, money, organization systems, technologies, psychologies, all are in flux and all must somehow be organized to a common end.

John was raised on a farm hardly different from a patch of land in medieval Europe or ancient Chaldea. His education was not scientific or technical, but moral and practical. The Bible and the stories read to him by his mother were the decisive influence on his youth. The moral stature of his mother had more influence on him and Wayne than any technical expertise they later acquired. What makes John's story compelling is the significant events he set in motion, what they say about the United States, and the light the Rollinses' rise sheds on the future.

* * *

I wrote John Rollins's history with the understanding that I would not be censored, that the ideas that drive the story would be my own, that any materials I required would be provided. The Rollinses have been rigorous in adhering to our understanding and always open in their responses to my questions.

My sources consist entirely of taped personal interviews and newspaper accounts. I am grateful to those who took time from their busy schedules to talk to me: Henry Tippie, John Rollins Jr., Michele Metrinko Rollins, Grace Rollins, Randall Rollins, Gary Rollins, Jeff Rollins, Cathy Rollins Searby, Ted Rollins, Patrick Rollins—and John's four youngest children, Michele, Monique, Michael, and Marc. In addition, I would like to thank Dr. Nick Pappas for introducing me to the complex and deadly world of chemical waste; Andy Lubin for guiding me through the labyrinth of constructing a $145 million mall; Ned Davis for his insights into John's political career; and Eugene Weaver for clarifying the complex financial relations between various companies controlled by John. Thanks are also due to Doctors Charles Hatcher and Bhaskar Palekar, to Joe Seymour, and to James Mahoney for his account of John's relations with Richard Nixon. I'm grateful to Catherine (Kitty) Muir and Linda Prickett for their personal stories. Thanks to copyeditor Karen Druliner, researcher Pat Collier, and typist Debbie Lyall. Finally, I want to thank my wife, Ellen Pifer, for her transcendental editing skills.

This biography would have been woefully incomplete without the inclusion of John's lifelong business partner—his brother, Wayne Rollins, who died in 1992. Despite his absence, I have treated Wayne's voice as living and present, as indeed he was when sundry interviews with him were taped. These conversations were conducted by J. Don McKee and made available to me by Wayne's son, Randall. I am indebted to them both for this crucial material.

Memories fade quickly. Some of the people interviewed offered quite different versions of events. I have given weight to those that seem most accurate. All inaccuracies are, of course, my own responsibility.

Author's Note

As this book was going to press, I received news that John had died on April 5, 2000. He died in his office during a normal work day while taking his afternoon nap. Though he is gone, the economic empire he created still provides work for thousands and services for thousands more. He died, as he lived, full of plans for the future.

Hanging the Moon

1
John's World

John W. Rollins is a broad-shouldered, easy man with a wide forehead and a dolphin smile. Six-foot-two and now past eighty, a self-made multi-millionaire, he was raised in a three-room house, educated in a one-room school, and spent the mornings of his childhood following a mule down a furrow in the hills of north Georgia.

The farmboy's journey out of those lightless hills into our fluorescent present embodies the American myth. His generation may be the last historically situated to move so far so fast. Born in 1916, gifted with an ability to learn from his failures, by the middle fifties John had established his family in a grand estate in the chateau country of Delaware.

This house is set well back on acres of manicured lawn. At Christmas time, the long drive is lined with a thousand tiny lights and, on one evening every December, a constant stream of automobiles rolls up to the door. John's blonde wife, Michele, and his children cluster in the hall beneath an imposing staircase. Visitors enter through a small porch decorated to resemble a frozen forest.

John's guests range from the very humble to the socially exalted. Senators circulate. Delaware's governor shakes hands with building contractors, school teachers, clerks, and lobbyists. These are the faces of people who have done well in a hard world, faces that express more practical intelligence than youthful idealism. Engineers, jockeys, literary agents rub shoulders with lobbyists and lawyers and their wives. Sly foxes mingle with tough old badgers; the highly articulate mingle with the very observant. The dining room table groans under dozens of dishes as caterers add fish, fowl, Ukrainian sausage, and wild rice. The Christmas decorations are as opulent as Bloomingdale's, and every year they are different.

Taller and wider than his guests, moving easily among retainers, cronies, friends, and family, John resembles an old prince in a story by Boccaccio. Like many a Renaissance *condottiere* who started out as a common soldier and battled his way to privilege and a title, John has scrambled to the top. His is an iconic success in the American manner, a success that demands not some inner transformation of the self, but rather the exhibition of an astonishing energy that seizes on the main chance, that links every fiber of a tireless ambition to the future and its demands, a success that senses the current of history and ties into it. With a lifetime of hectic activity behind him, John might well have retired twenty years ago. But immense projects, some of them thirty years underway, keep him in his office. Letting go of the work would be letting go of life itself.

Stendhal once wrote that "nothing is a promise of genius—but obstinacy is a sign of it." It takes a very obstinate talent to walk out of those back hills and take on the world as if one were born to it: to conjure new industries out of thin air, restore ruins, steer several generations of students into higher education, advise a beetle-browed president, and list seven companies on the New York Stock Exchange.

John landed in Lewes, Delaware, after World War II. In those days, Lewes was a remote village on the bay with cozy summer homes lining the shore. John brought with him Kitty, his wife, and two children. They moved in with Kitty's mother, Isabel. Isabel's little house was separated from the bay by a dune and a few feet of beachfront. There were gulls, vacationers sunning among spiky grasses, and occasional hurricanes edging up from Florida.

John, then in his late twenties, had already taken some measure of himself. He was commuting to Towson, Maryland, where he managed three plants for Bendix Radio. Weekends he drove home to Lewes to fish the quiet inlets around Rehoboth with old Theodore (Dory) Bryan, a folksy philosopher who ran the local ice house. Hired by Glenn L. Martin Company to convert their Towson plant to peacetime production, John found the managers inflexible and jealous of methods that guaranteed their failure, so he quit. Dory had saved up a few dollars. So had John. Whenever he visited Lewes, there was no service for his Ford. This made him think a Ford dealership might be practical. Each then put up $500 of his own money, borrowed $10,000 from Sussex Trust and went into business. John recalls his main motive for going into business with Dory was to get the old man out of the local ice house, where the freezing temperature was beating up on his arthritis.

Isabel owned a lot that she leased to John. He converted the two buildings, previously a laundry, into a car dealership, with BRYAN ROLLINS painted across the front. The renovations the Ford Company demanded sopped up their $10,000, so he borrowed more. The only distinguishing feature on the place was a high post with a General Tires sign on top. Around back the usual gaggle of mechanics hung out, gloomily poking under the hoods of diseased cars. Out front the salesmen lounged, straightening up, buttoning their jackets whenever a customer approached.

About a year later, John picked up the Ford dealershp in Newport News, Virginia. He drove around to every radio station in the area offering sixty-five cents for the airing of a thirty-second spot commercial he'd recorded himself. The going rate was a dollar; they told him to get lost. "Well," he quotes himself saying, "put it on if you have an extra minute, and I'll pay you the money."

Figuring that sixty-five cents was better than making nothing at all, the stations played his ads every fifteen minutes. His low offer worked to his advantage. With his name airing several times an hour, listeners were soon familiar with the Rollins countrified persona: "Uncle Johnny Rollins, the working man's friend. Drive your old car in, your new car out, and count your savings."

In the first flush of victory over Germany and Japan, buyers lined up, ready to put down money for anything that hiccuped and had four wheels. Car production had been frozen, but now came the spring. John was like a born virtuoso handed his first violin. He had the touch, and his business began to expand with incredible brio. Within a few months, he began buying up auto agencies in Maryland and Virginia, borrowing as much as the banks would allow.

A veritable abyss of debt opened beneath his feet. But he danced lightly on ahead, making up in activity for whatever he lacked in hard cash. This yawning chasm of debt scared the pants off Dory Bryan, who was sixty and conservative and had never seen so much real money disappear so fast.

John was too new on the lot to comprehend the chances he was taking. He saw life pretty much as it came to him—one big, gut-wrenching gamble that would work if he hustled. He was a natural born salesman with an intuitive understanding of people. Ned Davis, a strong Democrat who has long served as a lobbyist for John's interests on the state level, recalls that if some farmer quit paying on the car he was driving, John wouldn't hesitate to walk out into the middle of a field and root him out from his hiding place behind a cultivator. Brash, optimistic, unable to hold a grudge, he just scrambled harder when things started to go bad.

With his direct manner and open enthusiasm, John kept the cars moving off his lot quickly enough to stay out in front of the finance agencies and banks. In 1947, when his brother Wayne got laid up with a bad back down in Georgia, John urged him to come north. He offered Wayne a dealership in Maryland to manage. "I had an awful time getting him to join me after I got started," John recalls.

Wayne finally pulled up stakes the year following. Once he'd unplugged himself from Georgia, Wayne knew he'd come to the right place. "Wayne was brilliant," John says. "But he wasn't a person to ever take a chance." If Wayne was all calculation, his young brother was all energy and intuition. Wayne found he could learn from John's mistakes, while John tried to listen to Wayne whose job it was to stop the younger man from rushing off some cliff.

Their great differences made the Rollins brothers suitable as close partners. John had always been healthy. Wayne's body was fragile. John was the spender, the gambler, devil-may-care. Wayne played his cards a half-inch from his chest. He hated parting with a penny. John spent whatever he could lay his hands on. The way he laid money out, it seemed he had no affection for it at all. John trusted easily. Wayne was slow to warm, a wary man. In a strong light, John's broad forehead resembled the globe of the world. Wayne was about as tall as John, but a lot less likely to declare himself. He lived often with intense physical pain. He was given to popping aspirin and Tums. Cunning at the bargaining table, he enjoyed drily making himself the butt of his own jokes, meanwhile stealing a march on the opposition.

In 1830 that brilliant analyst of the United States, Alexis de Tocqueville, admired the American's ability to do a dozen different tasks, while the European did only one. "Aristocratic nations," he writes, "are by nature too liable to narrow the scope of human perfectibility."

In many respects, both the Rollins brothers are old-fashioned, and Tocqueville's nineteenth-century language seems especially appropriate to them. They were born in a region so geographically distant that human history had barely scraped it. Their bucolic hills were remote from human time, affected only by the eternal cycles of nature.

Such men tend to have a high regard for appearances because they see that much that appears substantial to most people is only a question of style. For millions the past is marked by the biplane, the fedora hat, or Al Jolson's voice on a scratchy record. The Rollins brothers were aware that a farmer in overalls is treated in a different way than a man in a suit. Nature, untouched by art, would always disturb Wayne. He could never buy a piece of land without thinking at once how he might make it over.

The Rollins brothers were raised with an elevated ideal of the human person. Their goals were unmodern because they were absolute. The modern person is soon convinced that grace, eloquence, and good manners are masks behind which Darwin's ape appears. The boys' mother, Claudia Ann Rollins (née Nance—1886–1976) would have been appalled by such a degraded and corrupt view of the individual. Women of her generation sought moral perfection, perhaps because their men were so often morally crippled by frustrating hardship and the boredom of poverty. They took their instruction from ancient Jerusalem, not cutting edge Paris or Vienna. Claudia's religious faith was the bread of life for her children.

Her two boys grew up under a heavy weight of obligations—an invalid father, the Depression, Wayne's tuberculosis, neighbor children who hurled rocks, drunken and violent neighbors, an annual family income well below even the Georgia average. They still regarded themselves as better off than most of their neighbors. They never went hungry. Wayne describes a high school teacher he greatly respected in this way: "She was one that didn't listen to you." In other words the lady was deaf to excuses. And so was his mother.

Wilbur Cash writes in *The Mind of the South* that the Southerner has "perhaps the most intense individualism the world has seen since the Italian Renaissance." But the Southern woman of Claudia Rollins's generation placed greater stress on the family than the individual person. She tried to make her children understand that every person born into this mysterious world owes a debt. And that the debt is paid by doing one's best. Being envious is a waste of time. Time spent whining is time that would have been better spent working. For Claudia, any hint of complaining came close to desecration.

In the Georgia of John's childhood, society consisted largely of family—the Rollinses and the Nances, cousins, nephews, uncles and aunts. Setting aside the racial abyss, Americans from the South liked to imagine that everyone is somehow related. The Second World War dramatized differences. Americans were being killed in European countries and on tropical islands no one had ever heard of. The war yanked John out of Georgia and sped up his modernization.

After the war, everyone dreamed of getting back to normal. Before 1945, culture was being recast by the scientific spirit and its technology. After 1945, upheaval and constant change were the norm. Even to a sleepy town like Lewes, Delaware, where John wound up in 1945, he would bring change.

Few businessmen of John's generation could guess in 1945 that history was casting them as the principles in an American Renaissance. They were just trying to make a buck. But as they became increasingly dependent on technology, they transformed the provincial democracy Tocqueville has described into our present Tower of Babble in cyberspace. John's expanding line of credit was one manifestation of an amazing creative outburst. When the banks decided that he was good for their money, he joined the mainstream and began to feel the power.

John's life spans precisely those amazing decades when America, dazzled by the creative power of business, set about transforming all its institutions in the commercial image. Born in Claudia's Jerusalem, by middle age he'd adapted himself to the glitzy Las Vegas culture of our day. Born, it seems, with business in their bones, the Rollins brothers were among those who transformed the world into a consumer's game, a universal bazaar, a shopping mall culture the young take for granted.

Our best point of entry to John's distant past lies near the community of Ringgold in the Georgia hills where he was born. The century is young and the first thing we notice is the astonishing silence: no tractors, no cars passing, no jets hissing overhead, a world without machines. The only sounds are a light wind rustling the spring leaves on trees above the farmhouse and children's voices in a field.

2
Beginning

Just south of Ringgold there's a little valley that contains a few gray wood houses and a white church called Smith Chapel. The region appears designed by nature for its beauty, not the serious raising of cattle or the mechanical cultivation of cotton. There is nothing overbearing or outsized in the landscape. The valley is narrow and rises into low hills crested with pine. The hills have a nurturing intimacy, and the most distant horizon appears close and available, a short walk away. The fields wobble drunkenly, offering few flat spaces for the frustrated farmer to cultivate corn or plant acres of lettuce. A narrow stream, named Tiger Creek, trickles down the valley between grassy banks, muddy where the cows come to drink.

The Cherokee were driven out of these hills by President Andrew Jackson in 1837 and forced to walk to Oklahoma. The year following this Cherokee March of Tears, European settlers were offered free acreage by the government in the Georgia land lottery. So wagons came trekking in from the Carolinas or out of Tennessee.

Named after Hebrew prophets, Roman emperors, and American presidents, these newcomers were mainly of Scottish, Irish, or Celtic stock. They stare out at us from old daguerreotypes, their worn faces resembling those of desperadoes or starving poets. Everything west of the Mississippi and much to the southeast was still up for grabs.

Aside from that overwhelming force, mother Claudia Ann, John, and Wayne learned their self-possession from a vast family whose members were scattered throughout those remote hills. The people they cared about most lived near Smith Chapel, but over every rise were close kin born in gray clapboard houses like their own.

Claudia's grandparents, William Madison Nance (1809–1863) and his wife Statirah Elizabeth (c. 1820–1897) had made their way over from a farm near Athens, Georgia about 1850. A pitted, ancient photograph shows Statirah (pronounced Suh-teer-ee) in a lace collar and loose dress, her head tilted quizzically as she waits for the picture-

23

taker to finish his business and let her get back to hers. According to granddaughter Claudia, Statirah was short, stocky, and leather-hard. In the picture, her eyes are deepset, and her thin lips are pressed firmly together. The square, weathered face is scored by work and care. Her hair is thin.

One other photo of Statirah exists, taken shortly before her death. She sits with the family of her son Robert Wesley Nance (1856–1905), surrounded by five grandchildren. In fact Robert Wesley and Mary Emma had eleven children, nine surviving. The women in those days produced enough offspring to fill a small country school. Including those who died, Statirah had thirty-nine grandchildren; on the paternal side of the clan Moses Waters Rollins (1828–1900) and his wife Nancy Emily (1830–1906) would put nineteen in the field. Altogether, there were some fifty-six cousins scattered up and down the hills through which Wayne and John tramped daily.

Moses Rollins is handsome and patriarchal with his white beard and deepset eyes, but his wife, Nancy Emily, appears on the point of death. Statirah in her last portrait is ancient and toothless, tired beyond exhaustion. Her hair is a ghostly white. Two young girls in white dresses flank her. Lillie Dale, the older, stands on her left. Claudia Ann is to her right. Statirah's father-in-law, John Nance (1779–1862), had nineteen brothers and sisters. Hailing from Virginia, John Nance secured 460 acres in Catoosa County (just below the Tennessee state line). His property was worth $3,000 when he died in May of 1862. His will stipulates that his twelve slaves should not be sold to "produce separation of husbands and wives even if they sell at a sacrifice." The price of these souls varied from $250 (for Wensted) to $1,200 (for Emons). One lot of bacon went for $360, and twenty-two chairs for $8.

Statirah's husband, William Madison Nance, died in 1863, aged fifty-four. She worked the farm alone. In 1881, when she was about sixty, she wrote her son Robert in Garland, Texas, asking for help. Her letter may well have expressed a certain desperation, because Robert set out for Georgia in the hard month of December with his wife, Mary Emma (1864–1938). Sixteen-year-old Emma was in the final month of her first pregnancy. Her niece, Ida Carpenter, describes Emma as "a pretty woman. She was short, a very pretty woman. Very neat. She had the most pride and, believe me, everything was kept clean around Aunt Emma."

The grinding trek across Texas proved too much for the infant son who was born dead on the west bank of the Mississippi, December 8. Naming the little stillborn Shalem, after Emma's father, the parents wrapped their baby in a shawl and buried him by the wide river before crossing over.

When Robert died in 1905, a month before his forty-ninth birthday, Emma inherited the same 250 acres Statirah had labored on as a widow. She was thirty-eight. Left with nine children aged twenty to two, she inherited the hard work as well. But she had the children to help. The Nance family constituted a working platoon—Lillie Dale (1883–1952), William Madison (1884–1946), Claudia Ann (1886–1976), Mary Lou (1888–1962), Bertha Statirah Nance (1892–1973), John Marvin (1894–1980), Robert Elkin (1897–1922), Scott Edgar (1899–1969), and Lloyd Franklin (1902–1982), for the most part a long-lived bunch. In a world without welfare, children were Emma's safety net. She didn't have to tell them what to do. It was work, or starve.

Tough and well organized, Emma was valued in the community as a talented nurse. Her niece, Ida Carpenter, recalls Emma spending most of one summer with Ida's mother, Martha, who bore twins, one sickly; soon afterward, she nursed back to health "Bill O'Donald, who came down with typhoid."

Emma never saw her hometown again. Her father, just once, made the long trip from Texas to visit her. Ida relates how Emma "lived up on a hill. And back then the little boys wore a blouse and pants with buttons all around the top. And she was a-setting on the porch putting buttons on [the trousers of her five boys] when she saw her daddy a-coming. And when she saw her daddy [Shalem] a-coming, she was so glad to see him she jumped up and scattered buttons all the way down that hill."

John and Wayne's mother, Claudia Ann, was eighteen when her father died. An early photograph was taken about the time she began teaching school. There were no teachers' institutions, and John assumes she taught because she could do it. She began teaching because she was a reader and able to master whatever she set her mind to. The photo shows Claudia staring straight into the camera with the steady composure of someone who, despite her extreme youth, expects nothing to come easy. All the individuals in these old photographs exhibit an impressive seriousness. Their shoulders are square, their bearing straight. Claudia's young brother, Lloyd, is the one exception; he leans casually against a Model T Ford in an English cap with a wide grin years ahead of its time. All the young Rollins women are solemn—though Claudia's straight-at-you expression doesn't mask her intelligence or her wit.

Claudia's brown hair is thin like her mother's and Grandmother Statirah's. She combs it straight back with a severe part down the center. The bow on the neckcloth that circles her throat darts off casually to one side. She appears more rough-and-ready than her younger sister, the glamorous Mary Lou, who wears a pretty lace blouse with a perfectly arranged bow tie. Claudia shows up again in a photo with the family of John Franklin Rollins (1862–1937), her husband's father. Snapped in front of John F.'s house, she stands next to her brand-new husband, William Henry Rollins (1889–1945). Staring down the camera, Henry has the tense look of someone anticipating a flu shot. In both his wedding picture and the family photo, Henry's aggressive expression and black bow tie are identical. Claudia, already a teacher, wears a school marm's imperious severity. Her hair is arranged in two wings that rise over her high forehead. The waist of her dress is tightly cinched. One imagines there wasn't a lot of time for fashion in those backwoods, but all these women had at least one good Sunday outfit in a period when you were nobody if you didn't dress up to the role. Claudia may well have thumbed through a *Sears Roebuck* catalog to pick out the pattern. Her dark dress is finished with full sleeves and a lace inset that runs beneath the high collar.

In her wedding picture Claudia sets vanity aside and wears rimless spectacles. Perched on her nose, these improve on her severity. Not only is she a reader—a fairly uncommon pursuit in that part of the country—she also plays the pump organ, though where she learned music John has no recollection. Claudia has the no-nonsense expression of a woman who will be listened to, and her sons will listen carefully.

The most fabulous and popular character in the extended family was Henry's father, John F. Rollins. Known as "Uncle John" to the community at large, John F. made a deep impression on the Smith Chapel region. Tall and rawboned with a forgiving sense of humor, Uncle John was married to tiny Roxie Tatum who never cracked a smile. The couple donated land for the local Methodist Church at Smith Chapel. Then John F. designed and built it around 1913.

There exists a vital link between grandfather and grandson John. Frank F.'s generous, observant nature, and often wry take on the human condition is replicated in the younger man. From the first, these two were drawn to each other. Grandfather John F. was an active force, after all, while John's own father was confined to his bed with a failing heart.

Wayne recalls that John F. could estimate exactly how many board feet of lumber a building would require by just glancing over a blue-print. He was musician, local historian, builder and accountant. Once he'd got the church erected, John F. maintained the records and led the singing. Although he was deeply engaged in the lives around him, and even ran for political office, he was not afflicted by any great ambition. He was the kind of American Thomas Jefferson had in mind when he envisioned an ideal democracy. John F. exemplified Old Testament wisdom grounded in a world where traditions are fixed and rituals are a point of honor.

Most of the snapshots of John F. and his family burned up when his house caught fire in 1932. The last existing snapshot of John F. shows him, with hair snowy white, peering beetle-browed into the lens, his face deeply etched and full of character. His daughters chided him for not wearing a tie when he ought, but he preferred to fasten the top button of his shirt and let it go at that. In this final photograph, it looks as though someone may have drawn in a tie over John F.'s white shirt, in one final effort to make him thoroughly respectable. John has never wavered in his loyalty to the Republican Party and John F. probably had something to do with that. John F. complicated his life greatly by attaching himself to Lincoln's party in a Dixiecrat South. Below the Mason-Dixon line, Republicans were regarded in the same league with snake oil salesmen, traitors, or worse. But the Rollins family had split during the War between the States and John F. followed the Republican party's antislavery philosophy, though his father, Moses, enlisted in the Confederate 12th Cavalry, the Georgia Dragoons, in 1862.

Wayne remarks, "I was a Republican by birth. My father was Republican and [his family] went North to fight for the Northern army. And my mother's folks had slaves and they were in the Southern part. So I don't know how I could say I was born Republican. But I'd always voted Republican."

The Republican party of the thirties hardly resembles the Republican party today. In John F. Rollins's lifetime (he died in 1937), the American far right was dominated by the Union Party and had few ties with the Republicans. The Union Party was led by such worthies as Father Charles Coughlin (a priest who excoriated Jews and blacks) and Gerald L. K. Smith, a garden variety rabble-rouser and deputy of Governor Huey Long.

Wilbur Cash describes the politics of the Old South as "a theater for the play of the purely personal, the purely romantic, and the purely hedonistic. It was an arena wherein one great champion confronted another or a dozen, and sought to outdo them in rhetoric and splendid gesturing. It swept back the loneliness of the land, it brought men together under torches. . . ."

Grandfather John F. Rollins had the democratic gift of disagreeing without making enemies. Alone in his backwater, he sailed with a tiny coterie of Republicans against the hierarchies of power that dominated Southern politics. He was probably quite aware of the sinister internal contradictions of the Democratic Party in the South. The party hacks devoted themselves to the interests of absentee planters and the owners of factories by employing a racist rhetoric to enlist the support of poor whites. The ignorant were pincered between their own racism and the merciless "stretchout" system—simply "downsizing" by another name. Cash observes that the stretchout policy violated Southern tradition. "To be wrenched out of the old, easy-going way so long native to the country, to be required to exhibit more energy than the climate allowed for . . . to be deprived of one's dignity as an individual and made into a sort of automaton; to be stood over by a taskmaster with a stop-watch in his hand . . . to be everlastingly hazed on to greater exertion by curt commands and sneers . . . that was . . . wholly intolerable." Both Rollins brothers would soon find themselves a part of this system as they scrambled to survive in a declining Depression economy.

The Southern dissenter was either a Republican (and therefore associated with the Yankee), or a voter for some regional demagogue like Pitchfork Ben Tillman, Hoke Smith, or Cole L. Blease. Wilbur Cash quotes Blease, Governor of South Carolina: "Whenever the Constitution comes between me and the virtue of a white woman of the South, I say to hell with the Constitution!"

A Populist like Governor Blease might bellow and fulminate against the landed interests and the mill owners, but he did next to nothing for the workers who voted him in. To help the workers achieve political power would alienate Big Money and split the Democratic Party into warring factions. A Democratic Party in pieces would make the Negro vote count. Among poor whites already pushed to the social margin, that was unthinkable. Frozen between their hatred for the mill and cotton bosses and their fear of the black man, they voted against what they feared most—equality.

In the South of Grandfather John F. Rollins's heyday, political realities and economic interests were at loggerheads. Cole Blease represented the populist deadend in its purest form. His constituency locked him into the straitjacket of a racism that made progressive legislation impossible. By declaring for the Republican party, John F. avoided the demagoguery that passed for politics. His reasons for remaining a Republican influenced both Rollins boys. Wayne and John voted Republican even as they dug ditches and toiled in factories. It was a very un-Southern thing to do.

John F. believed it was the Democrats who dragged the United States into foreign wars. He fully expected Franklin Roosevelt would do just that. Dying two years before Hitler attacked Poland, he didn't live long enough to see Roosevelt vindicated by the defeat of Fascism.

Europe during the thirties produced a number of political parties convinced that the best thing to do with an opposing idea was to shoot the person who expressed it. John F. regarded violence as a snare and a delusion. His strong, humorous nature made him a natural leader, popular with the young, a gadfly to the puffed-up. Though Republicans never won a major election in Georgia, he was nevertheless elected to a term as highway commissioner in his local county.

While John was powerfully drawn to this grandfather, Wayne attached himself to Grandmother Emma Nance, Robert's widow. Possibly the healer in her was attracted to a child so delicate and intellectually precocious. The earliest snapshot of Wayne (he looks about five) shows a neatly dressed child on the steps of his front porch, wearing a hat with a round brim. (Years later he would be named the Best Dressed Businessman in America by *Women's Wear Daily* on a "best dressed" list that included Cary Grant.)

Victimized by treacherous ailments throughout his life, Wayne had to nurse along a body that could barely keep up with the hectic pace set by his will. John, on the other hand, was a healthy, rambunctious boy whose energy and gift-of-the-gab got on Emma's nerves. She probably observed in him a powerful ego that needed a lot of honing. She kept him hopping, setting him chores and ordering him about. He felt he was always picked on.

Like all children, the brothers were not quite what they appeared. Wayne had a quiet, contemplative manner. But his sometimes sickly appearance masked a will of iron and an acute intelligence. He loved hunting and would continue to go on bird shoots throughout his life. John was so energetic only a twelve-hour work day damped him down a little.

The boys shuttled back and forth between their various relatives' farms. They visited, they worked, they slept over. Emma's treatment of John often hurt his feelings. Here she was ordering him around like some sergeant major at boot camp, while his brother got the gentle handling. "She thought he was the greatest person in the world," John recalls. "She'd say, 'Oh just let JW do it; he's strong as a horse!'" The memory of her rough handling brings a rueful expression to his face even today.

"She could get you souped up to do things, my grandmother. I don't think I ever did a thing for her that I didn't resent doing. People talk about women's rights. All my life, women have run everything."

Grandfather John F. died when John was twenty-three, but there had been years enough for the older man to pass on what was most important for the boy to absorb. John F.'s property lay a couple of farms south of the Nance fields. Three of his children married Nances. Ida Carpenter's description of their mutual relations suggests how entwined these two self-respecting families became.

"Wayne's daddy, William Henry Rollins, had a brother, Fred, that married Claudia's sister, Mary," Ida recalls. "And Henry's sister, Bessie, married Mack Nance. Henry was married to Claudia. So three of the Rollinses married into the Widow Nance family. And then my mother [Martha Nance] was a first cousin to those, and my daddy's mother and Wayne's grandmother were sisters. So that made me [Ida] related to the Rollinses, and we're double cousins and some of us are triple cousins. And anyone had to be raised up in the community to know them all, and get it all unraveled."

The Rollinses and Nances had good reasons for their mutual attraction. In early America families teamed up for the trek overland, and then set up communities together. Once settled in, the choice of eligible young men and women was limited. Many of the neighbors around Smith Chapel were disreputable, to say the least. When an entire community is poor, self-respect is a powerful determinant of class status. The self-respecting attend church, they don't drink, and they take learning seriously. They know the devil loves hard liquor, boredom, and getting all wrapped up in the opposite sex.

John remembers his grandfather warning a local moonshiner, Bayless Elliot, that if Bayless persisted in selling bad whiskey to his boys, John F. would put the law on him. The Bayless whiskey recipe—as John improbably reports it—was five gallons of watered down moonshine, a can of Red Devil lye, and a bushel of horse manure, drained off after steeping. The manure lent Bayless's truly superior moonshine a "nice brown color." This lip-smacking concoction was sold in quart Ball jars in the woods after dark.

Bayless lived with his mother, a broad-hipped, implacable female who affected wide hoop skirts and a deep glower. When the sheriff appeared at the end of their dirt road, Mrs. Elliot would plant herself on a stool over the trapdoor where Bayless stashed his whiskey supply. The sheriff wasn't up to demanding a widow woman raise her skirts for his inspection. So he'd always back away empty-handed.

"Now Bayless," John quotes his grandfather, "you're killing my boys with that rotgut you sell. So I'm gonna ask you to study on what I'm saying. You keep selling those boys whiskey, I'm gonna have you in the chain gang."

How John F. moved Bayless's mother off her perch over the trapdoor, John doesn't recall. But the Sheriff uncovered the moonshine and Bayless was chain-ganged. For two years he sledgehammered rocks for the state of Georgia.

"And the first person he sees when he gets out is my grandfather," John relates. "I was with him picking cotton near the road and Bayless comes up on his horse. And he says, 'Uncle John, how are you?'

"And John F. says, 'Why, I'm fine, Bayless. I missed you while you were away. I sure hope you don't have to make that trip again.'"

"'Never will,'" says Bayless, without a flicker of resentment.

"Which taught me," John concludes, "that if you look a man in the eye and you tell him what will happen unless he mends his ways, he seldom retains much animosity."

Both the Rollinses and the Nances exemplified the self-respect of yeoman farmers—those hardworking landowners sandwiched between deracinated, broken-spirited whites, downtrodden blacks, and la-de-da absentee plantation owners. When Wilbur Cash describes the yeoman-farmer of the Old South, he comes close to describing Grandfather John F. Rollins: "These men took from aristocracy as much as, and no more than, could be made to fit with their own homespun qualities; and so what they took they made solidly their own, without any sense of inadequacy to haunt them into gaucherie. The result was a kindly courtesy, a level-eyed pride, an easy quietness, a barely perceptible flourish of bearing, which, for all its obvious angularity and fundamental plainness, was one of the finest things the Old South produced."

Complicating this idealized portrait that John F. fits so well was the old man's loyalty to the Republican party. It took strength of character to adhere to Northern politics in a Southern community—where any notion imported from up north was looked on as inspired by the devil himself.

A generation earlier, the government of Georgia had posted a reward of five thousand dollars to anyone who brought in the abolitionist, William Lloyd Garrison, to stand trial on charges of inciting black men to revolt. During the thirteen years before the Civil War, five newspaper editors who held liberal ideas were shot to death in various Southern states by men who, in their insanity, were unable to distinguish between a point of view and a live human being.

The cultural divide between South and North was a chasm so wide that even that brilliant Bostonian, Henry Adams, couldn't see across it. Adams met the son of General Robert E. Lee at Harvard as a student and imagined he was seeing a "typical" Southerner. His description, which follows, represents the kind of North versus South generalization the Rollins brothers never indulged in as they moved up from hardscrabble farming to modern business. Wayne and John were too busy transforming themselves from boys who saw no farther than the fields they ploughed to men whose influence (and money) would revolutionize the service industry, advance the cause of African Americans, create the first practical hazardous waste disposal sites in the United States, and advance medical research.

Henry Adams describes Rooney Lee as a fine example of the best the South could produce:

> Tall, largely built, handsome, genial, with liberal Virginia openness to all he liked, he had also the Virginian habit of command. . . . For a year, at least . . . the most prominent man in his class, [he then] seemed slowly to drop into the background. The habit of command was not enough, and the Virginian had little else. He was simple beyond analysis; so simple that even the simple New England student could not realize him. No one knew enough to know how ignorant he was; how childlike; how helpless before the relative complexity of a school. As an animal the Southerner seemed to have every advantage, but even as an animal he steadily lost ground.

Generalizing with genial abandon, Adams concludes: "Strictly, the Southerner had no mind; he had temperament. He was not a scholar; he had no intellectual training; he could not analyze an idea, and he could not even conceive of admitting [contradictions]."

Bizarre it is to observe a Yankee mandarin describing a Southern gentleman in the same terms the Southern gentleman of that day used to describe the black man. But Adams's version of the "animal"

Southerner hardly matches the picture presented by men like John F. or his grandson, John W. Adams may have found them no less impenetrable than Rooney Lee, but eventually these yeoman-farmers would not only "analyze" ideas, but solve problems no one had even defined yet. The only higher degrees they received from universities would be a string of honorary doctorates late in life. Their school days concluded, Wayne went on to get a smattering of college chemistry, while John got what formal training he could through correspondence courses.

Ida Carpenter remembers the Rollins boys (in the early twenties) running around in overalls with "hickory-striped" shirts, the mud squishing up between their bare toes. Yet they enjoyed some strong advantages over contemporary children. Few youngsters today get their first immersion in the English language from the King James Bible. Even fewer have an in-house Scheherazade like Claudia, who read every evening by candlelight to the assembled family. They grew up free from the commercial devastations of the tube and psychobabble. They were left to invent their own amusements and dream their own dreams.

For years, John rose at 3 A.M. to accompany his grandfather a dozen miles to the cotton gin mill where they waited in line two hours to have their load reduced to bales. "With cotton at 5 cents a pound, you pick 500 pounds and that's $25," John says. (A lot of money for a family whose annual income was seldom above $100.) The slow ride behind the clopping horse, the closeness he felt to the older man, John F.'s wry remarks and easy humor—these childhood impressions are indelibly inscribed in John's memory. It was this learning at leisure that formed him.

The stories Claudia read at bedtime taught that constant application and absolute honesty perform miracles. No one was perplexed with double standards. Knowing her own mind, accepting her hard life without complaining, Claudia led them out of their ignorance without damaging their faith in themselves.

Self-esteem comes close to pride (a word long out of fashion). Because he knew the South well, William Faulkner created stories that give pride high priority. A faded and worn workshirt becomes a symbol of honor when it is washed spotless, starched, and ironed.

Wayne recalls, "My father had a lot of pride. Back then men wore hats all the time. He would never wear his hat without brushing it before he put it on. You never did see him when his shoes weren't shined. That was unusual out in that country."

"My mother had a lot of pride. A year or two before she died in 1976, when she was ill, the doctor over there—a distant cousin of ours in Ringgold—said, 'Mrs. Rollins, you don't have to get up, and dress, and put your . . . corset on, and all that just to come over here to see me. Just put on your robe and come in the back door.'

"And she said, 'I will not! I'm not coming out in public like that!'"

3
Hard Lives

Claudia's generation, born late in the last century, lived among the men who'd fought in the defeated Southern armies. Her grandmother, Statirah, told her how the Confederate "guerrillas," outlaws apparently, would suddenly come out of the woods and take "everything. Come by and drive the cows off, and take and drive off with the best horses, the pretty mares." There were neighbor girls, the Fagleys, who "loved these soldiers. They'd lay around with them."

Smoked hams were hidden "up in the loft where they had planks laying across the joists [so you couldn't see the meat]. When I was a child," she recalled, "I saw those hickory tree saplings you could twist without breaking where grandmother [Statirah] hung her meat."

Grandmother Statirah thought that the Fagley girls told the soldiers about the hiding place. The soldiers knew exactly where to look. And then another time the soldiers walked in on them at dinner, commandeered the table and gobbled up everything without a word of thanks. The Nance family were strong supporters of the Confederate cause. But these soldiers were perhaps free agents of some kind. Claudia recalls, "My grandma hated them with a vengeance."

The Nances were folks at the top of the local social hierarchy, but whatever wealth they had was lost after the Civil War. The whole family would laugh over Statirah's big trunk full of Confederate money, turned into worthless paper in 1865. Claudia says, "She had hundred dollar bills, and they was stacked and tied together . . . in the trunk. And the one row put on top of others. And it wasn't worth nothing. Now I've heard her tell that."

The Rollinses were divided from the Nances over the war, but they couldn't manage to stay away from each other. Both the Nances and Rollinses were strong-minded people who had come out into the wilderness because they were independent. Among them were some more given to boxing each other than debating. Politics was the one subject never discussed at dinner. Wayne recalls that "Feelings ran too deep."

The Rollinses' association with the Union cause was never accepted by the Nance clan, and Claudia was very much a Nance. With the same precision that a physicist knows his equations, Claudia knew right from wrong. Years later she would refuse to go down to the basement of Wayne's house because he had a pool table down there. Nor would she enter a room where alcohol was served.

By today's indulgent standards, Claudia's youth was intolerable. Her extraordinary intelligence and high-spirited nature were tightly constrained by the hard life she led, by her Old Testament ideals, by her husband's illness. She lived as most American women had lived in rural communities all the way back to pre-Revolutionary days. She could hold everything she owned in two hands—her Bible, shoes, work clothes, Sunday clothes and a few trinkets. While men hunted and argued and sometimes shot or knifed each other, women expressed their deeper emotions in church. The rest was silence.

As a child Claudia probably went barefoot, providing it wasn't Sunday. Around her, the fields and skies were quiet unless wind tossed the leaves. The human voice calling out had more power in that world without machinery. The jet flying high overhead had not yet been imagined.

The Rollinses' three-room house, with its tiny fireplace and Home Comfort wood stove in the kitchen, had no electricity. No one in that part of the country had plumbing. Wells were dug for water, and sanitation consisted of the pit under the outhouse. In the fall the family dug another deep pit near the smokehouse and buried jars of preserved vegetables and fruits under layers of straw. "We used to buy day-old bread," John says. "We'd say it was for the pigs, but we'd eat a good portion ourselves. Just sprinkle water on it, put it in a paper bag and heat it in the oven." They were certain never to starve, which put them ahead of generations of Europeans subsisting on a similar economic level. The price was unremitting physical labor. "If ever you slept past four, my dad figured you were sleeping in," John says.

So every day started before sunup and the slogging continued until sundown.

We had a mule and a mare. We had up to three to five cows. It varied. Because that was where we got our money to buy salt and pepper and stuff like that. Because I sold the buttermilk when I was a kid, going door to door [in Chattanooga]. We always kept two hogs. We'd butcher them every year. That was our meat for the whole year. We'd wait till it came cold weather, because you had no refrigeration or anything. We had to get a cold spell, and then we'd butcher where we could hang the meat up. And then we'd make our sausage, and fry the sausages and put them in those Ball jars. And pour the hot grease in around them. And seal them. You could open those in August and they'd be just as nice as could be. The grease would congeal around and hold them. And we'd do that with the tenderloin. We'd cook it the same way and put it in there.

So during the summer, when we were raising crops, we could have sausage, tenderloin. Mostly sausage. Plus, another thing we used to do, we'd put the sausage in a cloth bag and smoke them. Mother would take cowfeed sacks, wash them and make our underwear from them as well. When you smoked, the hickory smoke going up, it was delightful. It forms kind of a crust. Takes quite some time. You have that smoke going all the time while you've got the meat in there. You also have your hams, and your shoulder, which you will eat, spaced out over the year. And you kept your ham for when you were working in the fields in the summer time.

Henry Rollins was a big man, six foot two, 260 pounds—too heavy, Wayne says, to ride a cultivator. The long tongue of the machine tipped up when he sat in the seat. Wayne began following their mules, ploughing the small, uneven fields when he was ten. Young John was soon tagging along after him. John remembers chopping down woods to enlarge their fields, recalls the way the cut roots snapped painfully back on his shins when he ploughed the virgin land, the mule swishing its tail in his eyes.

(Years later, when Wayne's sons bought a mule to pull a wagon to use as a hunting platform, he said, "it was the stupidest idea they'd ever had." And they began to understand his lack of enthusiasm when a low-flying jet passed over and the animal broke free of the wagon and ran off into the woods.)

The Ringgold community was not exactly burning with educational zeal. Claudia seemed to be the great exception. Farmers who spent fifteen hours a day in the field could see little reason to learn Latin. They wanted their kids out in the fields through harvest time, September and most of October. But Claudia foresaw a time when clear heads would matter more than strong hands, and she believed children should spend more time educating themselves than in tilling the soil.

Arguments erupted. Claudia held her ground. Henry, who didn't care one way or the other about education, sided with Claudia because, in John's words, "My dad always thought my mother hung the moon." When Henry insisted his wife was right, one of Claudia's cousins attacked him with a knife. Henry got a hand on the cousin's throat and pinned down his arm so he couldn't use the knife. But others siding with the cousin pulled Henry's overall jumper over his head and dragged him upright. "So this fellow cut [my dad] across the head," Wayne recalls. "And across his face. Tried to cut his throat, and cut him across the stomach. It was serious. He like to have bled to death. We don't ever see people go and get in fights any more like they used to. Used to be, every ball game you saw a fight."

Gushing blood, Henry walked home. John still remembers the moment his father walked in the door. A neighbor drove him over bumpy backwoods roads in a Model T Ford to the nearby town of Cohutta. There he was doctored, then moved to the home of a relative in Cohutta where he recovered from his wounds.

If Claudia's frustration was intense, she could do little more than curse the cows (as her niece Ona Mae relates) and sublimate her fury in church. Religion back then was the best path to sanity, and Claudia was a spiritual woman. In her hard life, the church offered the brightest light.

John believes his father never really recovered from that knifing at the school. Claudia had to give up teaching to work the hilly acres of their farm—the eighty bumpy acres Henry bought from his father about the time he married, a narrow little valley that was a strait jacket on advancement.

Henry was in his early thirties when his heart began to fail him. Wayne says the first attack came in 1927 when his father was thirty-eight. Ona, his niece, says he was in the fields "pulling sod" when he collapsed. After his recovery in Dalton at the Methodist Parsonage, he "was never able to [work] after that." Grace, whom Wayne married in 1931, says it occurred shortly after their marriage. Wayne recalls how his father suffered too from "a double rupture hernia." Working in the fields became a torture for him. A man of incredible will, with a wife and two sons to support, he pushed on. Wayne recalls how his dad "would have to go lay flat on his back and put his feet on a tree" to relieve the pain and press his innards back through the torn wall of his abdomen. Wayne, still a child, felt the presence of death in the fields. "The danger of gangrene," he says, "was always there."

The boys' grandfather, John F., had the wisdom to stay emotionally uninvolved in the injustices of the world. But his son had a short fuse and tended to see things in absolute terms. John describes his father as "a man that had no sense of humor. None. He was always very firm. It was his way, or no way.

"Once, when I was harrowing, I thought he'd left us alone. And I said, 'Dad just doesn't have any damn sense!' Only he was walking right behind me in the ploughed ground, so I couldn't hear him. And he kicked my ass up right between those mules with the side of his foot." On another occasion, when Wayne sat on the wagon dreaming and oblivious to his father's calls, Henry lost patience and flung an ear of corn that hit the boy so hard it knocked him to the ground.

Frustrated by a body that was so early failing him, Henry was forced to accept the pain as part of some inevitable order. Watching his health deteriorate with so little accomplished, he had every reason for fury. His wife, if not his children, understood why he exploded.

In the thirties, medicine was decades away from open heart surgery. No one knew enough to warn Henry that his diet was a killer. Worse, he'd been born into a family with a history of heart failure. Henry drank half a gallon of milk a day, consumed quantities of butter, and loved the fat part of the pork.

The Rollins diet was hardly different from the food Americans had put on the table a hundred years before. Volnay Ashe, an Englishman quoted by Henry Adams in his *History of the United States,* describes meals served in a Kentucky cabin in 1806. Adams says Ashe is not entirely trustworthy, but the Rollinses' childhood lends credence to Ashe's report, for he writes:

> I will venture to say that if a prize were proposed for the scheme of a regimen most calculated to injure the stomach, the teeth, and the health in general, no better could be invented than that of the Americans. In the morning at breakfast they deluge their stomach with a quart of hot water, impregnated with tea, or so slightly with coffee that it is mere colored water; and they swallow almost without chewing, hot bread, half baked, toast soaked in butter, cheese of the fattest kind, slices of salt or hung beef, ham, etc., all which are nearly insoluble.

Ashe then describes the horrendous drinking habits of the early American, "who drank nothing but whiskey, which soon made him more than two-thirds drunk." The Rollinses' neighbors also employed alcohol to escape the monotony of their lives and the tedium of their own thoughts. In her family, Claudia banned anything that remotely resembled alcohol. Let relatives pickle themselves in drink, nobody within shouting distance of the Rollinses dared show a bottle.

In this world of scarcity, excess nevertheless lay in wait for the weak and the bored. Local females tended to dwindle into sticks or puff up into mountains of flesh like poor Mrs. Epps, who lived just down the road.

Wayne well remembers how the Epps family used their backyard for a toilet: "we'd see those girls run around to use that, and you'd see them just as plain. . . ." As for their father, Jim Epps, the husband of fat Mrs. Epps, "He'd read some books and kinda thought he was a lawyer. He never did go to law school." His wife finally got "so big that when she died they had to knock out one of those windows. The door wasn't big enough to get her out. So they took her out the window. I'd say she weighed over three hundred pounds."

What frustration, what fury led Mrs. Epps to dig her grave with her teeth? And after her death, what lonely desolation led her young sister-in-law to suicide? Wayne says that the young woman missed the old lady so much that she went out to the barn, tied a rope around her neck and hung herself from a rafter. Her body was discovered there by John who cut her down. Recalling the moment now, he says, "You do what's got to be done."

The society in which the Rollins brothers grew up was hardly Arcadian. History had thrust them back into savage nature, and only the church and its Word afforded them a larger view. Less fortunate were their illiterate neighbors, the Elliots, the Epps, the Schulers, and Fagleys. The Rollins and Nance families were aware of their superiority. Alcohol was a forbidden substance. They were never foul-mouthed or in desperate need of a bath. Their dialect may have been unintelligible in Boston, but they had ideals, religion, and ambition.

Their family might hold itself above certain disreputable neighbors, but they were hardly exempt from the same hard life. Wayne and John recall their father, like some fairy tale giant, hefting two hundred-pound sacks of feed, one under each arm. But after his heart gave out, he dwindled overnight into a helpless invalid. After that first savage heart attack, he lived on for sixteen excruciating years, barely able to negotiate the porch steps. The slightest effort caused Henry pain.

His condition was only made worse by the local doctor. Confronted with a patient who now weighed 275 pounds, the doctor "put him on a diet of soda crackers and buttermilk. And then," John says, "they kept him on that until it ate the protein in his heart and his kidneys, which brought him down from 275 to 180. The doctor was having marital problems, and right in the midst of this cure, he killed himself. He committed suicide. Dad wanted to be well. So he did exactly what the doctor told him. But then he found a new doctor who said, 'Gosh, you've got to have a balanced diet. Your body is eating itself.'"

During his final years, Henry looked after his grandson, Randall, who remembers him as an affectionate man who loved to sing and was not ill-humored. Henry never reconciled himself to his failing body. But when he finally died in 1945, he must have been ready to give up the long struggle. He was then fifty-six, a grand old age for someone with a heart three times normal size. His wife and both sons were with him. "He just ceased to be able to breathe," Wayne recalls. "It was in daytime . . . about two o'clock."

All through the interminable illness that became Henry's life, Claudia and her boys had to keep the farm going somehow. Like Grandmother Statirah, like her mother, Emma, Claudia spent a great part of her adult life as a widow. Much of her youth she cared for her invalid husband. She was the third generation of women in her family to be faced with doing a man's field work, and the boys joined her as soon as they were strong enough. They worked out of their small, L-shaped house hammered together from rough pine. Cupboards were unnecessary; aside from a church-going outfit, there were no clothes to store.

No one owned a radio but many could pick out a tune on a guitar. A piano was regarded as a local treasure. Most evenings Claudia read aloud to her family by candlelight from the King James Bible, as well as *The American Magazine,* and stories by Zane Grey, Scattergood Banes, and Horatio Alger. More than anything, she wanted her boys to understand the powerful link that ties true achievement to the imagination guided by moral behavior.

If the Bible gave form and substance to their imaginations, it was the Horatio Alger tales that established their unconscious agenda. These novels acquired an even greater power by virtue of the silence and darkness surrounding reader and listeners. There was only the kerosene lamp burning, and the enlivening rise and fall of their mother's voice as she turned herself into the characters from the book.

On his first day at the tiny local school, Wayne was given a daunting lesson in adult solidarity. Playing "horsie" with a child his age, he fastened a string bridle to his friend and galloped him around the schoolground. When his horse galloped away with the string, Wayne shouted to an older child, "Catch him! Catch my horse!" (In Wayne's account, this second child is Bayless Elliot, the future bootlegger of John's story.) Child number two ignored Wayne's order. So Wayne lit into the older boy with a mind to punishing him for not following orders. He found himself getting more than he could give. "I was gonna whup him for not catching my horse. But he whupped me."

Wayne complained to his teacher. She called in Elliot and gave both boys a whipping for fighting. Wayne went home and complained to his mother about the teacher. Unfortunately for him, the teacher happened to be living in their house. As if the tiny Rollins abode weren't already crowded enough, Claudia often had teachers board with them.

The teacher Wayne had tattled on was Rio Bandy, a pretty young woman and distant cousin of Claudia's. "I told my mother about the boy who wouldn't catch my horse, and how we had a fight, and how Mrs. Bandy whipped us both. Mother just marched me out back and whipped me again. So I got three whippings the first day of school."

The boys discovered immediately that getting into trouble at school meant worse trouble at home. Claudia was Wayne's teacher at the school during his third and fourth years, and he recalls being enormously relieved when she quit the job. "She punished me a whole lot more. . . . And I didn't feel like I got a fair deal. She expected more out of me than she did the others."

Those Georgia hills were no environment for the development of finer sensibilities. Wayne showed signs of possessing a delicate disposition, but a disposition forged by circumstance and his mother's discipline to include an inflexible will. He would mature into a quiet man with a reflective nature who loved nothing better than besting an opponent in a business deal.

No one has much to say about Wayne's inner life. He seldom expressed his feelings to others. He once told his wife, Grace, that his greatest pleasure in later life was just coming home after work and settling down in their study with something to read. Given the quality of his mind and his often fragile health, a more forgiving childhood might well have turned him into a scientist or professor of agriculture. But necessity narrowed him, and he bent his considerable intelligence almost exclusively to making things work.

Nevertheless, Wayne had a touch of the artist. He never bought land without foreseeing its improvement in his mind's eye. He detested developers who reduced fields and hills to stubble, lumber companies that clear cut, contractors who lay down cracked sidewalks

and, when nothing would sell, walked away from their failures. He
wanted a landscape to yield richness for both the eye and the spirit.

What worried John at school was surviving the long walk home.
The grade school population at Smith Chapel was about a dozen children. Three of the boys would entertain themselves by running him
down like a dog after class and making him their punching bag.

He knew better than to go whining to the grownups. What he
needed was a good weapon. He found it in the eight-pound crockpot
his mother packed his lunch in. This crockpot had the density of
sandstone. The bullies always picked him off in the afternoon, by
which time he'd finished off its contents: dried beans, a piece of ham
and a biscuit. On his way home from school, the crockpot nestled in
a tin lunch bucket at the end of a strap. He decided to go after them
with this weapon, one at a time.

"I figured to make it so expensive on one that he wouldn't want to
fool with me the next day. And I'd take that bucket with the crock
and hit him smack on the nose. So then the other two whipped my
ass. But the next day I'd get another one, which made him a lot less
anxious to join in again. And I did that until I got them down where
they didn't do it any more."

These kids from the north Georgia hills—the Eppses, the Schulers,
the Elliots—all made a habit of throwing stones. There was nothing
uncommon about a fist-sized rock flying at you out of a dark wood.
Their cousin Robert Nance was in such a pitch of terror that he
wouldn't leave the house alone, and Wayne was given the job of es-
corting him to school every day.

In this carnage among the kids, the worst offenders were the Epps
boys—sinister, violent, and not very bright. One day an Epps boy
flung a stone that flew off course and coldcocked his own brother.
The kids were too frightened to tell their father the truth. Old Man
Epps ran around the community in a white-hot fury, interrogating
every child he could lay his hands on. Each put on a face of wonder-
ing innocence.

Old Man Epps lorded over all his children, even his eldest son, a
man no longer young—balding, in fact, and going gray. The old fellow often lined up the whole clan on a hilltop to dress them down.
They had to stand with their hands behind their backs, silently ab-
sorbing his long-winded wisdom.

Once, when he announced that he was going to whip Jim, his gray-
ing eldest, the man objected, "Paw, Ah'm too big to whup!"

"Well, you sure ain't too big to eat," rejoined old Epps. "And yore eating at my house as I recollek. So yore not too big to whup neither." And without missing a beat in his solemn adjuration, old Epps backhanded the heretic, slapping him to the ground with a single blow. The fallen son shambled back to his place in line while the patriarch continued his sermon on the mount.

Henry Rollins was likely to fly off the handle occasionally, but Claudia was more even-tempered and impossible to fool. If she chose to, her sons agree, she could charm a skunk off the back porch. She had a knack for arranging events and a way of putting things that somehow kept them hard at work doing what they least wanted to do. Nor would she hesitate to pick up a switch if either boy crossed her.

Grandma Mary Emma Nance (Claudia's mother) was less subtle. Her level glance told you at once that she was not to be trifled with. After her husband died, she had nine children to keep in order and get to church on Sunday. "They all used to live on a hill with a spring at the foot of it," John recalls. "And every time you showed up, she'd hand you a bucket and tell you to bring it back full."

Between Claudia and Emma ran the electric tension that often crackles between mothers and daughters. "My Grandmother [Emma] always made slighting remarks about my dad. She believed her daughter had married beneath herself," John says. There came the day when Claudia decided she'd had enough of her mother's innuendos. Imitating Claudia leveling with Emma, John speaks in her stern voice: "Now mother, I always enjoy your visits. But I want you to know that Henry Rollins is my husband. He is the one providing for me and this house. And never, when you're in my home, do I want to hear a remark that's adverse to Henry Rollins."

4
The Source of Dreams

Grandmother Emma Nance's living children were preceded and followed by the dead. Her last child she named Craydon Angel, born dead ten weeks before his father's death, victim of Emma's anxiety and overwork. There was never starvation but the climate was often violent, fever was common, the crops were infested with insects for which no chemicides existed, the flies and mosquitoes swarmed everywhere, and the boys were required to do the work of two men on any European farm.

Emma's husband, Robert, was "a great person to joke," Wayne recalls. "But he didn't let the managing of things [at home] interfere with his hunting too much." Robert died because he went hunting in the rain with a bad cold and contracted TB. As his tuberculosis worsened, the children cared for him and for Emma, who was carrying her last child. She was brought to bed with her husband mortally ill in the next room.

Widowed in 1905, Emma still had nine children to care for—the youngest still a baby, the oldest Lillie Dale, aged twenty-four. The year her father died, Lille Dale had been married five years and long out of the house. That put the responsibility for running the farm on her brother Mack, twenty-one, and sister Claudia, nineteen.

Claudia's later life, her responsibility for a stricken husband and tiny farm, bore a close resemblance to her mother's and her grandmother's. Almost every family around Ringgold had suffered similar early deaths and disease. A pattern emerges. The women become the caretakers and examples of responsible behavior. The men make an art of escape, not excluding death. But with an invalid father in the house and a gimlet-eyed mother, Wayne and John had less wiggle room than their male cousins and neighbors.

Wayne would remember with chagrin his mother's dream to add one more room to their small dwelling. "I only wished we'd been able to fix the house up," he says. Apparently, Henry had chopped down pine trees, then sawed and planed them into planks that he stacked against the side of the house. Everything was prepared for the renovation. But he toppled over in a field one morning and was brought home to stay in bed for the rest of his life.

Wayne remembered his mother shedding tears only twice in her life. One was the day they had to sell that lumber to make ends meet. By then Henry had been long bedridden and the Depression had clamped down like a vise.

"I planned," says Wayne, "to do things that would make it possible for us to live better than she did. Because mother had a hard life. Daddy was bedfast. And she'd have to wait on him. He would have those very serious heart attacks. One of the hardest things she ever had to do was to learn to give him shots. For some reason that was kinda beyond her capabilities. I remember her getting an orange and practicing to be able to give the shots because we couldn't afford to have anyone to stay. A nurse or anything. . . . She dreaded it. That's the only relief he could get—a shot of morphine when he would have those real bad heart attacks."

Years later, Wayne kept a book, *The People of Georgia* by Mills Lane, in the library of his Atlanta house. The author describes Georgia about the time that the Rollins brothers were growing up in Ringgold as "A miserable panorama of unpainted shacks, rain-gullied fields, straggling fences, rattletrap Fords, dirt, poverty, disease, drudgery and monotony that stretches for a thousand miles. 'As poor as a Georgian,' back then was a popular figure of speech."

The income of the Rollins family was about half the state average. A New Deal study in the thirties found tenant farmers living in "unpainted, four room shacks with 80 per cent of the houses supplied by well water, with an average income of $73; $309 for the average family. No money was available for home improvements or repairs. Malnutrition, pellagra, rickets, and hookworm along with strong drink insured a sort of universal lassitude."

In economic terms, the black population advanced while the whites regressed from 1865 to 1920. This is not to say that the blacks surpassed or even drew even with the whites. But they did emerge from slavery to tenant farming. Henry Grady, the editor and orator, said of Georgia's manufacturing capacity in the late nineteenth century: "Only the corpse and the hole in the ground are produced in Georgia."

Every family around Smith Chapel was entirely dependent on that uncertain economic engine, the family farm. Born into an timeless agrarian system, the people scraped their food off a few bumpy acres. The Rollinses were distinguished from their depressed neighbors only by pride, religious scruples and self-discipline. Their incomes were more or less identical.

Learning to work long hours and to run a farm at an early age would not have been enough to harden the brothers for the world-blazing success they later enjoyed. The true source of their achievement, their unrelenting effort and drive, is found in Claudia's steady character and love of learning. The Bible may not jibe with Darwin's science, but it has all the moral force that *The Ascent of Man* lacks. John still smiles with pleasure when he recalls his mother's reading sessions.

"If you want to be successful," both brothers like to say, "just work as hard as we did." Many people worked hard, of course, and got nowhere. John and Wayne were successful for any number of reasons, but it was crucial that their path lay down the center of that great commercial highway the United States was traveling. They had the intelligence to stay on course, and the grit not to be swept aside by adversity, failure, and false counsel.

Like Ben Franklin, they saw the path to wisdom in practical activity. Ben Franklin's father, like Claudia Rollins, read each evening to his children from the Bible. In his autobiography, Franklin recalls his father quoting this passage from Solomon: "See'st thou a man diligent in his calling, he shall stand before kings; he shall not stand before mean men." The Rollins brothers were familiar with these words too. Like Ben Franklin, they "considered industry as a means of obtaining wealth and distinction. . . ."

On the other hand, Claudia did not teach her sons as Ben Franklin believed, that it is a "convenient thing . . . to be a reasonable creature, since it enables one to find or make a reason for everything one has a mind to do." For Claudia, reason should be the slave of moral necessity. She read the Horatio Alger stories in that light. On every page a simple (or simplistic) moral truth moves its hero toward money. Alger teaches what Tocqueville observed: "To clear, to till, and to transform the vast uninhabited continent . . . the American requires the daily support of an energetic passion; that passion can only be the love of wealth; the passion for wealth is therefore not reprobated in America."

No fiction writer has written before or since with such open admiration for money. Those who denounce Alger (and who does not?) fail to mention that he lived in a time when economic power deserted the land and entered the machine. Technology and Business (with a capital B) married and their offspring was enormous wealth. Alger contemplates with placid satisfaction what money buys: respect from others, a sense of accomplishment, freedom. Prosperity is the new form that honor and self-respect assume. In his books for boys, Alger speaks as openly about the pleasures of money as contemporary children's authors (Judy Blume comes to mind) dwell on the pleasures of sex. In any case, it was Alger's understanding of success that supplied Wayne and John with a vision for their future.

Alger's characters often sound as if they were modeled on John Rollins because he modeled himself on them. In *Brave and Bold*, Robert Rushton, Alger's fifteen-year-old hero, has "inherited from his father an unusual amount of courage and self-reliance, and if one avenue was closed to him, he at once set out to find another."

John learned how, as he says, "The boy would go out searching for his fortune, and it always came out good. He was honest and he was sincere and he worked hard and he became successful later. The guy trying hardest was always the winner. I didn't know enough to disbelieve it."

The Alger books reflected precisely the nickel-and-dime economy that Rollins boys inhabited. Whenever Wayne earned a dime or a quarter, his Grandmother Emma said it would be best if she took care of it for him. She didn't want him to come crying to her how he'd lost it. She'd then pin the coins into the hem of her petticoat. Whenever the boy spotted something at the store he wanted, Emma objected that she would have to lift up her skirt in a public place to get his money. For the sake of her modesty, Wayne gave up on impulse buying. To his surprise, he soon had saved enough to open up his own bank account. He realized then how he never missed what he never bought and was now sitting on a substantial pot of money.

The Alger books (there are dozens of them) offer a young person's guide to business practice—everything from accounting to trading and check writing. Alger's cheaters never prosper. The reward for honesty is always hard cash. The children of rich men are rotten. Those who make their own money are good, generous and true. Only evil men squander money.

Alger's young hero, Robert Rushton, supports his mother because his father has been lost at sea.

> He was now able to earn six dollars a week, and this, with his mother's
> earnings in braiding straw for a hat manufacturer in a neighboring town,

supported them, though they were unable to lay up anything. The price of a term at the writing school was so small that Robert thought he could indulge himself in it, feeling that a good handwriting was a valuable acquisition, and might hereafter procure him employment in some business house. For the present, he could not do better than to retain his place in the factory.

Alger's style looks stiff and pompous by modern standards. In fact, it has all the qualities of a decent business letter. No youngster today would get further than the first paragraph of an Alger story. Yet a century ago boys were snapping up these books in which, on every page, the hero is threatened with loss of life, limb, or money.

Alger's world was swept away by a new literature that taught that morality is the weakest resource available to people, and the pursuit of money a delusion. Faulkner's Snopeses were created by a Southerner of genius to show the depravity of people who grow rich. Similarly, Scott Fitzgerald's Gatsby supports his romantic dreams with money from organized crime.

Had they read them, there was nothing in these great works of modernist literature to inspire farm boys like the Rollins brothers. This was reading for the well-to-do, a leisured elite who could repent the rise of commerce in lives upholstered by commerce. It would have been impossible for Claudia to teach her boys that striving for money was vulgar, that defeat and loss and ambiguity are more admirable than putting three square meals on the table and paying the doctor's bill.

Claudia's faith was rooted in Jerusalem, not Paris or New York. Alger's heroes captivated her because they were moral, brave and practical. They succeeded though they held honor higher than gain. Providence always rewarded them for their industry. Alger's world was plotted much like the Rollinses. Robert Rushton's mother wove objects for sale; so did the women around Ringgold. In fact, John's earliest job would be supplying the bedspreads that neighboring women tufted. At home, his sister-in-law, Grace, was fabricating hooked rugs, then splitting the fifty-cent price with John who sold them.

Wayne and John were teenagers when the Depression arrived. As Wall Street went belly-up, little changed in northern Georgia, where the economy was a local affair. People lived off the land, sold what it produced, and sewed and hammered together what they needed with their own hands.

The inspiration that John felt when he heard about commercial

success was an American faith undermined in the cities where strik-
ers were being beaten and modernism flourished. But John stayed
true to Horatio Alger's creed. In time he even became chairman of
the Horatio Alger Society, an organization founded to bring recognition to successful businessmen. John enlarged its scope to include
a well-endowed program that aided students who excelled despite adversity. The companies that John himself organized had, by 1995, created jobs for over 43,000 people.

Georgia farmers were as ambitious as their brethren in other states.
But in what field could they exercise their ambition? The idea of borrowing money to buy more land was foreign to their way of thinking.
Borrowed cash was tainted with the sin of usury—a first step to moral
ruin. The idea of being educated for some profession lay miles outside their experience. Children were needed for planting and har-
vesting. Booklearning only swelled their heads and put them beyond
understanding.

These red dirt farms were chopped up quickly when a head of family died, and the land was parceled out among survivors. The Nances
and the Rollinses were being divided and fragmented into poverty
along with everyone else. Statirah's land, 140 acres passed on to her
by her husband, William, was sold in 1898, "in front of the courthouse
door" in Ringgold, "for the purpose of paying debts and making dis-
tribution among the heirs." The land was divided among eight families. In other words, the heirs were consigned to smaller farms and
lesser lives. Henry bought his eighty acres from the family, but it was
never enough to produce an excess. What the stone-throwing Eppses
and the sad-eyed Fagleys didn't have was the disciplined self-respect
the Rollins boys got with their mother's moral instruction.

Wayne learned just how much his mother objected to whining
when he was ten. His father, not yet stricken ill, had gone over the hill
one Sunday to visit Laura Nance, who was ill. In a world without tele-
phones, a buggy trip over wretched roads was the only means of communication. By dinnertime Henry was still gone. Claudia suggested
that Wayne should do his father's chores as well as his own. Finding
himself stuck with all the milking, feeding, and corn-shucking, Wayne
began to complain, half under his breath. He was sick and tired of
his father sneaking off "on purpose," he muttered, doing it just so he
could stick Wayne with all the work. Believing himself alone in the
barn, talking only to himself, he spewed his resentment—flinging the
shucked corn into a pile.

His mother stood outside for a time, listening to his furious muttering. Then she strode to a plum bush and snapped off a thorny branch "about six foot long," as Wayne recalled it. "I was standing in the crib door shucking the corn, and she just whipped me long ways. Straight down my back with that thing. I can tell you, she didn't hear any more out of me. She took all the complaint out of me with that one whipping."

More humorous than grim, Claudia was a woman of strong convictions. "She had an opinion on everything," John recalls, "but no one ever heard her complain." According to her neighbor, Ona Mae Carpenter, the only creatures she ever cursed were the cows when they wandered into the wrong pasture. "But," Ona adds, "maybe I shouldn't repeat that."

"People had a lot stronger feelings then," Wayne says. "Sometimes I wonder if nowadays we don't really feel strongly about anything." During his youth, men used to have fistfights at the polling place. One year Andy Epps and Morgan Martin beat each other bloody. The next time the voting booths were set up, Grandfather John F. asked Andy if he was going to provide the same entertainment again. Epps replied, "Hell, nobody didn't put up no monument last time. Don't seem worth the work."

Henry Rollins held a grudge as well as any man. John remembers the day his father laid hands on the cousin who'd cut him up over the school issue.

Dad was out trimming the hedge row when this cousin who'd knifed him passed in a wagon with two mules. Dad had a scythe in his hand, and he stepped out and he hooked that scythe around the neck of this guy. And he said "You son of a bitch, I'm going to cut your head off." And he meant it! But the guy let out a banshee yell and called for my mother. You could hear him all over that countryside.

She came out and stood on the porch, and she said, "Henry, you don't want to do that."

He said, "Yes, I do. I'm going to cut the son of a bitch's head off. He's a coward. He had those people hold me and cut me up. I'm going to cut his head off." And he was determined.

And mother said, "Well, I guess, if you want to do that. Have you ever thought, if you're in the chain gang, who's going to look after the boys and I? And they'll put you in the chain gang. They'll put you in a chain gang maybe for life for cutting a man's head off. You can do that. But you have to make the decision on that. If you care more for the vengeance than you do for the family, that's a choice you have to make."

This guy said, "If you let me go, I'll never pass your house again." My father just removed the scythe from around the man's neck and quietly walked off. And that man took off down that road whipping those mules going straight out, and I never did see him ever pass the house again.

John had expected to see the man's head fly off. "That," he says, "would have been normal for that part of the country."

5
Ideas and Onions

What news of the dazzling twenties was heard in the Georgia hills below Chattanooga? At best, distant rumors. The disillusionment that blighted Europe after the First World War turned Americans into isolationists. A clever generation, bored sick in Chicago and Minneapolis, sailed overseas and was labeled "lost." The European twilight had sufficient energy remaining to turn young Americans into artists and writers struggling to overcome the Puritan blandness back home. Writers like F. Scott Fitzgerald and Ernest Hemingway brought the twilight home with them. Europe's dimming legends inspired William Faulkner and Eudora Welty to reinvent the South.

Flannery O'Connor, who lived in Milledgeville, described what she saw around her and was accused of turning Georgia into an hallucination, surreal and grotesque. Her critics had not grown up in Milledgeville, where miracles and murder were as common as pellagra, ringworm, and fried chicken.

Few in Catoosa County read *The Great Gatsby* or *The Sound and the Fury,* but they didn't find life boring or bland. They were the desperate poor, doomed to live out the epic the writers they didn't read were trying to describe. Their road out didn't lie through the fields of high art.

Their books were the Bible and the *Sears Roebuck* catalog—that true book of the future. First published in 1925, within a decade the catalog was being mailed out at the rate of some 30,000 copies daily, a 1,200-page bible of commerce, depicting everything from whalebone corsets to air pumps. Those precise descriptions of dinnerware, plumbing supplies and cattle feed constituted a genuine American literature. (And in a few years it would be designated as such—"Yes, I believe we have some literature on that item.")

The catalog promised a bright future, relief from baggy underwear stitched from sacking and from boots that never quite fit. It offered instruments for body and spirit. Mr. Sears sold more pianos and organs than he did bathtubs. Few backwater villages around the turn of the century lacked a local musician. Jazz was already drifting up the Mississippi from New Orleans whorehouses to St. Louis flophouses and Chicago bars.

In communities like Cohutta and Smith Chapel, live music still flourished in a thousand churches, white and black. Claudia was part of this world of homespun music-making, playing hymns on the pump organ for her Methodist congregation. Grandfather John F. Rollins, known for his powerful bass, led the congregation. In dim living rooms and summer porches neighbors were singing together for the last time, before the radio arrived to do their singing for them. Sears initiated the age of passive entertainment. Communal music hung on in the African American churches longer than anywhere else. But America's communal music would soon be a thing of the past. Technology would replicate and even generate the music of the future.

Around 1900, well over half of all Americans lived on farms, but the balance shifted rapidly during the Rollins brothers' childhood. By 1925, the cities were filled with restless folk off the farm looking for jobs. Wayne and John were among those who would ride into Chattanooga searching for work, just as the Depression arrived in full force.

Wayne was seventeen when the Crash came in 1929. Already by 1927, the Northern mills, unable to compete with low wages down South, initiated a stretchout system. Those who survived the drastic layoffs handled more machines and took home less pay. The price of cotton fell like a stone. Warehouses became overstocked. Shutdowns and wage cuts multiplied.

The thirties were a period of blight and fury, particularly in the South with its rickety cotton gins and oversupply of labor. Only two percent of the population in Georgia had tractors, three percent had indoor plumbing. During these years, the average income the Rollinses managed to glean off their land amounted to no more than the income for an individual Georgian—only $73. After buying flour, lard, kerosene, and simple medicines, no money was left for home improvement or equipment repair.

The Rollins brothers had a powerful advantage. They had little to lose and they had learned to expect the worst. To call yourself a free man, all you had to do was crawl out of bed before sunrise and work till dark. As long as nature cooperated, even a widow with a whole platoon of children needn't starve. Grandma Emma had proved that, and Claudia's grandmother Statirah before her.

So the Depression, when it hit, was hardly noticeable in a community long used to scraping its existence off the land. But it severely crimped any hopes Wayne and John had for bettering the family's condition. Wayne recalls that when the richest cotton man in the region died, he left $5,000.

In the twenties, H. L. Mencken famously lambasted the South for being "The Sahara of the Bozart," decrying (from his office in Baltimore) a region where "a poet is now almost as rare as an oboe-player, a dry-point etcher or a metaphysician. It is, indeed, amazing to contemplate so vast a vacuity. . . . Nearly all of Europe could be lost in that stupendous region of fat farms, shoddy cities and paralyzed cerebrums." Mencken's view is supported by the likes of Georgia governor Allen Candler who said in 1901, "Do you know that you can stand on the dome of the capitol of Georgia and see more Negro colleges with endowments than you can see white schools? I do not believe in the higher education of the darky. He should be taught the trades. When he is taught the fine arts, he gets educated above his cast and it makes him unhappy." (The passage comes from Mills Lane's book on Georgia in Wayne's study.)

Mencken also wrote that "The tone of public opinion [in the South] is set by an upstart class but lately emerged from industrial slavery into commercial enterprise." This class is indeed the class that produced the Rollins brothers, though Mencken's use of the word "upstart" throws more light on his lethal snobbery than the complex evolution occuring in the South. His "upstarts" might better be labeled "self-starters."

Mencken describes Georgia as "a state with more than half the area of Italy and more population than either Denmark or Norway, and yet in thirty years it has not produced a single idea. . . . The North," he adds, "is also stupid and obnoxious. But nowhere in the North is there such complete sterility, so depressing a lack of all civilized gesture and aspiration." Mencken quotes with approval the English actress Fanny Kemble Butler who married a slave owner and wrote of Georgia's poor whites as "the most degraded race of human being claiming an Anglo-Saxon origin that can be found on the face of the earth—filthy, lazy, ignorant, brutal, proud, penniless savages."

Martha Berry, who lived in north Georgia and founded Berry

School in 1902 (later Berry College) saw this "degraded race" with more sympathy. Wayne Rollins used to pass the gates of Berry College as a young man. He sometimes dreamed of studying there. But he would only be recognized there long after Martha Berry's death, when he was invited to sit on the Board of Trustees—a man of the world untouched by anything remotely academic.

Martha Berry's view of the people in Georgia was not confused by theories of race. Berry describes hill people so poor they dressed in rags, their "eyes dull from poor diets." She talks about bad nutrition, not the decayed nature of Anglo-Saxon "blood." She notices that the mountain children love stories and want to read.

Martha Berry understood what Claudia knew—that stories interpret life and make it significant. Berry records a mountain child's comment after hearing the story of Jonah and the whale. "That's the all-timest whopper I ever heard!" The child is delighted by the incredible story because it departs from reality. The gates to the imagination lead through the suspension of disbelief; Berry made it her life's work to open them. She wanted the children she taught to be able to say one day, "I myself was Jonah, and I escaped the whale."

Berry College is laid out in groups of buildings set far apart in broad fields under tall trees. Berry charmed Henry Ford into putting up gothic stone buildings on her original eighty-three-acre campus. The college would eventually spread out over 26,000 acres. The school began accepting girls in 1909, the year that Berry almost destroyed her health through money raising. She talked the reclusive architect, Captain John Gibbs Barnwell, into designing one of the most elegant stone chapels in the state, because she believed that buildings with tall spires would give her students "cheer and courage." She wanted "the boys surrounded by fine things so they can absorb them and become part of them."

Berry would have agreed with Mencken's view that "an impulse that deserves respect . . . is the impulse to seek beauty and to experiment with ideas, and so to give the life of every day a certain dignity and purpose," but she would have laughed at his notion that, "You will find no such impulse in the South."

The South had already produced Allen Tate, John Crowe Ransom, and the Agrarian movement. But in the real agrarian outback, Martha Berry dealt with children who grew up tilling fields and chewing on roots in winter. Like Claudia Rollins, Berry stuck to basic texts because she had to work out basic problems—ignorance, bad hygiene, hunger, not enough love, too much disease, early death.

There was a powerful current of puritanism in these extraordinary women. They put moral probity before everything, including caste and class. They had little patience for ideas that didn't yield practical results. The Bible was their Doctor Spock. They perceived life as a parable; otherwise it would have been intolerable, lacking color, mystery, wisdom. No one told Claudia that the U.S. Government printing office had dozens of do-it-yourself documents that detailed everything from milking a goat to having a baby, each available for a dime. The Rollinses were not materially better off than their neighbors, but they were superior in one respect. Claudia established a spiritual order for her family founded on belief in some higher power, on love, honor, and laughter.

Mencken was a city man who felt uneasy around livestock, country people and fields saturated with manure. His admiration for European high civilization caused him to look with dismay on the grubby United States. Commerce and technology were already turning his country into a vast suburb linked by asphalt and airwaves. The nation could not make up for two thousand years of civilization in a fortnight. Its first order of business was collapsing time and space so it could communicate with its far-flung territories. Little wonder technology was its first love. The Rollins boys travelled first by wagon, then in a fifty-dollar Model T over roads so poor that the trip from Dalton to Chattanooga seemed interminable.

Wayne says his father had "a tendency to fix something temporarly— or wait on it. That always bothered me. The time is now; it isn't tomorrow. I think if you wait till you're ready, you never will do anything." John exhorts along the same lines. Years later Wayne would place a sign in his office that read "NOW!" And he would always go into a slow burn when one of his workers said, "I'm going to start this on Monday."

"What's wrong with *now?*"

Like rock climbers on an exposed face, John and Wayne dealt always with immediate matters. Seize the right handhold, move into the best foothold now, and soon you're at the top. Not sullied by theoretical notions, clarified by practical work, they could see for themselves what was important, what was time-wasting.

In his early teens, Wayne had delivered milk for his uncle. One day he accidentally let the cows get into the onions, which gave their milk an unpleasant taste and odor. One of his uncle's customers, an Irishman named Mahoney, soon canceled his standing order. Wayne figured he'd better visit and find out what went wrong.

Because he was so insistent, Mahoney's wife reluctantly let him into the kitchen. But she whispered that it would be good for his health to stay far away from her husband. Mahoney, an enormous, reddish pale man, hated the taste of onion in his milk. Bread soaked in milk was his favorite dish. The taste of onion had put him in a fury.

Nevertheless, Wayne decided it was better to face Mahoney than to tell his uncle what had happened. He insisted he wanted to see Mahoney. Mahoney's wife finally relented, but suggested he come back after dinner. Her husband, she said, tended to be calmer on a full stomach.

When Wayne returned after dark and edged into the room, he felt like Theseus facing the Minotaur. Mahoney immediately began to shout at the top of his voice. He'd be damned before he put up with onions polluting his dinner. Wayne whispered that he understood completely. Mahoney waved his arms and went on bellowing. Wayne murmured his apologies. He had been careless. It was unforgivable. It would never happen again. He went on apologizing until the Irishman fell silent.

"After I admitted I was wrong all he could say was, 'Okay. Let's try again.' It's odd how many people who are wrong won't admit they're wrong even though it could put everything right."

Wayne recalls his Grandfather John F. gazing across a bleak landscape in northern Georgia one evening and remarking, "A rabbit crossing that land would have to carry his food with him." John F.'s grandchildren would soon be crossing over into an era of the most radical change in the history of the planet. The food they carried was of a spiritual sort, supplied them in childhood—a survival kit made of no tangible material but harder than a blacksmith's hammer.

Wayne says, "I guess in a way probably the Depression contributed much to our family staying together the way we have. We stayed [together] on the farm. Now we're living in a different time. With communication and transportation as it is, the children scatter all over. It's much harder to raise a child now than it was when I grew up. I'm not one of these people that believe they've got it soft now."

During his own childhood there was no such thing as child psychology. Weak and feeble youngsters sickened and died. The rest were pitched out of their trundle beds at four in the morning to milk cows and plod all day behind a mule. Failure was ascribed to God's will or alcohol. The sick, the sad, and the too-smart-for-their-own-good were granted no saving euphemisms. There were no victims, just losers.

Wayne was bound by a moral code that could be described as Practical Puritan. To break your word was to destroy yourself. As a rule, he left women to heaven and reserved his moral demands for men. Later, when he owned several ranches, he discovered one of his managers living with a woman out of wedlock. Following the manager's example, two ranch hands had quietly sneaked women into their quarters as well. Wayne ordered them all to move the ladies off his property pronto. The men offered no objection, but they ignored his orders. Wayne's response was to fire all three of them on his next visit. So much for the sexual revolution.

In later years, on the other hand, he made the admirable and attractive Madalyn Copley the chief operations officer of Rollins Broadcasting—the only woman to hold such high position at that time in Delaware. After Madalyn was hired as the company's controller in 1949, she advanced quickly. This was in the fifties, decades before women began to press hard on corporate glass ceilings.

There were crucial years when simple survival was no easy matter for Wayne, much less wild success. Like others in his extended family, he'd been stricken with TB and removed from the classroom when he was ten—old enough to know about death. His uncles, Theodore and Oscar, had both died of the disease. "I'd seen them just strangle," Wayne remarks, "till that blood would come out. So I took my sickness seriously."

Three times a day Claudia prepared raw eggs in whole milk flavored with vanilla. "I can remember sitting in the sun on the south side of the house in a chair." The boy would laze about grandly, sipping this grog from a tall glass under Claudia's watchful eye. After a summer, fall, and winter had passed, they realized that he'd recovered.

In Wayne's view, that year of tender loving care was dangerous in another sense. It weakened his will. When he went back to school he was a year behind his schoolmates. He was thrown in with "those remnants [from among his former classmates] who didn't pass because they never did study. I fell right in with them. They got to be my buddies. I guess that is where I learned one of my important lessons about associates—that you have to be careful you don't associate with the people who are not gonna accomplish what you want to accomplish."

In the seventh grade he was still with "these same sorry people. I

don't know that they were *sorry*. But they sure weren't interested in
getting an education. So I didn't do well in the sixth or the seventh.
Then I went over into high school and I didn't have the background
that I needed. But there I had two of the roughest teachers that I ever
had in school.

"There was Mrs. Bankston, and another tough one was Missy
Owens. She taught Latin. I had to get two years of Latin in one. She
just made me do both. She didn't give an inch on anything. She was
one of those that didn't understand. She didn't want to understand.
That's why I learned her lessons." In other words, Missy Owens understood very well indeed. It's not hard to imagine the boy tendering
his excuses while she gazes at him with a flat, sardonic expression, her
eyes fixed on his eyes, not buying a word of it.

6
Bubbling Optimism

Once Wayne and a cousin were trying to get rid of some cats that were infesting their farm. They filled a large sack with cats and drove to a distant field where they turned them loose, hoping the felines would scatter into the wood. But the cats had no sooner dashed into the field than half a dozen dogs dozing under the trees snapped to attention. "[The dogs] were just laying up there. And when I turned these cats out, they come roaring out of there. And they ran the cats, I guess it was a thousand feet, up to a sharecropper's house. They ran them up and ran every one of them into the house.

"And as we came back from Cohutta, [the sharecropper's family] had them sacked back up. One of those gals were standing beside the road and she said, 'Here's your cats back.'"

The best sport was generally provided by relatives and neighbors playing jokes on each other. Fishing and hunting were not called sports. To hunt they usually went with Uncle Fred. The word "entertainment" didn't exist. But you could keep an eye on the Epps girls across the way—or, as Claudia recalled in 1975, on the local girl who was "just crazy about Frank Henson." At the time, John was little more than a toddler.

She'd never had a date in her life, [because] she was as ugly as home sin. She couldn't have a sweetheart. And Frank Henson, I don't know howcome that he asked her for their first date. But he come in, and of course we didn't ever pull our shades down out on the farm.

And Wayne said to me, "I wish you'd go out there and look and see Frank sitting there, and her a-hugging and kissing him." Because he'd sit this way, and she'd just swing around his neck and then she'd kiss him. And Frank'd say, "Ha ha, ha ha." But he never did touch her. Never did unfold his hands. He'd just sit there. And J. W. [John] heard us talking. And he decided that the next time they was coming that he would get his little chair and sit behind the door where he could see. And he got this little chair and he was sitting there a long while. He wanted to see them kissing. Finally, he got out from behind the door and he come in and said, "I never did see a thing in the world. I sat there and they never did even kiss or nothing." He was just so disgusted he didn't know what to do.

Church on Sunday was the high point of the week for Claudia. There were sermons; weddings; funerals. You could always count on death—and the young were as often carried off as the old. Ida Carpenter (born 1905) recalls the funeral of a neighbor, old Mrs. Sharp with a certain pleasure:

> I remember very well they had three long benches on each side up at the front of the church called Amen corner. And my daddy and Uncle John F. Rollins sat on the front bench and stood up to sing. The whole congregation did, and Uncle John Rollins, Wayne's grandpa, led the singing. My daddy sang the bass and the congregation joined in. And I remember just as well what Uncle John and my daddy was singing. They knew the two songs by heart. One of them they sang was "In That Beautiful Land Where the Angels Stand." And Uncle John come out on that lead and Daddy would come in on that bass. "We shall meet—shall meet." And the congregation helped sing. And the next song was "Jesus, Lover of My Soul." Now that was sang without any books. But they just sung it, and I thought they sung real good. I was just a little girl but I remember it all.

For a time Claudia had a sharecropper on their land to do the work her bedridden husband could not. Wayne remembers meeting some of the old ex-slaves who had worked on his grandfather Nance's plantation. But again, "We never did discuss politics at our house because they were Republicans on the Rollins side, who left the South to join the Northern army."

When Wayne graduated from high school in 1930, he was seventeen and class valedictorian, with a grade point average of 96. His mother cried when he made his speech in front of the student body. His title: "Tonight we Launch, Where shall we Anchor?" She cried out of pride, and because she knew his schooling was over too soon. With a family to support there could be no thought of higher education.

Wayne married the year after he graduated. His bride was Grace Crum, the daughter of a farmer with property just across the state line in Tennessee. Grace had grown up in a three-room house on a farm much like the Rollinses'. Nothing surprised her except maybe the Rollins family's expressiveness.

"My family," she says, "loved each other, of course, but we just didn't show it. We were never loving. We never had deep disagreements, but we just weren't affectionate. The Rollins family, they were just open, and you soon learned to do the same thing, and really show your emotions."

John, thirteen years old when Wayne married Grace, moved into the kitchen to sleep on a daybed. He loved his new sister-in-law from the first, an affection that would endure over sixty years. Despite the crowded cottage and the sick father who grew yearly more childlike and dependent on his wife, the family lived—more or less on top of each other—without complaining. Claudia had long since given up her dream of having the house enlarged.

Grace was young and tough, ready to take on her share of the ceaseless labor. She had a farm woman's uncompromising and realistic eye. Her nature combined a powerful independent streak with a fun-loving disposition. Her sometimes grave manner belied a love of cutting up, dancing, and dating boys with convertible cars. She was composed of elements not often mixed together in the same person, dead practical and mad for fun. If anything, this attracted Wayne, who never liked anything too simple. Grace proved difficult to win over. She'd never go along easily and didn't mind opposing him just for the fun of it.

When he first presented himself at her door, Grace regarded him as a very poor candidate for her affections. Wayne was younger than she, and too serious, in her view. He didn't have a car. Worse yet, she was, as she puts it, "desperately in love" with another man. Wayne might be academic top dog at the Ringgold High School, but that didn't cut him much slack with Miss Crum. She wanted to ride in a fast convertible car, to feel the wind in her hair, and to have a real house with a garden and no pigs in the near vicinity. More than anything, she wanted to escape the farm, and any fool could see that Wayne was a farmer born and bred. So Wayne had his work cut out for him. If Grace's father, Jim Crum, hadn't come down so hard on his side, he might never have won her.

Grace's father was a very straight man, dark complexioned and raw-boned. He'd never bought so much as a loaf of bread on credit. You didn't deserve what you hadn't paid for in cash: that was his attitude and was the attitude of his neighbors. Jim pretty much ordered Grace to get serious about Wayne. And when he decided Wayne was going to be his son-in-law, Grace ran out of wiggle room.

"My dad was a good judge of character," she says. "I was going with this other boy. . . . But [my dad] just said, 'You can't go with him.'

"And I said, 'Well, what's wrong with him?'

"And he said, 'He doesn't have any countenance. He can't talk to me and look me in the face. Anyone like that I don't trust.'

"And," she concludes, "that boy turned out exactly like he said. He drank too much and never did amount to a hill of beans."

Married in 1931, Wayne and Grace planted corn, beans and potatoes. When possible, he also worked with a shovel on the county roads for ten cents an hour. In Georgia, every man paid a highway tax of five dollars or worked five days on the roads. Wayne, in effect, collected his pay from those who coughed up enough tax money to avoid the work.

Wayne and Grace lived two years in the family house while they constructed a place of their own on an adjacent forty acres he bought from Grandfather John F. Their first house, twelve by twenty-four feet, had two rooms. They cut the framing lumber and box sheeting themselves, and paid cash for doors, nails, and roofing material.

Meanwhile, brother John led his tiny high school to the statewide championship playoff in Atlanta where Cohutta (its student body numbered fifty) came in second in the state. After this feat, John was offered a basketball scholarship. Like Wayne, who could have accepted a scholarship for academic achievement, he had to refuse. The boys were their parents' sole source of support. By now Henry could do nothing except babysit his grandson, Randall, born November 5, 1931.

Randall remembers Henry so enfeebled he couldn't make it down the porch steps. Though his bad heart weighed like an anvil on them all, and put to the test Claudia's genius for self-denial, the sick man was accorded all the respect his wife felt a husband deserves. Helpless as a child, dependent on his wife for everything, Henry, they had to keep reminding themselves, could die from any overexertion. Even a bout of bad temper might kill him.

Wayne became the working head of the family with whom his mother shared all her financial decisions. As a teenager, he was the family money manager. He learned to make dull work more interesting by always trying to outperform himself. "If I was going to plow two acres of ground, then every time I ploughed it I tried to plough it quicker than before."

John, by this time taller than his enormous father, had to curb his coltish adolescence and buckle down to survival. Grandfather John F. Rollins and the Nance women had made a covenant of simple honesty. Claudia believed that a person who tells the truth has enormous power. He moves along a straight line to his goal. It's the habit of ly-

Baby John William Rollins about 1917, son of William Henry Rollins and Claudia Nance Rollins. (*Rollins Family Photo Collection*)

Claudia Nance's family in 1896. *Left to right:* John Ashbury Nance (with two dogs); *Standing:* Mary Emma (Scott) Nance, Claudia Ann, William Madison, Lillie Dale. *Seated left to right:* Robert Nance, with Bertha Statirah on his lap; Statirah Elizabeth (Weatherly) Nance; William Osborn with Mary Lou on his lap. Both Claudia Ann and Mary Lou would marry Rollins boys. (*Rollins Family Photo Collection*)

The Nance family in their Sunday best, about 1905. Claudia Ann is seated in the front row, third from the right, next to her mother, Mary Emma. Their father, Robert, had just died. (*Rollins Family Photo Collection*)

The Rollins family in 1911. Claudia Nance has just joined the family and stands next to Henry, *top row far left*. Seated are the parents, mother Roxie Elaine on the right and John Franklin Rollins on the left. The children (*counterclockwise*) are Theodore Roosevelt, Oscar Charles, Herschel Eugene (on his mother's lap), Edd Waters, John Frank Jr., and Walter Fredrick. After his mother, Claudia, John Franklin was to be the most powerful and benign influence in young John's life. (*Rollins Family Photo Collection*)

Double first cousins, Madison Nance (*left*) and John W. Rollins (*right*), age 14. Photo taken about 1930. (*Rollins Family Photo Collection*)

Amy Grace Crum, six years before she married Wayne in 1931. (*Rollins Family Photo Collection*)

John and Wayne with their father, William Henry, shortly before his death. (*Rollins Family Photo Collection*)

John in 1942, fondly holding his first child, John W. Rollins Jr. (*Rollins Family Photo Collection*)

John in front of his first Ford agency in 1949. The drab building with its single gas pump belies how much he had already accomplished. (*Rollins Family Photo Collection*)

Listing Rollins Broadcasting on the American Exchange. *From left:* John, Madalyn Copely, American Exchange President Edward McCormick, Wayne, and the indispensable Henry Tippie. Ms. Copely was the chief operations officer of Rollins Broadcasting, the first woman in Delaware with a corporate job at that level. (*Courtesy of the American Exchange*)

John Jr., Kitty (Rollins) Muir, Cathy Rollins, and Patrick Rollins campaigning for their father. (*Rollins Family Photo Collection*)

John when he ran for lieutenant governor of Delaware. Senator John Williams wanted him to run because he was too new on the scene to have made political enemies. (*Seawell-Paul A. Hesse Studios*)

John, in front of the Rollins building that brought both class and controversy to Wilmington's Concord Pike. (*John Carter/Delaware Today Magazine*)

Michele Metrinko as Miss USA-World, 1963–64. (*Official Miss USA-World Photo, Miss World Pageant*)

John W. Rollins Sr. and Michele Metrinko Rollins in their first year of marriage. (*Willard Stewart*)

ing that introduces a wobble in one's advance, and life is too short
for detours. The best defense is to go straight along the course that
conscience dictates.

The habit of losing no time trained the brothers to decide on a
course of action quickly. This particular habit laid the groundwork for
everything that followed. Grandma Emma taught Wayne that all he
had to do was work fifty percent longer to be fifty percent better. In her
view, the most well-rehearsed opposition could be overcome through
time and effort alone. Time was at least as important as talent.

Wayne was twenty-three when he landed his first real job. It was
1935, and the stretchout system was in full swing. The work he got in
a local thread mill was a piece of sheer luck. He was hired only because his Uncle Fred, gamely doing the work of two men, assured the
foreman that Wayne was ready to do the same.

Wayne understood that he had to make himself indispensable. He
made a point of coming early, finding tasks that needed doing (even if
it was only sweeping the floor), and leaving very late. To hang onto that
job, he did what Claudia, Emma, and Horatio Alger had instructed him
to do. The idea was simple but its execution took considerable stam-
ina. It required a submersion of the self rare today. As he would later
point out, once a habit has been established the will is free to seize on
a new task, harder and more complex than the one before it.

Wayne's first job was to operate a twister, a machine that wound
yarns into thread. The company had cut back so brutally on its work
force that he was obliged to operate four machines at the same time.
These twisters were antiquated devices that broke down constantly.
He had to repair the ailing machines while somehow keeping the others producing thread.

Sam Ray, his coworker, was supposed to operate an identical set of
four machines. But after a half hour or so, Sam would curl up in a
crate full of yarn and sleep until morning, leaving young Wayne to do
his work.

"I'd go over and I'd say, 'Sam! Sam, wake up!'

"And he'd say, 'I'm not asleep. Just resting my eyes.'

"Now that was my first job. I didn't know how people did. I only
knew I was supposed to work. I thought it was his boss's job to check
on him. But his boss had no reason to do that because I was running
his twisters as well as mine."

Waking just in time to greet the morning shift, Sam would make
himself presentable and put on a welcoming smile for the oncoming

crew. After a few months the company laid Wayne off. With things going so well they calculated one more cutback wouldn't hurt.

"That was my first experience of working for a company of any size.
And I thought, 'Gee, is this the way the world runs?' I was a very disappointed young fellow."

It took two weeks for the company bosses to realize they had gotten rid of the wrong man. Then they fired old Sam Ray and brought
Wayne back. He was now put to work on all eight twisters, which was
not exactly fair. Still, he had a powerful reason to keep going: every
time he glanced out the window at the yard below, he'd see fifty or
sixty unemployed men lined up. Years later he'd remember the sight
of the shift boss, Henry Egler, driving up each morning and parking
his car in the shed. Egler would walk past the long line of huddled,
silent men with his face slightly averted. Moving briskly, slowly shak-
ing his head, he would murmur, "Sorry, not today. Nope. Sorry. Don't
have a thing for you. Sorry."

By the time John graduated from high school in 1934, Wayne had
worked his way up to thread mill supervisor. He was earning enough
to buy some farm land just south of the state line below Chattanooga.
There he intended to build his parents a more spacious house. Later,
he and John would pool their money to buy Catoosa Springs. Wayne
intended to peddle water from the springs which contained seventeen different combinations of minerals. At the center of the springs
is a clear lake that mirrors the surrounding stands of evergreen and
maple. "There are four springs going into that lake," Wayne points
out. "One of those was arsenic water. 'Beauty water' was what they
called it. . . . It cuts down the red blood cells."

During the Civil War wounded soldiers were hospitalized at the
springs. A large hotel had existed there in the nineteenth century.
The Battle of Chicamauga took place about ten miles to the west in
1864. Catoosa lies at the heart of the region where the Rollins boys
were raised, a small region, comprising about ten square miles just
east of Interstate 75, marked off by Ringgold to the west, Cohutta on
the state line to the north, and Dalton to the south. Catoosa with its
evergreens, rolling hills and reflecting pools breathes serenity and
calm. Wayne would return there throughout his life. Claudia would
live there after their father died. Wayne's grandchild, Rita, would
come to a violent and sudden death there.

In his early twenties, John was a compendium of happy contradictions. A farmboy, a lover of inspirational poets (Kipling, Emerson),

an excellent athlete (runner-up in the statewide basketball championship), a born raconteur and stand-up comic, a wild-eyed optimist.

While John was still in high school, Grace had begun fabricating rugs to sell. She remembers him then as "just a big overgrown boy." If Wayne was reflective and more than a little remote, John was irrepressible and hyperactive, outgoing to say the least. He tried his hand at selling bedspreads. As a sales incentive, he gave away tins of Bruton Snuff. The cost of the snuff put him out of business. "My first lesson was that you've got to have more coming in than going out, or you went broke quick."

The Depression was at its bleakest. The lines of men outside the mills grew even longer. John had no choice but to join them, but he didn't stand there long. The bright thought came to him that standing in line was doing nothing. Unless you were actually accosting someone who had a job to offer you weren't doing anything. He tramped around looking for such a person and intercepted the owner of the Peerless Woolen Mill crossing the street. "Mr. Huchinson," he said. "I need a job. I have to have a job. My father's had a stroke. I've got to support him. And I'm trying to go to college at night."

Huchinson said, "Go up and see Hugh Hickey, and tell him I said you need a job."

Hickey was a sadist with a giant potbelly and sour disposition, an ideal representative of the era. He took immediate exception to John's smiling face and sent him to work under a rock crusher. His job was to toss out the crushed stone with a scoop as it tumbled down from above. "See how you like that," said Hickey, turning up the machine to its maximum velocity.

John soon realized there was no way he could keep up with the machine. The danger of being buried alive by the rain of stones was real. But after all the fuss he'd made, he believed his only recourse was to keep going till he dropped. Shovelling as fast and hard as he could, he breathed rock dust and spouted sweat. The machine overheated. Its metal guts seized up and it clattered to a stop. Thankful not to have been buried under a ton of stone, John crawled out and said cheerfully, "Is that all there is to it, sir? I really like this job."

This show of bravado earned John the worst jobs that Hickey could devise. So John went out of his way to ask for them. If there was heavy pipe to move, or a filthy boiler that needed scrubbing out, he'd be the first to volunteer. Hickey would get suspicious. He figured John must be angling for some advantage, trying to get away with something. The result was lighter work for a time.

Then Hickey came up with a real stretchout special. He put John with half a dozen other men in a ditch and told them he would fire the three that did the least digging at the end of each day. John, young and strong, outperformed the others and survived through the summer.

He was then hired away from the grotesque Hickey by the owner's son who needed a bottle washer at his dairy. When John sliced open his hand on a broken bottle, he was kicked up to assistant manager and moved out to live with the estate manager. The manager had four beautiful daughters and John was looking forward to living near these delectable creatures in their big white house. But he was led around back to a chicken coop and told he would sleep there. If he preferred it clean, he was welcome to clean up what the chickens had left behind before he moved in his cot.

Wayne, earning the princely sum of ten dollars a week at the thread mill, had picked up a secondhand car. It was his first vehicle, a source of great pride. John borrowed the car one Sunday to impress the youngest of the girls in the white house, and cracked an axle negotiating a pothole. This injury to his car caused Wayne so much anguish that for the rest of his life he was reluctant to let John drive any car he owned. Wayne loved automobiles as much as he hated selling them. (When he died he left a garage full of well preserved, if ancient, models standing idle.)

John regarded the car as a convenience merely. He disliked driving and hired a chauffeur as soon as he could afford one—but that moment still lay years in the future. A legendary car salesman in his day, he regarded driving as a waste of time in a life that would be too short for everything he intended to accomplish.

Like most working men in the thirties, John labored six and seven days a week, rising at two in the morning to check the milk trucks and laboring until six in the evening. When he had a free hour he laid quarry stone in a creek bed on the property.

One morning, exhausted, he fell asleep at the wheel and launched himself and forty gallons of milk over a high embankment and through a telephone pole. The severed pole took out the brand-new phone system installed the length of the valley. The truck was a total wreck. Milk poured downhill in a rain of broken glass. Though he wore no seatbelt, he was unhurt.

He trudged back to the office to get himself fired. He was ordered to sit outside on a bench and wait for the boss to do the honors. While he slumped there in woeful dejection, the president of the Dyer Cor-

poration, one George T. Smith, stopped and asked why he was looking so glum. "Not your style, is it?"

He confessed that he'd destroyed a company truck, spilled forty
gallons of milk, interrupted phone service throughout the entire valley and was waiting to be fired. After talking to him for awhile, Smith
stood up to leave. "Now my brother is the superintendent at Com-
bustion Engineering. Tell him I sent you. Maybe he can find something for you to do."

This piece of good luck landed John a job so bad that he wished
he was back with Hickey. The company hired him to secrete himself
inside metal vessels to grind the welds smooth. There he labored all
day every day, under a fine shower of metal dust. His only relief came
when he fired the boiler behind the plant and removed its ash out to
the city dump. Brooding over small fires at the dump were groups of
hoboes drinking sterno—an alcoholic concoction used to heat
portable stoves.

Dumping the ash one day, John picked up a rag of newspaper and
his eye fell on the following literary gem, which he will still recite to
anyone who wants to hear it:

> You may know your economics,
> Your philosophers and such,
> But all the knowledge
> You have gathered
> Won't amount to much,
> Unless you've got the courage
> Of the factory or the shop,
> And can climb the ladder
> From the bottom to the top.

Standing there in that field of ashes, his body and face saturated
with metal fragments, John felt that no job could be worse then this.
"And then," he says, "it hit me what a wonderful future I had. Because
no one had a worse job. And no matter what I did, it was going to be
an improvement. The only place I could go was up." Never has the
philosophy of optimism been more concisely defined.

Somehow, John found time to become president of the Industrial
Basketball League and eventually talked a station manager into giving him a job as a radio announcer so he could broadcast play-by-play
accounts of local baseball games over a Chattanooga station. It was
the era when baseball truly was the national sport. Every mill had its
own team and anyone with some ability could play. To broaden his

broadcasting venue, John started a poetry-reading program. And he was made a foreman at his plant.

Wayne always insisted that John was born lucky. John recalls himself as "kind of a smart ass, being a boss at that age. I wore a pair of coveralls and straw hat. There was a pipefitter, a monster of a man, who tried to give me some technical advice. I told him he was full of shit, and he smacked me halfway across the room. And lying there, I thought, 'Now do I get up and fight like a hero, or just lie here and pretend I'm knocked out?' I didn't stir."

It was company policy that any worker who hit a superior was automatically fired.

Soon I got a call to come up and see Mr. Fred Krouse. He was something of a genius. A self-educated man from Cleveland, who'd made outstanding designs for water-cooled boilers. He said, "Rollins, I hear you've been fighting."

"I said, "No, sir."

"Well, what happened then?"

I said, "I said something I shouldn't have said and someone smacked me good."

"What"s his name?'

I said, "Mr. Krouse, I'm not going to tell you. Because it isn't his fault. He probably just had a bad night, or I would have got away with it."

"You mean you refuse to give me the name of a man I'm asking for directly?"

I said, "Yes, sir. That's it."

He looked at me a minute. Then he said, "Get out of here, Rollins, and grow up!"

An attractive hometown girl he'd often eyed from afar stopped John on the street one evening and said she'd heard he was driving down home. Would he give her a ride to Dalton? Dalton was only a few miles south of his parents' farm. He said it would be his pleasure. As they bumped happily along in his Ford, she pointed out a roadhouse and suggested they stop for a little pick-me-up and some dancing. It wasn't his neighborhood, but he figured her insistence augured well for their immediate future.

"I was out on the floor dancing with her when she whispers, 'Oh dear me, there's my husband.'

"I said, 'Hold on. Since when are you married?'

"She says, 'Some time now, I reckon. It's just we don't get on none too well.'"

In those steep hills, young men don't appreciate strangers, especially a stranger pressing some local hero's wife to his chest. John recognized this husband as somebody that one of the Rollins cousins had run out of their neck of the woods. Worse, a sullen crowd had gathered and were examining him closely as he twirled the wife around. When the music stopped, she murmured something about having to go somewhere and was quickly absorbed into the surrounding wall of male bodies. John was beginning to feel claustrophobic.

He started to push his way outside, trailed by a crowd of glowering locals who pressed close around him in the parking lot. Then the woman's husband, hefting a knife, was extruded from the pack.

"And about the time her husband is pulling his knife, a small car pulls up with its radiator shooting off steam," John recalls. Attention was diverted from John as a platoon of very large men began to extricate themselves from this vehicle—two machinists he knew well, three boilermakers of equally mature acquaintance, and a pipe fitter with a lantern jaw.

"They were from my plant. I was never so glad to see a car full of drunks in my life. 'Trouble, John?' they said. 'Go away and we'll take care of this.'" Seeing no good reason to stick around, he left them to enjoy themselves in his absence. Escapes like this convinced Wayne his brother was born lucky.

By the time he moved on four years later, John had been elevated to the position of assistant to the superintendent. He was beginning to gain some measure of himself. If nothing else, he knew a lot about boilers, but he had no long-range plan. Complex, long-range ideas carefully worked out would always strike John as an elaborate excuse for not getting on with the job at hand. That some of his sudden flights of fancy required a lifetime to bring to fruition is true, but he apparently takes pleasure in solving problems that would drive many men mad. He has found that success requires an extraordinary patience and staying power. Some of his impulsive ideas have demanded years of tender adjustment, political tact, and millions in investment before they matured into working propositions.

7
The Precipice Is a Path

When John was twenty-three he applied for a government job as an ordinance inspector at the government's Watertown Arsenal in Massachusetts. It was a modest civil-service job that required a college degree. He submitted work affidavits that testified to his practical experience and records from correspondence courses taken and night school attended. He was turned down. He kept coming back over a period of two years. They gave up and accepted him the thirteenth time around.

Having battered his way through to his first decent job, he worked his way up to assistant assembly superintendent at $18 a week. John arrived having a lot more practical experience than his fellow inspectors. The bosses quickly jumped his grade from a junior to an associate inspector and selected him for special training, in case of war. His salary leaped from $1,620 to $1,800 a year. He can't recall all the companies he has since bought and sold, but that first pay raise is burned into his memory.

When he left the farm and learned the boilermaker's trade, John leapt across centuries. At the Watertown Arsenal, he arrived in a nineteenth-century world devoted to heavy manufacture and old-fashioned warfare. He was making his way past the stations of the industrial revolution.

The ordnance department was unprepared for war. Faithfully reflecting the isolationist sentiment of its people, the United States had washed its hands of Europe while England and France fed small nations to Germany to keep Hitler plump and happy. The people who didn't think war was inevitable included the leaders of the great European democracies. Neville Chamberlain fairly grovelled before Hitler. Franklin Roosevelt assumed the worst was coming, but his countrymen were loath to involve themselves in Europe's insanity. As an inspector at the arsenal, John stood in line to shake the hand of President Roosevelt, the first of nine presidents he would eventually meet.

The atmosphere at the arsenal was uneasy. "We could see how ill prepared we were," John recalls. "We had nothing. In 1940 the U.S. had seven 37mm antiaircraft guns and a single 90mm." After Germany overran Poland, Belgium and France, it seemed inevitable that Britain would fall next. The United States began to ship tanks and planes to Britain behind the backs of its own citizens. John went to Lukins Steel as deputy chief inspector and was then picked by Booz Allen & Hamilton to work for the Crosley Company as their chief expediter. He was promoted to director of planning for the Air Corp's Quartermaster Division. With the war now spreading around the planet, his job was to procure metals for airplanes, tank turrets, bomb releases and various technical devices employed to make war.

At Lukins he found plant production was bogging down in government forms and reports. Struggling to cut through the red tape, John worked out a supply route that was bureaucrat-proof. Instead of filling out an array of forms in quadruplicate, he told his people to mark the defects on the steel itself. He shipped back defective material minutes after it arrived, employing the same vehicles that trucked it in. This simple innovation cut a turnaround of ninety days down to three, and his division received a series of awards for its high production figures.

In charge of his own department, John quickly realized how workers' initiative was undercut by poor organization. He was astonished at the creative energy some workers expended in devising complicated ploys in order to do nothing whatever.

"Every time I walked out of my office there was this one man, and he'd damn near run me over with his wheelbarrow. That must have gone on for a year. Finally, I started thinking—how is he at my door every time I come out? So I trailed him. And he was going around, hauling that same load all day. He'd just stay out of sight. And when I opened the door, he'd head right for me. He actually had me thinking I should give him a raise."

Both Rollins brothers had complete faith in the redemptive nature of work. They would agree with the Chinese sage who said that employment of the will keeps one open to the influence of heaven. Slacking off on the job expressed a distrust of life and closed doors that open into the future. Their credo was, "Always do more than people expect."

Wayne's and John's rural faith in self-reliance, their pull-yourself-up-by-your-own-bootstraps optimism, is expressed in the old-fashioned rules that make up "The Berry College Code." Claudia would have approved entirely. "I promise at all times," the first sentence of the code runs, "to keep my *clothes,* my *body* and my *mind* clean. I will always cultivate these habits which will help me to become *strong physically, mentally* and *morally,* but I will *spurn* those which will harm me." "Order is Heaven's first law," says the Berry College Code.

Cut off from Europe and the past by the Atlantic, the United States of the late thirties seems from our vantage a land vastly innocent. In Europe entropy was god. Paradise lay in the senses alone. Idealism had degenerated into Bolshevism. In the short stories he wrote after the First World War, Ernest Hemingway describes how meaningless any activity whatever appeared to men returning from the battlefields of Europe. Men like John and Wayne Rollins reflect an understanding of things diametrically opposed to the defeatism across the sea.

The Second World War turned loose the surging energy bottled up by America's long isolationism. The nation's response to fascism was to wake up to the world. Young and old streamed off the farms into the cities, the factories, the barracks. Technological invention was given an enormous boost by the threat of Adolf Hitler. Young men who would have been confined to the farm a generation earlier were turned, virtually overnight, into managers, parachutists, foreign-language experts, engineers, biologists, and ball turret gunners. Those who knew nothing but the strip of ploughed field where they'd grown up were picked up like chessmen and put into play on the stage of world history. At the same time, demagogues all over the South fell silent, because the greatest demagogue of them all had surfaced in Berlin. Hitler made even those avatars of southern reaction and racism, Senator Bilbo and Little Ed Rivers, look like small potatoes.

The war was the catalyst that rocketed Americans into responsibility for the disorganized world they would rather have ignored. The productive capacity organized along a conveyor belt by Henry Ford now became universal. Manufacturing enough machinery to put down Hitler and Tojo demanded an economic engine of gargantuan proportions. Technology will always inspire dreams of absolute mastery, and only unconditional victory was acceptable to the warmongers. The war economy (which business would later inherit) was created in the space of a few months.

For anyone with a flair for organization, it was a glorious time to be alive. Every trade, science, art and commercial institution was linked to a single aim. The nation state was enjoying its last big splurge. But for the first time in history, the state depended more on machines than manpower. More than the military, the economy was the nation's source of strength.

The bombing of the U.S. Fleet at Pearl Harbor led to a desperate scramble as factories across the nation retooled for major conflict. Suddenly, no one was interested in college diplomas; experience alone counted. Technical expertise that took half a lifetime to acquire in peacetime was now passed along in days or weeks. The whole nation underwent massive basic training. Playing his own vital part in the war effort, John moved up rapidly from Lukins to the Crosley Company in Cincinnati as director of planning. Crosley was switching from refrigerator manufacture to the fabrication of gunsights and proximity fuses.

Planes were being grounded because of a shortage of critical steel, manufactured in Knoxville, Tennessee, used for bomb releases. Because of the delays, John went down to Knoxville one Friday to meet with the sales manager and get the steel moving north more quickly. The manager claimed he was too busy to see him. John walked upstairs and banged on the door of the head of the company, Dick Vanbanshoten (a name he would find it impossible to forget).

Vanbanshoten said he was willing to do whatever it took to move things along. John said, "If you'll just run the steel, I'll have trucks in here and have it made into bomb releases the next day."

Vanbanshoten said he had steel, but it wasn't the steel ordinarily used to fabricate bomb releases. A chemical analysis would have to be made. But that would take days. John looked at the steel and said it looked fine to him. He thought it might even be better than the usual run—more alloy, less carbon. He guessed he was getting a superior steel for the same price. But he wasn't entirely certain. He decided to take the risk.

The steel was shipped. "I was feeling very cocky and proud of myself." But the government inspector looked at the bomb sights and wouldn't pass them. "Wrong type steel," he said. The man had been a paper carton inspector before the war. He knew what he was looking for, but not what he was looking at.

John was hauled into the head office and told he'd bought the wrong steel. Did he have any idea what he was doing? John protested he'd gotten better steel for the same money.

"How did you know that?"
"I looked at it. It's high alloy."

"Well, that's right. It is. But what would you have done if you'd been wrong?"

"I don't know."

"Get out of here, Rollins."

When he'd been elevated to director of planning, John Rollins found himself responsible for thousands of different aircraft parts. His salary rose from $3,900 to $5,000 a year. The work was vital to the war effort and probably would have kept him from the draft in any case, but with a wife, children, and two parents to support, he was fully exempt.

He left Crosley in 1943, and went to Bendix Radio in Baltimore. Not yet thirty, he was put in charge of three plants, seven days a week. With the war raging, his can-do style worked well. In dangerous times the supreme realist comes into his own, while bureaucrats get in the way. But as the war in the Pacific began to wind down, priorities shifted. Company politics came back into play.

He left Bendix, where things were bogging down. He found himself doing the work of the man who was supposed to be his boss. "He'd come in three hours after I'd arrived and hand his secretary his glasses to clean. I never had enough hours in the day and I was running like hell. And he'd go to lunch about 11:30 and come back at 2:30, and then go home at 4:30. I just got tired of it."

John moved to Glenn L. Martin, another Baltimore company. They needed someone to organize their conversion to peacetime operations. Ed Foster, his boss at Bendix, begged him to stay on, saying he wanted to make John the company's head of sales. Even after John left, Foster kept mailing him paychecks.

"Damn it, Ed, I'm not coming back," John would say and send back the checks.

"No, no, you're coming back," Foster insisted. This ping-pong of checks in the mail went on until Foster fell victim to company politics and was fired.

Glenn Martin interviewed John for the position of vice president in charge of manufacturing. In John's view, the conversion of these companies to peacetime manufacturing consisted of replacing efficiency with politics. Glenn Martin had run into trouble with its financing and fallen out with the banks. Their closed-door policy made it impossible to converse freely with the brass. He felt it was time for something new, something completely different.

Still in his twenties, John was tired of working for other people. He

had an idea he might start a business of his own, but he didn't have
a clue what business. All the money he'd saved had gone into Catoosa
Springs, the land he'd bought with Wayne. Henry Rollins died in the
last year of the war. Claudia began to travel back and forth between
John in Delaware and Wayne in Georgia. Her permanent home was
a little house built on a rise above the Catoosa Springs.

A photograph of Henry and his two boys sits today in John's inner
office. All three men are wearing suits. The breast pocket of Wayne's
coat is crammed with pens and pencils. The faces of both young men
radiate a restless energy of the sort exhibited by Roman statuary, or
Holbein's portrait of Renaissance merchants. Their father wears an
uneasy look, as if he already spies death approaching in the middle
distance. Forced to forgo his brief years of physical well-being for the
life of an invalid, he must have reflected on the claustrophobic nature of human fate. His sons look charged up and ready to make up
for everything the old man was denied.

In about the same time it takes a college undergraduate to earn a
degree, World War II gave John an education in modern plant management. Like his brother, he made a habit of arriving an hour before starting time and going home an hour after the last whistle.
When Grandma Emma had said spend twice the time and you'll be
twice as good, the boys believed her.

John maintains today that anybody who worked the hours he did
would do just as well. But few have his enthusiasm for long hours, or
his ability to discover in some picayune job an opportunity for invention and self-improvement. Most people would feel demeaned by
the routine work he did in his youth. But what both brothers brought
to the job, besides their drive, was imagination. Wayne's first work in
the thread mill was pushing a broom. But he pushed it with efficiency
and grace and it's amazing how soon a job well done draws favorable
attention.

Disorder, John realized on the farm, was forever gaining. A man
might choose to see this as a curse, or an opportunity. The greatest
disorder inevitably surfaced in the people one had to work with. "A
critical factor for making it in almost any field is understanding
people—what makes them tick, what motivates them," John says.
"Youngsters in a small community get to know and understand all
kinds of people much better than their 'city-slicker' cousins. Lives of
people in smaller towns are more open. In the city, even neighbors
are anonymous.

"In a small town a young man or woman can try their hand at work early in life." The small town, he concludes, is a great arena for "generating good work habits, and acquiring common sense." The small town he is talking about is, of course, virtually extinct.

His experience at plants like Crosley and Glenn Martin made him aware that bureaucracy was often the worm in the works. John instinctively organized his workforce to offset the weaknesses of some with the strength in others. He could study a room full of faces and get a pretty good feel for their collective capability. He had a gift for cutting to the heart of a problem in an organization, and everyone who knows him well remarks on this.

Back on the farm, everyone had figured John for a great big, likable farm boy who would have a wonderful time going nowhere in particular. He was too gabby and full of good humor. His peculiar genius for picking out the best line of action in a complex field of events was not the sort of thing that sticks out like musical talent or good looks. Randall, John's nephew, remembers the day John left home in an old rattletrap Ford. He'd made all kinds of absurd promises—said he'd come back, like one of Horatio Alger's heroes, and put his parents in a big new house, and buy his mother more clothes than she'd ever dreamed she'd have. Randall still smiles when he recalls the wild-eyed optimism, and then John driving off in a cloud of dust.

Those back in Georgia must have been astonished when news came that John was snapping up car dealerships all over the Mid-Atlantic. How was he doing it when he didn't own a plug nickel? What marked him apart from most businessmen was his disinterest in money as such. As a wage earner, he'd spent every penny. When he started up his first business, he operated by borrowing whatever the banks were willing to lend. From the outset he treated money as a tool, never as an end in itself. It was the game that interested him. He thrived on the challenge. Where others saw a precipice, he saw a path. Climbing a cliff demands a person who can concentrate fully on the moment while keeping in mind what lies ahead. It's also important not to look back.

8
High Explosives

Wayne never could adapt himself to the midnight-to-sunrise grave-yard shift. Born with a farmer's internal clock, he hated sleeping during the day. He couldn't do it. He was plant manager, but the boss told him the manager on the day shift would have to die before he could take his place. "I don't think that anyone should be waiting for a fella to die," Wayne says. "Unless maybe you're an undertaker."

In 1942, he got work at the Hercules Powder Company. Hercules mixed high explosives for the war effort. They sent him out to Kanka-kee, Illinois, to learn how TNT (trinitrotuluene) was made, then back to Tennessee where he was put on the line. Having studied briefly at the University of Chattanooga, Wayne knew a little chemistry. He never found time to complete the course for credit, but the mixing and manufacture of high explosives didn't offer too great an intellectual challenge.

TNT is composed of toluene, a substance resembling diesel fuel, nitrated to resemble picric acid, dried into flakes for storage, then melted down to pour into shell casings. It explodes under pressure. To illustrate its power, students were taken to see a pound of the stuff exploded. "They'd put a pound of that dust in a bag and put it in one of these big three-hole toilets . . . That toilet just disintegrated. There wouldn't even be a splinter left. Just dust."

The plant consisted of sixteen assembly lines, each housed in a separate building made of earthen walls poured into wood frames. The storage area was spread over 24,000 acres, and the finished product was stored in bunkers under mounds of earth. Wayne recalls that each line produced 2,400 fifty-pound boxes of TNT a day, so that the factory total was 38,400 boxes, or some 960 tons of explosives every twenty-four hours. If his memory serves him well, the plant was producing 336,000 tons of TNT every year. At the time several such plants were contributing to the rain of fire falling on Berlin, Hamburg, Dresden, and Tokyo.

To keep from blowing themselves up, the workers had to conform to an order more absolute than any monastery. The manufacture of TNT meant wearing wool clothing even on the hottest summer days. In theory, wool didn't spark and reduced the danger of an explosion. The factory floor was pure lead. This oxidized so quickly they had to scrub it continuously with steel wool to keep it bright. The brass fittings and risers were being polished perpetually, the interior continuously repainted. Nothing could be left lying around, no lunch buckets, ladders, pop bottles, rolls of fire hose.

In front of each building, signal flags indicated which crews had been awarded best housekeeping, best safety, best TNT quality, and most quantity. There was a separate flag for each category. Wayne was soon made line foreman and decided his building should win all the flags simultaneously. And somehow, he got his workmen so juiced up that they did. He was quickly advanced to supervisor of two lines, then three. By the end of the war he was running the entire plant. That he broke every record in the nation for TNT production helps account for his rapid rise.

Like his younger brother, he increased production by breaking through the procedural runaround. After being mixed in ovens, the hot TNT was cooled and "flaked" in a tower. Dumped into the tower, it cooled as it fell. Wayne figured he could cut down the cooling time by dropping the TNT through the tower from a higher level. The government wanted the final cooling stage to take place in a storage box. But this took more time. By quick-cooling the material in the tower, Wayne ran his production figures way up.

One Sunday, he was working with a man called Big 'Un Howard, "six-foot-six, and rough as a cob." Big 'Un had been in the moonshine business before he began making TNT. Wayne got Big 'Un all fired up to break the record. They were going full tilt, running up the steps to the higher drop point with their boxes of TNT, when the supervisor, R. King Stone, appeared on the scene. Wayne told the supervisor he was trying to break the record and suggested he might like to be part of an historic event.

Stone didn't know enough to realize he was breaking the rules. He got the spirit and was soon running up and down as fast as he could, pouring the mix into the flaker. Then, "Lo and behold, we're joined by a government man, the safety inspector, Sharp. And Stone says to Sharp, 'Grab a box, come on, Sharp! We're gonna break a record today.'"

And break the record they did, coming in twenty-five percent over the previous winner. But their success made the engineers on the project suspicious. The engineers were known among the workers as the "slide rule gang," or "the semi-hemi-demis," because they sliced every problem into quantified bits. These gentlemen calculated it was impossible to make TNT that fast and demanded an official investigation. Mr. R. King Stone was shown a number of graphs proving their point and asked to arbitrate the matter. The graphs indicated that some rule had been broken, some redline exceeded.

Wayne assumed it was all over for him. "I knew when they called me up to explain, I was going to tell the truth." And after the "semi-hemi-demis" had presented their case, he was ordered up to the front of the room. "So I went up there and I sat down in front of Stone. But I believe he'd figured it out while I was making my way to the hot seat, because he suddenly bellows, 'Hell, I don't see anything in this! Let's all stop wasting time and get back to work. Case dismissed!'"

Wayne tried to get his process made official procedure, but the paper he wrote outlining his improved method was ignored. Because pumps often burned out and halted production, he designed a new valve that would keep the plant producing if a pump went down. His design was swallowed by the bureaucracy. Experiences like this soured Wayne permanently on government efficiency. He came to believe that government process and efficiency are antithetical terms. "I've been burned more than once by government bureaucracy. That was only the first time I was exposed to it."

The high wages generated by war industry made it possible for both Rollins brothers to save money. While the money paid them abruptly increased by ten and twentyfold, the concept of disposable income was alien to their upbringing. John, a born big spender, adapted instantly to modern economic thinking. Wayne was far less flexible. He put every spare penny he'd saved into property, though he knew from bitter experience how hard it was to make a living off the land. But land was in his blood.

The agrarian ideal had been out of phase with the rising tide of commerce for a century by then. Wayne's father-in-law, Jim Crum, had eked out his existence on forty acres, never adding another square foot to the property, religiously paying for every nail and two-by-four with hard cash. When Grace married Wayne, she expected they would spend the rest of their lives on the land.

In 1933, Wayne's last year as a full-time farmer, his income totaled $153. "I got beat into the ground so bad that I've been trying to get even ever since. You could look back at my parents' generation and see they'd never accomplished very much by farming. I didn't realize

that at the time. I did later. We'd have been better off to have given
our farm away, gone to Indiana and rented a farm, than to try to make
a living on our own farm. The soil, the size, that rough ground, never."

Like most American farmers, Wayne was given to some brooding
over resources. He was convinced that "there'll be a shortage of water quicker than there will be a shortage of food." After buying
Catoosa Springs, he was always irked that he'd missed buying Yates
Spring at the head of Chickamauga Creek, which flows into the Tennessee River. Yates Spring eventually became a source of water for all
of Catoosa County.

He was soon forced to quit farming, but farming never entirely quit
Wayne. He grew vegetables on the lot adjacent to the house he and
Grace built on a $200 parcel of land in Lakeview near Rossville, Geor-
gia. Years later, a millionaire many times over, he was still trying to
grow corn in Florida, though it never worked out and he always lost
money.

Grace spent the Depression tilling the soil and hooking rugs. Then
she got work as an inspector at the textile mill during the war. With
the surfeit from two incomes, the couple bought four hundred acres
for $50 an acre in Cherokee Valley. There they raised hay and corn.
As for Catoosa Springs, Wayne and John (who put up half the money)
planned to bottle and sell its mineral water as soon as the war was over.

By the end of 1945, Wayne was bottling water full time. Even before
the war was over, he and his son Randall were delivering Catoosa spring
water to Atlanta, and as far north as Cleveland, Tennessee. They soon
pushed on into Alabama and Florida. But no matter how much water
they sold, their profit margin proved as sluggish as an old alligator.

"The product doesn't cost you anything. You only have bottling
and transport. But everything is always the same whether you sell one
thousand or ten thousand gallons. The problem of the water business
is volume doesn't get you any more margin. It costs the effort to deliver this gallon of water, to bottle it and everything—the same thing.
The product's not costing you that much. But you got that same cost
of the truck and everything. If you put another man and another bottle, you just can't change your margins." In other words, the business
was not like manufacturing or a service industry where greater sales
mean lower costs per unit, which in turn create higher profits.

Had the five-gallon bottles been less awkward to handle, Wayne
might have dabbled in spring water longer. "They didn't weigh that
much, but you lift by the neck to your shoulder, and that continual

twisting did something to my back. Also, a lot of customers lived up a flight of stairs. We were up and down all day, a lot of work."

He woke one morning to find his back paralyzed. The slightest movement caused excruciating pain, and his left leg was frozen. His family eased him into a car and drove him to a chiropractor. At a hospital in Atlanta, he found himself in the same room with the famous golfer, Bobby Jones. Jones had a similar injury. Wayne, always wary, decided against an operation. Jones went under the knife, and was paralyzed for life.

Worried that his brother was not getting good medical attention, John arranged an appointment for Wayne with a highly regarded neurosurgeon in Baltimore at Johns Hopkins. John recalls, "I had just begun to make a little bit of money, and I knew some doctors at Johns Hopkins, so I took Wayne in there. And we had the chief neurosurgeon with us and Wayne says, "Doctor, I know a chiropractor who puts these discs back in.

"And I thought, oh my goodness, here I've been trying to make like I know a little something, and my brother gives a testimonial to the chief neurosurgeon on some chiropractor."

John's attitude toward the chiropractor's profession reflects that of H. L. Mencken who wrote,

> Six weeks after he leaves his job at the filling-station or abandons the steering-wheel of his motor-truck, he knows all the anatomy and physiology that he will ever learn in this world. Six weeks more, and he is as adept at all the half-Nelsons and left hooks that constitute the essence of chiropractic therapy. Soon afterward, having taken post-graduate courses in advertising, salesmanship and mental mastery, he is ready for practice.

John was caught off guard when the head neurosurgeon said, "'You know Mr. Rollins, I've done a lot of these operations, and I'd try anything before having one. I'll give you a brace prescription. If you can get by with that, fine. Meanwhile, you go ahead and visit that chiropractor.'"

Wayne had escaped the knife, but he continued to suffer excruciating pain. At thirty-three, he feared he'd end up like his father, bedridden for life. The pain was short-circuiting his ambition, draining his energy. When he used crutches to move around he suffered excruciating bolts of pain through his neck.

He began to plan a visit to Jerusalem. Grace says he'd always believed in God, but he never talked religion. With his private and essentially inscrutable nature, Wayne was not given to sharing his deepest convictions with anyone. Whether he suspected he was being tested by some higher power, or was the chance victim of bad luck, he never said.

The journey to Jerusalem was canceled after he hurt his back again. He climbed a ladder to bolt a mailbox to a tall post. Termites had eaten out the post underground, and it broke off and landed on top of him. He was paralyzed again.

He'd made visits to a chiropractor in Tifton, a Doctor Shaw, who gave him ether to relieve the pain so the doctor could "realign" his vertebrae. It was a procedure (Mencken's "half-Nelson") he had grown used to. Now Doctor Shaw suggested that he sleep on a plywood board covered with a single sheet. He was confined to this plank all through the spring of 1946, reading and staring through the window of his house at Catoosa Springs.

Wayne had a reflective side to his nature that undoubtedly helped get him through this period. Many people have remarked on his wisdom (a word not often associated with businessmen). Dr. James Laney at Emory University, whom Wayne befriended fifty years later, says that the first thing he noticed about Wayne was his eyes. Dr. Laney says, "They are not hard eyes. But they are very appraising eyes. You have the feeling that there's a lot of experience and wisdom and canniness there. . . . His capacity to reflect on his early life and draw very telling parallels to the present day is just stunning."

Raised in a society where any kind of heartfelt self-expression in a male was regarded as frailty, Wayne was never one to express his feelings in words. Like the rest of his family, he was more liable to turn what he felt into humor. His son Randall says that "You never knew what he really thought." Yet there are indications that his months of pain and enforced idleness drove Wayne to reflect on the meaning of existence.

He describes a fight he saw between a squirrel and some snakes, a battle that made a curiously profound impression on him.

> We used to have big post oak trees out in front, two or three of them. And that's where I saw the squirrel. I heard all this noise. And this old mama squirrel—snakes had got up and got in there after her young ones. And she got those snakes, bit them and killed them, and pitched them out of the tree. I went out there and looked. I didn't know what all that commotion was. She was just whipping that snake back and forth. She bit through him and killed him.
>
> And that's when I first learned about [squirrels]. They have a highway, just like we do, that they travel. They come down, jumped on mother's

house. You could hear them just patter, patter, patter, of a morning early going across that way. And they went the same way all the time. . . . Most of the time I tried to be up by that time. But they'd wake you up.

Beneath the surface of this simply told tale another meaning emerges—of some deadly force faced, beaten back, and overcome. Wayne's deepest feelings always operated undercover. He expressed them in images recovered from nature and the surrounding landscape. "I just love land and taking it and seeing what I can do with it, how I can improve it. There's an old stone church that was here during the Civil War. I just love to see what you can do with it, how you change it. I guess maybe I have the ability to see what it will look like after you change it. Certainly it makes it more valuable. But the biggest thing I approach it from is, 'How can you make it more beautiful?'"

Later in life he took to attending plays in London when he could get away. Much to Grace's discomfort, he insisted on renting rooms in ancient hotels with balky heating systems, because he was attracted by their Edwardian facades. But he was most himself when he set out to transform some wilderness tract into a cultivated field where nature and art colluded.

When Wayne found he could rise from his plywood board and walk a little, he joined John in Delaware. It was 1947. John was doing well and invited Wayne to join him. "It was always hard to get Wayne started on a thing," John says. "But once he got going, he was a blue streak."

Wayne's future didn't look particularly bright. His back was healing slowly, and he was in no mood to risk the little money he'd saved. His little brother had always been rambunctious, quick to assume big risks. Now it was young John who hired him to manage one of his auto agencies.

John drove his salesmen hard. Unless he kept tabs, they tended to drift away and end up in bars or in air conditioned movies on hot afternoons. The trick was to keep them hustling, making contacts, pushing the product. He always gave big bonuses, prizes, ran contests. Wayne occasionally suggested that maybe John should slow down and consider where he was going. "Go after the things that will make or break you. Separate the incidentals from the fundamentals. That will get you to the root of the problem."

But John says it's always much easier to formulate than to actually operate. Pick out a goal and keep moving, and you'll end up doing something right. Think about it too much and you end up very thoughtful. His preternatural energy, gift of gab, and business sense made him one of the most effective salesmen in the state of Delaware.

Perhaps because hoisting heavy jugs of water had weakened his back, Wayne figured it was practical for him to sell the lightest product in the universe—radio waves. John had barged in and out of radio stations for years, beginning with his sportscasts and poetry readings in Chattanooga. In Delaware, he bought air time to advertise his car sales. The idea of owning a station appealed to him. Why buy time when you could sell it?

The brothers operated easily as a team. The war had separated them, but now Wayne's injury had the happy effect of bringing them back together again. Wayne spent over a year running John's dealership in Princess Anne, and tried to talk himself into going into debt. By then John owed the banks many thousands. Wayne realized he would have to stake everything he had on his first station.

Perhaps the brothers' lack of sophistication was their greatest asset. What they actually did would probably be considered sheer madness by most. They knew almost nothing about cost control. Wayne didn't even bother to bank his checks. Like a peasant who stuffs banknotes into his mattress, he let the checks accumulate in a desk drawer. John hardly concerned himself with his mounting debt. He allowed himself a salary of twenty-five dollars a week. As long as he could out-hustle his interest payments, he was in good shape. That meant going full throttle every day of the week. Around 1948 he picked up another dealership in Princess Anne. Soon thereafter he was selling two hundred cars a month. By 1950, he was buying other dealerships and needed a plane to get around in, so the company acquired a little Beechcraft Bonanza and a pilot.

John ran this entire operation out of a single checkbook that he never bothered to reconcile at the end of each month. He had no experience in financial control, and the first accountant he hired was more interested in strong liquor than balancing figures. It was not until 1952, seven years after starting his business, that the brothers realized they could no longer continue without a first-class controller and reached outside the state, hoping that somewhere out there existed a brilliant accountant willing to live in their seaside town where the major excitement was provided by waves falling on the beach.

9
Going for Broke

Between the broad waters of the Delaware River and the wide Chesa-peake Bay a long, flat peninsula plunges due south like an excla-mation mark. The period at its terminus is Tangier Island. On Tangier they speak a curious dialect that sounds like the last re-maining version of Elizabethan English. The peninsula is cut into Delaware to the east, and Maryland to the west, and severed at its waist by an engineering marvel, the Chesapeake Canal. The region north of the canal is part of the northeast corridor, connected to the historic centers of Boston, New York, Philadelphia, Baltimore, and Washington. South of the canal are green fields, part of an Arcadian world of picturesque towns, woods, rural ideals, and down-home habits.

Maryland absorbs over half of this idyllic land. Virginia has grabbed a slice from its southernmost tip. Delaware's hundreds of jewel-like fields support wandering streams, woods, cloudscapes and marshes lined with whispering reeds. In 1945, when John arrived, it was pris-tine, as near as could be to an enchanted world.

Above the canal, the little city of Wilmington and the University of Delaware in Newark quietly turn their backs on each other. Both are intellectual centers, the first inhabited largely by chemists, bankers and lawyers; the second, at once a university village and a factory cen-ter. In the thirties, Newark was still a rural town where some Wil-mingtonians bought summer homes. Today its inhabitants are the professorate and their students, workers at the Chrysler auto plant, and people who commute to Wilmington and Philadelphia.

Further north, near the Pennsylvania state line, the reticent du Ponts live quietly on their estates in a hilly region reminiscent of the French *chateaux* country. Initially, their genius had made the state a region of dangerous explosives and well ordered greenery. The fam-ily produced great businessmen whose wives and children luxuriated in landed estates and fabulous gardens. Over time, the du Ponts wisely transformed their company from a gunpowder factory to a chemical concern and made money past mortal reckoning.

The family arrived in the United States direct from France, arriving in Newport, Rhode Island, on New Year's Day, 1800. Pierre Samuel was a philosopher hired by the infamous Talleyrand to work for the French King's mistress, Madame Pompadour. Pierre's son, Pierre Eleuthère, described himself as a "botanist." The family brought with them an enormous library and a grand piano. But their destiny was commerce. A century later their great-grandson Pierre would bark gruffly, "No man can amount to anything if he smokes cigarettes, wears a *pince nez* or plays the piano."

The Rollinses brought neither books nor pianos to Delaware. John began his first business because he couldn't get service for his Ford. Pierre Eleuthère, the first du Pont to do business in America, began work with a government contract to manufacture gunpowder. The order came from President Jefferson himself. Jefferson happened to be a friend of his father, Pierre Samuel du Pont de Nemours. The closest the Rollins family came to producing philosophers was Grandfather John F. who couldn't look at mankind without laughing, and Emma Nance, who made a kitchen-science of efficiency.

In 1945, the historical wind came from a new quarter. The high civilization that gave the du Pont family its best customers had blown itself to pieces, largely with DuPont powder. The Rollinses, by contrast, emerged from a more benign world where old-time religion was more persuasive than high culture.

Pierre Samuel had fled France to escape the guillotine. He intended to discard a corrupt and vicious land and design a better society in the wilderness. The Rollinses escaped from the wilderness into a postwar America poised for world leadership. They might be compared to rustic Etruscans stumbling into the suburbs of Rome on the brink of empire.

If John had set out to make millions he would hardly have begun his career in Lewes, Delaware. There only a dreamy unconsciousness reigned. He too was unconscious back then, and Lewes reflected his own state of mind. The streams flowing out into Lewes Bay were laden with fish. Lazy waves broke on mostly deserted beaches. The atmosphere was balmy, life indolent. Children sat on front-porch steps consuming watermelon while their mothers hung long lines of laundry in backyards. It was a place a Southerner might feel at home. The weather and the seasons were variable within temperate limits. Hurricanes were few, tornadoes unknown. If Heaven has a landscape, it probably resembles something like the southern Delaware of John's first acquaintance.

Grandfather John F. had died eight years before and John still missed him. When he befriended the sixtyish Theodore (Dory) Bryan, he may have seen him as John F.'s alter ego. Dory lacked John F.'s wisdom, but he was easygoing and contented with an existence on the margin of life. "He was great fun to be with. I loved him," John says.

John talked Dory into going into business with him and they picked up that first Ford dealership on the road out of Lewes. John painted Dory's name before his: BRYAN ROLLINS.

The Ford company was clawing its way back from a generation of declining sales. In the teens and twenties, Henry Ford had made mass production the American way. When he jacked up the pay of his workers to five dollars a day, he was cursed by big-money men all over America, but that pay hike proved a brilliant and decisive calculation. His workers now earned enough to buy the cars they were building. Thus Ford established the groundwork for the mass market that would turn the United States into an economic dynamo. Many visionaries are narrow-minded and Henry Ford was very narrow-minded. He was also irascible, mean-spirited, and opinionated. His most famous dictum was, "History is bunk." Having created the assembly line system that demanded a vast buying public, Ford then did everything in his power to stifle his own invention. An intellectual prisoner of his own parochial past, he was never able to comprehend the complex forces that brought on two world wars and the Russian Revolution. "Damned foolishness," he cried. "Do you want to know what's the cause of war? It is capitalism, greed, the dirty hunger for dollars." His was the kind of remark that satisfies without throwing much light.

Dead certain that good old Yankee horse sense could forestall the Great War, he sailed on board his famous *White Ship* to call on European politicians. He informed them that wars are unnecessary and bad for trade. The polite incredulity of the European heads of state infuriated him. They were thinking politically as Europeans always had, he was thinking economically as Americans naturally will. These Europeans were all tangled up in history and filled with notions of pride and vengeance and *lebensraum*. He thought in terms of markets.

Horrified by the specter of the technological future he'd set in motion, Ford hankered after lost simplicity. When he was told that a new generation of consumers wanted cars that had style and elegance, he flew into a rage and said he'd promise "any color, so long as it's black." By the end of his life, he'd become a Midwestern Luddite who took a crowbar to his own creation. Overhearing that a department in his own factory had hired mathematicians to do cost analyses, he picked up a sledgehammer and joined the workers he sent to smash up the office.

Until Henry's grandson took over in 1945, the Ford Company, not surprisingly, had been skidding downhill. Henry II put the company back on its feet—a stroke of luck for John Rollins. That was the year he borrowed his way into the car business, opening a Ford dealership on a dirt lot in Lewes. He recalls that Lee Iococca was then a clerk in Ford's fleet department.

The tremendous outpouring of optimism after the defeat of Germany and Japan quickly froze into the Cold War. Normalcy turned into neurosis. The bomb made the United States a superpower but in almost no time, Stalin had the bomb too.

The Cold War culture ran against the American grain. We now had a government that polluted pristine deserts with atomic waste, investigated the politics of film stars, and subsidized a CIA that, like a snake swallowing its own tail, seemed permanently unaware of what the other end was up to. A troublesome world again dragged the United States into the nightmare from which our nation had been organized to provide an escape.

The genius of the American people, however, turned even the Cold War into a business opportunity. The export of fancy weaponry became a major industry. Easy credit, as John instinctively knew, was a force not unlike the propellant that fires a rocket into space. John bought his business on credit and sold his cars on credit. Everyone in business had begun to borrow, hedging on an apparently limitless future. The nation was transforming itself into a giant Sears Roebuck with something for everybody.

Technology and the arts (in the form of advertising, market research and mass entertainment) gave business a tremendous boost. Government, swarmed over by thousands of lobbyists, grew ever more obliging. John had stepped boldly into the vacuum that pent-up demand created. New autos were flying off the assembly line, barely pausing on his lot before they drove smartly into the customer's garage.

Within two years, things were going so well that John added a

Princess Anne dealership to his Lewes original. Then came Radford, Newport News, Roanoke, Washington D.C., and Wilmington, Delaware. It was like stringing pearls; he just kept adding.

John had been selling since childhood when he peddled Cloverine Salve and buttermilk door-to-door for twenty cents a gallon. He began to experiment with ways of making his sales force efficient. "I did a simple thing. It always worked. I had them list their names on the board with the top salesman always number one. When number one fell off he was erased and moved down. And they hated like hell to see another guy above them on the board. And we'd bring those boards up-to-date every day."

He also used silver dollars. "Winners always got a prize every day. I always had incentives. But you have to follow up. We used to have the John W. Rollins Truck of the Month Club back when trucks were hard to sell. They'd fight like hell to get their names on that. You have to know where a salesman is, and you have to know who he calls. You have to help him. A man selling can get into a slump just like a baseball player. It undermines his confidence. You say, 'Let's sit down, you and me, and visit a little bit. Maybe I can help. Let's see what's been happening.' Of course the salesmen always lied like hell. But you could get them close to what they promised."

His secretary at the time, Dorothy Harrison, remembers the hours as horrendous. "Work with Mr. Rollins was nothing like it was before he came along. I mean sometimes we'd start at five in the morning and go till after dark in the winter, and till dark in the summer. I'd come in around 8:00 and get through at 6:30. Then I'd go back at 8:00 [at night], though I wasn't told to."

John recalls a workday that started at six o'clock and ran to eleven or twelve at night. His children didn't see much of him. He had four: John Jr., James, Cathy, and Patrick. He tried to keep pushing ahead with his correspondence courses too. His wife, Kitty, who typed up his academic essays, recalls, "John wasn't any beach buzzard. He was just all business."

"When I had dealerships spread over the country," he says, "I'd still try to get home Friday and Saturday night. But if you're going to take every one of your kids to every baseball game and choir practice, you'd better be rich. Money was hard to come by, and I was the whole organization in the beginning."

His frenetic pace soon wore out old Dory Bryan. Ned Davis, a longtime friend of John's in Delaware, says Dory was "an old school, mossbacked businessman. And at some point John told him, 'Dory, we're not getting anywhere. We need a line of credit to build up our inventory.'"

So Bryan put in another $10,000, borrowed from a local bank. Then he went on a short vacation to Florida to give his nerves a rest. But by the time he got back, John had spent every penny of it. And back in the forties, $10,000 was a veritable fortune. Davis recalls Dory was badly shaken. "Hell, I can't go on with this man! He's reckless! One of us is going to have to buy the other out. And I know he doesn't have any money, so I've just got to make him an offer."

According to John, this story is pure fabrication, part of the gossip still bandied about in lower Delaware. Ned says that Dory broached the subject as delicately as he could. "John, now we're good friends. But this isn't working. One of us has got to buy the other out." Local legend has it that he got no further than that. John leapt into the air and clapping his hands exuberantly, cried, "Great! How much do you want, Dory?" According to Ned, John had been trying to figure how to buy Dory out for months without hurting his feelings. Now all he had to do was borrow a whole lot more money. The way John tells the story, Dory, who was in his sixties, sold his share because he hated leaving Lewes. "I'm a hometown boy, John," he said. But it's possible, whatever spin is put on it, that their partnership gave Dory some sleepless nights.

Always hyperactive, John quickly turned himself into the king of cash flow by moving a tremendous inventory with great skill, even after the postwar passion for cars was sated. If being hugely in debt bothered him, he showed no sign. He likes to say he was too ignorant to know how much trouble he was in. He would continue to operate that way for a generation. In the late forties, he borrowed $26,000 and transferred the money to a small local bank. It was the first time he'd ever made a deposit of over $1,000. "That banker thought I was the greatest guy in the world, but it all came out of there the next working day."

He was impatient with analysis. From an accountant's vantage point, his techniques must have appeared wildly irrational. But his intuitive sense of the game kept him winning. "Once you had one [dealership] it seemed they were ready to sell you another, so I just kept buying."

He almost went broke in the late forties trying to outdazzle the competition. He began selling cars with a total service contract so generous he almost lost the shop. "If something went wrong they didn't even have to bring the car back to me. I had to go out and find them."

The finance company wouldn't repossess trucks and cars on his re-purchase agreement. That left John to fight it out with delinquent owners. "I was chasing down people in three states." He then had to buy the cars back, recondition them and unload them secondhand. "I kept seeing those headlights coming in, and all I wanted to see was tail lights going out." This was around 1950, when Ford was running into some trouble with its new models. The public found them dull and uninspired. Only raw energy kept John afloat.

In the fifties, he bought a Dodge Plymouth agency in Washington D.C. that was "not worth a damn. The Chrysler products went to hell. They just weren't selling." He'd fallen into a trap when he applied for the Ford dealership in Washington. His hotshot reputation preceded him and the local dealers went in a delegation to Detroit to complain there would be too many dealerships in town. Ford accepted their argument and withheld his contract. That left him with a big lot full of Dodge cars that no one would buy.

Success had already begun to dull Detroit's edge. They were beginning to engineer cars that fell apart on schedule. "Planned obsolescence" was the term. Having bought thousands of these loosely constructed rattletraps, the American public was in revolt. The marketing vacuum created by this crisis of confidence sucked in the Germans and Japanese. They began shipping over their tough little cars, VWs and Toyotas that lasted. Like ticks on a shaggy dog, the foreigners had come to stay.

Stuck with his Dodge dogs, John describes himself as a "rat in a trap. I just wanted out. I didn't care about the cheese. I forget how I got out. I might have just locked the doors and walked away."

10
Radio Time

Wayne likes to say that before he went into the business the only thing he knew about broadcasting was that you needed a microphone. True to form, he patted the outside of this particular animal with great care before he bought the beast. To prepare himself, he visited twenty-eight stations over a two-year period. John had already spent a small fortune advertising his cars before Wayne involved himself with broadcasting. Everyone was telling him that radio was an obsolete medium soon to be erased by television.

Because conventional wisdom in 1951 foresaw the end of radio, stations would never again be so cheap. Owners were running scared, terrified they'd be stuck with hundreds of thousands of dollars worth of useless technology. (In those days $100,000 was the equivalent of about $1 million today.) The Rollins brothers were offered WNEW in New York City for $300,000 in the early fifties. By 1991, that station was valued at thirty million. But in 1950, owners trying to unload their stations considered Wayne an innocent, and a godsend.

If John was always ready to plunge into unknown territory, Wayne wanted to see the thing from every possible vantage before he spent a dime. It irked him that he could never reduce the element of chance to zero. Business, like life, is always a gamble. For all he knew, this radio business was simply throwing his life savings down a rathole. John did not doubt that even if they lost every cent, they could simply start over. Make it all back. He saw a world full of golden opportunities. To Wayne the cosmos looked like a trap set to spring.

To get his foot in the door, Wayne knew it would cost him every cent he had, plus all he could mortgage. He was putting up money he'd saved over decades. He was not young either—thirty-four, no spring chicken. This madness had taken three years of preparation. He finally picked a station in Radford, Virginia, where his brother

94

had one of his Ford dealerships. He began to canvass the community to see if merchants would be willing to buy radio time.

Wayne, who had the combined talents of a statistician, a stand-up comedian, and a fox, always boiled his ventures down into very basic terms. This served to make it sound simpler than it was. "The one thing that's always dominant in my mind is controlling expense," he'd say. John, on the other hand, said, "You have to spend money to make money."

The thousands of new concerns that fail each year give some idea of how difficult business success is. Where do you find customers? How do you keep them coming back? What technology will work best for you, and how do you stay out there on the cutting edge?

During the late forties live studio performances were still a vital force in broadcasting. Local stations generally built sound studios for local musicians, actors, comedians. Radio was a powerful force in the promotion of local talent. You got to know your favorite performers over the air. To see them in person you went to a club or theater. Radio energized the imagination in a way that television cannot. Modest careers thrived from Boston to San Diego. Nashville became the center of country and western music. New York's theater scene was enhanced by radio. NBC had its own symphony orchestra conducted by Toscanini. Musical comedy and the pop song achieved a sophistication that the famously "cool" medium of television had no way to follow up on. So while radio enhanced the age-old worlds of live performance, television soon erased this last surge of live popular expression in America.

Wayne's career was given its initial impulse by the energy and optimism of his younger brother. To buy the Radford station, Wayne was able to scrape together $12,500. Wayne handed John the bundle of uncashed checks he had in a drawer. He'd sold his interest in Roanoke Lincoln-Mercury to John for most of the money. According to John, he then added $25,000 to Wayne's $12,500. He would act as president of the new corporation until 1956. Wayne was then allotted half the shares and became president with John serving as chairman of the Executive Committee.

To most broadcasters, buying into radio broadcasting in 1950 looked like suicide. Television was the future. The Rollins brothers decided to gamble. They perceived that the largest American audience without any voice on the airwaves was African American. At that time blacks were still confined to the back of buses and had little representation on the air. The comedy team, Amos and Andy, were white men wearing blackface. An enormous population with a distinct culture of their own had no electronic voice.

During the late forties and fifties, the most popular radio shows were weekly half-hour programs written around comedians like Jack Benny, Fred Allen, Bob Hope, Burns and Allen. Celebrities like Danny Kaye, Al Jolson, and Enzio Pinza (of *South Pacific* fame) were written into the script to take advantage of their success. The jazz age and the era of the big band reached its apotheosis in the same period. Benny Goodman, Tommy Dorsey, Artie Shaw were succeeded by Claude Thornhill and Stan Kenton. Louis Armstrong, Django Reinhardt, Duke Ellington, Art Tatum, and Eddie Condon became public figures. Because there were so many venues available, these performers were less cramped by the demand for commercial glitz so congenial to the bland demands of television producers.

More to the point was the fifties revolution that was bred by men like Sam Phillips, the record producer, who went out looking for a new music. Resistance to African American music in the industry was endemic until then. The Rollins radio network habitually put the leading black musicians on the air. The evolution of Rhythm and Blues to Rock and Roll was led by such talents as B. B. King, Little Richard, Ike Turner, Roscoe Gordon, Muddy Waters, and Bo Diddley. Their music fed directly into the Presley phenomenon, and inspired white musicians like Buddy Holly. There was still massive resistance to this music in the South where the gyrations of Elvis the Pelvis and his like were perceived as the machinations of the Antichrist.

These reactionary fears were not unreasonable. They were an acknowledgement of the link between art and politics, the power that an apparently inchoate power like music has to change social reality. The popularity of a Louis Armstrong or Little Richard fed black pride and black consciousness: "If the white community wants *them,* why doesn't it want *us?*" The freedom marches of the sixties and the politics of Martin Luther King did not spring full-grown from Rosa Parks's refusal to sit in the back of the bus back in 1954. African American demands for social equality grew as much from the energies released by music as the preachers at the Ebenezer Baptist Church. The Rollins network was a crucial instrument in the creation of all that followed, the most extensive network for black culture that had ever been set up.

By 1960 the advent of television was changing the nature of American music. Driven by mass appeal and the manipulation of that mass, it became a more purely commercial art, its popularity linked to hype. Unique musicians, supreme instrumentalists like Bird Parker or Oscar Peterson, began to fade from view. In an entertainment universe supersaturated with technical means and confused by the drug and rock culture of the Haight, musicians, like those astronauts already circling the earth, became ghosts in the machine.

Wayne's stations were brought on line all through the fifties when the ferment was at its height. His brilliant program manager, Al Lanphear, took full advantage of an African American culture. Black artists and their audiences were freed from their confined preelectronic world of tiny clubs and backwoods bars.

In short, John and Wayne had keyed into seismic social change. Managed by an African American staff trained from scratch, the Rollins stations brought along new black talent struggling to get noticed. These included the performers mentioned above and many others like Nat King Cole, Eartha Kitt (who began recording in 1950), and Aretha Franklin.

The first studio Wayne constructed (in Radford, Virginia) was a room twenty by thirty feet, big enough to contain a jazz group or country band and an audience of fifty. Tape recorders didn't exist. Except for 78 discs and an occasional wire-recording, everything broadcast was live. In the early years of radio anything recorded was regarded as meretricious, not fair to the listener. Only sounds sent out as they occurred were even legal.

The Federal Communications Commission had at first refused to certify the Radford station (which was white) because, their engineers claimed, its 250-watt transmitter didn't "cover" its area. John and Wayne drove up and down every street in town to test the signal. It was clear as a bell. After a lot of futile wrangling over technicalities, John went to see the FCC's chief engineer in Washington. He had to travel from Philadelphia where a party crowd had somehow ended up in his room and kept him up most of the night. He'd also imbibed more than he should have. He drove three hours to Washington with a bad hangover and arrived feeling distinctly green.

For some reason John's weakened condition put the FCC's chief engineer in a jovial mood. He said that Bloody Marys were the best remedy for alcohol poisoning, and joined John in the cure. They both felt much better by dinner time and John left with the certificate to broadcast from Radford in his briefcase.

The evening the Radford station went on the air coincided with Wayne's thirty-seventh birthday. A ceremony featuring a speech by the mayor was held at the Radford State Teachers College. John had

invited a contingent of his car salesmen who swarmed over the Hotel
Tyler and kept the bartender hopping.

With most of their life savings riding on the venture, Wayne and
Grace were in a state of high anxiety. Wayne had bet every cent he
had on the basis of a few conversations with local businessmen who
said they'd probably pay for a commercial if it came to that. Experts
in the industry let them know they were making a bad mistake. But
as John observes, "No matter what you set out to do, there's always
someone who'll tell you it can't be done."

John, who invested twice the money that Wayne had scraped together, was in excellent spirits. The station wasn't even on the air yet
and John talked as if it was already a great success. Not only would
the signal saturate Radford, the transmitters were powerful enough
to reach the outlying townships of Christianburg and Blacksburg too.

The celebration went on into the small hours, growing increasingly
rowdy, moving back to the hotel around midnight. Toward morning,
a hotel clerk woke John and said he had an emergency in the lobby.
A man had appeared in the lobby wrapped in a newspaper who
claimed John could identify him. John admitted the person looked
more or less identical to one of his sales managers. The manager said
he could explain everything. A young woman had invited him to her
room. When the lady expressed a powerful desire for more booze,
he'd mentioned some booze stashed in his room next door to hers.
She suggested he get it. Wishing to make his absence from his new
friend as brief as possible, the manager calculated that dashing next
door stark naked would make the most efficient use of his time. Unfortunately, he forgot the key to his room was in his trousers pocket.
He tried to get back into the woman's room but she'd locked the
door. No matter how desperately he banged, she wouldn't open up.
Picking up a discarded newspaper to gird his loins, the manager tried
to make himself decent before descending to the lobby. John sent
him back to his room. In the morning WRAD went on the air.

Wayne decided his stations would survive only if he cut back the
number of people needed to run them. He hired Fitzgerald Mc-
Daniel, a broadcasting engineer, to design an easy-to-run station. Mc-
Daniel came up with a studio that allowed the announcer to double
as engineer. With help from his eldest son, Randall, Wayne did most
of the construction himself, hiring labor only when absolutely necessary. Later, when he could afford one more hand, he hired Norman
Glenn.

Glenn remembers how the fire they lit to clear brush around the Georgetown, Delaware, facility got out of control when a wind came up suddenly. They decided to attack the flames from two sides but soon lost sight of each other in the heat and smoke. After five hours in the burning summer sun, battling flames and smoke, Glenn had no idea if they were making headway or the fire was totally out of control until he saw Wayne's blackened figure looming through the clouds of smoke and realized they'd beaten it.

Georgetown went on the air in March of 1951. According to Glenn, the Rollins brothers were already "well known people in the state." John had been advertising on radio for years, and the publicity would serve him well when he decided to run for political office in the summer of 1952. He was elected lieutenant governor of Delaware that November with Wayne working as his campaign manager.

Wayne was dubious about John's success because, in his opinion, his brother was too frank. In a passage commending Machiavelli as a patriot, Burkhardt uses words that fit John Rollins nicely: "The danger for him does not lie in an affectation of genius or a false order of ideas, but rather in a powerful imagination which he evidently controls with difficulty." Instilled in both Wayne and John by their mother was a fine sense of just where reality stops and affectation begins. And such people will always have trouble running for political office because the public always demands an affectation of sincerity at every moment. John claims he won his first race, in part, because (as Senator John Williams remarked) he hadn't been around long enough to make a lot of enemies.

Much of Wayne's advertising revenue in the early years came directly from John. Wayne himself sold air time to every business owner in Radford before WRAD began broadcasting.

11
Like Stepford Wives

In the late forties, John was among those who set out to transform the nature of commerce. In 1945 the notion of a "service industry" was vague at best. The idea that services (rather than products) might comprise an industry required a new way of thinking about what commerce could be.

John was the least theoretical of men. But he knew from bitter experience that want ads for salesmen included the phrase, "Car required." Back in Ringgold and Chattanooga, he found himself perpetually out of the running for good sales jobs: "In those days I couldn't even afford a bicycle, much less my own car." He perceived that companies, in effect, made the car more important than the salesman. "When you interview a typist," he says, "you never figure on telling her to bring her own typewriter." He thought same should apply to salesmen. Drawing on this simple logic, he built an empire.

Until almost midcentury, leasing cars and trucks was virtually unknown. Car owners are often irrationally attached to their machines. Primitive ownership was the ideal, but practically speaking, machines are tools, not status symbols. John's concept went against the prevailing Madison Avenue approach in which machines were given false values to promote their sale. Cutting through the romantic haze created by admen, John asked companies to shed the transportation problem entirely. He pointed out that salesmen inevitably add twenty-five percent to their mileage when they use their own cars. Simple arithmetic told him that many companies would be better off leasing than paying mileage. "Back then," he recalls, "you'd have these companies with the most bedraggled bunch of cars you could imagine. Because they belonged to the salesmen. I was one of the first to begin leasing a whole fleet of cars to companies like Monsanto Chemical."

Even a good idea is hard to sell when it goes against convention and resistance was strong. He might argue that a machine was no better than its function, but the idea of buying "use" was too abstract for most people to easily accept. They wanted "something" for their money. Leasing a vehicle for its performance alone was like buying air. He appeared to be selling something weightless, invisible, and odorless.

John argued that every person on their sales force would have a car in mint condition all the time. He was selling the only necessary thing about a car, its work. If the machine broke down, he'd foot the repair bill. If it blew a tire, he'd supply a new one. The worst aspect of any labor-saving device is the amount of labor it sucks up. He suggested that companies with their own fleets should turn over the problem of maintenance to him. If he took care of the licensing, repairs, tires, bodywork, buying, selling—entire departments could be eliminated. No longer would salesmen tack on added mileage. Nor would they hesitate to drive the extra mile because it was not their own car they were wearing out.

John was making a quantum leap from machine to virtual machine. He was offering to disengage his customers from the gadgetry that increasingly enslaved them. He offered ideal cars that, like Stepford wives, never grew old. He made the automobile's function his product, removing buyer and seller from their negotiating nightmare.

By selling activity instead of an object, he was in on the ground floor of what soon became the service industry. This was an important step into what became the postindustrial world. A later generation of business people would simply *give away* the product (Netscape software, for instance) and charge only for the service it demanded. John set out along this evolutionary road in the forties.

In the growing bustle of rapid and constant change, the merchant found himself married to technology. Business was driven by mechanical reproduction, electronic replication, the evolution of technical means. It was Darwin's world with the machine as its metaphor. Business took on the evolutionary character of biological science. Whatever machinery was most congenial to the market thrived. Technology could advance the design of only what sold. The evolution of science, too, was increasingly integrated into the business of selling.

In 1932, the Rollins brothers still worked the family farm and a year's work netted Wayne $137. Twenty years later, John found himself able to borrow a million dollars. Thirty-two years after that, Tom Blank, a consultant in Washington, remembers walking into John's office after some bad publicity had caused a precipitous drop in

Rollins stock. John looked up and said, "How do I look for a man who just lost $23 million dollars in one night?"

The Rollinses may be compared to time-travelers who step out of a horse-drawn wagon and discover themselves on board a space craft. The slow, circular tread of nature has been effaced. We live in a virtual machine that technology renders more ethereal, more abstract with every passing year.

Wayne always felt a twinge of frustration that he could never return to the land, but the tiny economic engine of the farm was being dwarfed by the commercial dynamo. Just as the farmer has been replaced by agribusiness, so the theater has been replaced by film, and now the film is being erased by television and the ascendant technology of the computer. Replication is the key to growth (economies of scale). In transport, in medicine, in information technology, the story is everywhere the same.

When he bottled water at Catoosa, Wayne realized that success in modern business depends on exponential reproduction. Neither water, land, nor live performance lend themselves to duplication. A family restaurant will succeed as business only when it turns itself into a franchised chain called The Family Restaurant. Colonel Sanders, who once mixed up a batter used for frying chicken, has been transformed into a logo and made immortal. The film star will fade quickly unless her image has the market power of a Marilyn or a Madonna. Her person becomes irrelevant.

In 1945, with Germany flattened and Japan in ruins, Americans looked forward to an era of undiluted happiness. Good had triumphed; totalitarianism was defeated. Overnight, the line that ran from life to death was reversed. Every sort of killing invention was transformed and adapted to civilian use. Mountains of army surplus were sold to civilians—everything from pup tents to pursuit planes. Tank lines became truck lines. Horatio Alger himself could not have devised a more morally appropriate ending. The war gave technology a boost and now there was radar, sonar, synthetic rubber, plastic, nylon, and atomic power. The human mind was married to the machine. The humanities were backpeddled. Psychological testing used on soldiers became a marketing tool. John had grasped the importance of promoting his product back in the thirties when he used Bruton Snuff as his marketing tool. He had gone broke, but his instinct was on target. Give comfort, sell the good life, and your product will fly out the door.

As early as 1920, an ad for Libby's Foods shows a young girl at a table reflecting to herself in these words: "It hurt—that sudden flash of seeing herself as others must see her. A drudge—that's what she was. One of the army of women past whom the world whirls gaily, while [she] grows older and more faded and colorless. Till finally one morning [she] wakes up [to] realize that [her] chance to play has slipped away forever."

The Libby's ad writer hit on the great theme, the enormous message that business would convey to the world: our product will bring you a better life. Earlier John used Bruton Snuff to create a link in his customers' minds between the bedspreads he was selling and pleasure. Today the pleasure principle undergirds business—pleasure for everyone, great and small, domestic and foreign.

The Rollins brothers grew up with a mule's tail swishing in their eyes, ploughing the earth, and planting seed. Such men are not attracted by abstractions. They want as few political impediments, as few regulations as possible.

In the thread mill and the plant producing bomb releases or TNT, they saw technology in a state of rapid evolution. In the Krouse boiler factory, John had seen Fred Krouse reinventing the product in front of his eyes. Improving a device was improving your life. Both Rollins brothers were consummate realists. They moved up rapidly from hard labor to assembly line work to procurement, from shift bossing to ownership and, finally, the business of business itself. Never questioning the value of the job, they gave it everything they had.

John, setting the pace, converted himself into a member of that new class described as socially desirable by Bernard Shaw in his preface to *Major Barbara:* "Rich men . . . with a developed sense of life . . . not content with handsome houses; they want handsome cities. They are not content with bediamonded wives and blooming daughters; they complain because the charwoman is badly dressed, because the laundress smells of gin, because the seamstress is anemic, because every man they meet is not a friend and every woman not a romance."

12
Everything but the Kitchen Sink

The Rollins brothers' radio stations diverged radically from the mainstream but found solid support from mega-advertisers like Lever Brothers. By 1964, Wayne had about 500 employees, and he tried to know them all by name. Once the company had gone public, in September 1960, Wayne assured investors that Rollins Broadcasting was "part of the infrastructure of the affluent society." All the same, beaming radio signals into four million black homes constituted a radical political act.

Almost single-handedly Wayne had given many of the best black artists and not a few activists a wider access to their community. At the same time, a financial analyst wrote (in *Television Magazine,* September 1964), "Few operators have ever approached the medium with the sophisticated market research, programming and sales techniques of which Rollins is capable." In John's view it was their music, news-every-half-hour, sports-every-half-hour, that did the trick. That the voices of Jesse Jackson, Martin Luther King, and Malcolm X were broadcast over these stations lends a provocative slant to the report of the company's "fat profits."

When Wayne first entered the field, radio stations, under pressure from television, were supposed to go bankrupt all over the country. Wayne's solution to the money squeeze was to redesign operations and reduce staff. He kept salaries low, with the understanding that profitability would lead to expansion, and expansion would translate into higher wages and more jobs for members of the African American community.

He decided to employ African Americans to manage all the stations designed for that community. In those days few had management experience, and he trained them from scratch. By the time Rollins Broadcasting went public in 1960, the Rollinses had nine stations—a limit imposed by law—and two television outlets. For better or worse, the United States had turned its airways into highways of commerce, and the airways soon resembled the cluttered main streets of America, where a thousand competing merchants lend public life the energy of a carnival and the intellectual content of a raffle. Wayne never set out to bring enlightenment. He survived by selling air time. He would probably have fired any station manager who set out to "educate" his audience. Neither of the Rollinses had any desire to preach to or somehow improve their audience. Nevertheless Rollins Broadcasting took part in the movement for social progress that culminated in the freedom marches led by Martin Luther King. Their stations helped greatly to give a stronger feeling of community, the sense they shared an important culture. For a minority just beginning to assert its equal rights, nothing can equal the powerful sense of identity that only culture can give.

Because the Rollinses' minority stations had the highest financial return of any stations in the nation, the Federal Communications Commission investigated them in January of 1968. Wayne called the U.S. Secretary of Labor's office "absurd and careless." Rollins Broadcasting was charged with violating federal wage-hour laws. The government's suit claimed the company's records were inadequate. What most irritated Wayne was that his system of reporting to the FCC was being copied by other broadcasting companies because his company had put together a 400-page manual on the subject. In the end, the government dropped the case. But there were lawyers to pay, and the episode contributed to Wayne's disgust with government inspectors who misinterpreted their own regulations and then made him pay for it.

Wayne, as John often remarks, hated wasting money. Even when he was worth many millions, he spent very little on himself—though he had an affection for designer suits and classic cars (parked in a basement under his offices). One of Wayne's managers recalls how Wayne once took his Chicago managers out to dinner to reward them for superior work and discovered he didn't have enough cash to pay the bill. His vice president, Madalyn Copley, had to dig the money out of her purse. The managers suspected that the restaurant they had chosen was too high-priced for his taste, and maybe that was his way of letting them know it.

John recalls that even when their company was grossing millions, Wayne still insisted on "approving every expense over twenty-five dollars." He could not tolerate waste. Late in life he granted vast sums of money to research institutes and colleges around Atlanta, but he always designed his contributions to multiply many times in value through matching grants.

John could not have been more different. It's difficult to imagine another entrepreneur with his track record saying, as John does, "I never had a plan. I just ran like hell on whatever track I was on." He never paused to reflect on the Grand Canyon of debt yawning beneath him (until it threatened to swallow him alive in the seventies). By the fifties, he was flying 250,000 miles annually to keep his leasing operations going.

According to Randall, John traded the Bonanza for a two-engine Beechcraft around 1950. Edmund G. Chamberlain was his pilot. In September 1953, the pilot flew Wayne's top engineer, Russ Chambers, to Washington. Chambers was on his way to his father's funeral in Tennessee. Approaching Washington National, the plane developed a fire behind the instrument panel. To avoid traffic, Chamberlain elected to ditch in the Potomac River. The plane hit the water and sank immediately. Chambers wrestled the door open underwater and made it to the surface where an Air Force boat pulled him out. The pilot drowned. The brothers were devastated by their young pilot's death, and set up a fund for the education of Chamberlain's children and living expenses for the family.

When sales fell precipitously in the middle fifties, the brothers decided it was time to give Ford the full benefit of their long experience. So they went to see Mr. Charlie Beacham in Chester, the gentleman who had taught John the business in the first place.

They drove into the parking lot, clattered upstairs and presented themselves. They were clad in nicely tailored dark suits. John sported a homburg. Charlie asked what he could do for them and they launched into their prepared text. While they spoke, Charlie Beacham stood looking out the window, gazing down on the parking lot where their Lincoln was parked.

They had strong opinions, based on their own market research. Well, maybe not so much research. Strong feelings. Because their Fords were not selling as they should. And they knew why. In fact, they knew what was wrong with the Ford Motor Company. They knew how to improve sales. First, there were too many black cars. Americans don't like black cars. Blue, yes; black, no. There weren't enough cars with four doors. Americans liked doors. Ease of entry and exit. Also, the cars lacked power.

Wayne and John came to Charlie Beacham with their criticisms in the same year (1955) that the infamous Edsel was under design. The company that Henry II had put back on its feet ten years before was in trouble again. Robert McNamara was Ford's CEO at the time, a brilliant numbers cruncher. He had pushed the Falcon, a direct descendant of Ford's early cars. The Falcon sold fairly well because it was cheap. Unfortunately, it looked cheap too. Its metal skin resembled that of a beer can. The Falcon perfectly embodied McNamara's lack of intuition.

The Rollins brothers sensed Ford was on the wrong path. For one thing, Chevrolet was producing a better car than Ford. A Chevy two years old sold for $200 more than a Ford of the same vintage, and in those days $200 was a considerable sum. In the nineties, Lee Iacocca wrote that McNamara almost destroyed Ford by pushing so hard for a car that didn't make enough for the company. He claimed that McNamara handed over millions of Ford customers to General Motors, that Ford was helping to sell GM's big cars, because they didn't produce any of their own. Ironically, this was the time when Ford unveiled the Edsel—the most ballyhooed automobile ever designed, and the greatest defeat the ad industry suffered at the hands of the American consumer.

John and Wayne knew nothing about the Edsel. But they were trying to sell Ford cars out in the marketplace, so they had strong opinions. Beacham listened to them in silence. He sat quietly, staring through the window at the parking lot. When they were done, he turned and asked if the Lincoln in the parking lot belonged to them. They acknowledged it did. And what about the driver in the black uniform and cap? Him too, yes. Beacham contemplated the car and the driver for a considerable spell.

"Well, I can tell you what's wrong with *your* business," he said. "I saw you drive up in that big, black Lincoln—I mean you boys aren't even driving a Ford anymore. And you've got your lot boy dressed up—what's that suit you've got him in? I thought you hired him to wash cars and shine up your inventory, and all you've done is put him in a black suit. How much good is he doing you driving you around the countryside in a black suit? And look at John here. A fella from Georgia, and you come up here wearing a homburg hat? In a big black Lincoln? And a lot boy dressed in a black suit? I can tell you what's wrong with you fellows. You've stopped growing and you've started swelling."

"And the only thing I can say," Wayne remarks, "is we had sense enough to believe him. And John—I can still see him—he puts that hat up back of the seat. And he says, 'Well, I guess I won't need this homburg. You just go back to Princess Anne and I'll catch the plane for Norfolk.'

"And it was just like Mr. Beacham said. It all straightened out. He just turned us around. Headed us in a different direction."

After Beacham's lesson, they quit listening to the excuses of their salesmen. "We did pretty much the same to them that Charlie had done to us. We told them we didn't want to hear any more. And I remember, they told us that the customers down in Norfolk weren't the same kind of customers as in Pennsylvania. And John can be pretty crude sometimes. And he said, 'Don't tell me that damn stuff. They still eat, shit, and have babies, don't they? Just go back and sell them cars.' Once John threw away his homburg hat, he came on pretty strong."

Wayne compared John's management style to that of a Scottish collie herding cows. An ordinary collie, he said, "just eats up a cow that gets out of line, and makes things so unpleasant the poor creature wishes she'd never been born. But the Scotch collie is all over the place. He just runs up on this side and down on that side and keeps them together. So he never has to bite any of them."

As for Ford, the company stayed its course with its Edsel and lost more money with the car than any previous model in history. And Walker Percy in 1966 had one of the characters in his novel, *The Last Gentleman*, drive an Edsel "to commemorate the last victory of the American people over marketing research and opinion polls." The Rollins brothers took Beacham's lesson to heart. Their plan was not to create a need but to fulfill it. Their dealership, which had been 187th in the nation, moved up to 44th for numbers of cars sold.

Wayne liked to say that the easiest person to sell something to is a salesman. Thus he considered John's talent for making a sale his greatest weakness. About the time Wayne moved up from Catoosa to work for him, he remembers how John was shown thirty fine-looking automobiles by a dealer in Philadelphia. The cars shone glossy black under the bright yellow lights. John made a deal on the spot. He was on his way to Florida with Kitty and the kids, so he passed the cars along to Wayne who was running the Princess Anne dealership.

He'd just left town when it began to snow in Maryland. Snow was followed by a warming rain. As the snow melted, so did the paint on the cars. They stood revealed as ancient yellow taxi cabs. The black overpainting fell off in long strips. Wayne was left to slog it out in the wet snow, trying to sell a line of cabs painted like zebras. It seemed to Wayne that John was never coming back and Wayne meanwhile couldn't sell a single taxi.

The week John blew back into town, the car market abruptly lurched to life. For six months Wayne had been stuck with those cabs. A month after John returned from Florida, he'd sold every one at $1500 per unit. "That was how he was," Wayne says. "He always seemed to have luck on his side."

During the great fifties tungsten scare, everyone agreed that a shortage of that metal would run up the price of television sets astronomically. John dashed out and bought a thousand TVs. But the panic degenerated into rumor and rumor dwindled into hot air. So he hired a woman to sell the TVs. Having accomplished the task with skill and dispatch, she disappeared with the cashbox. John didn't work very hard to find her. He figured his time was better spent pursuing business than seeking justice.

For reasons obscure to Wayne, John then bought a whole field full of school buses. They were all parked on the grass somewhere up in Pennsylvania. None of them had engines. John had a deal worked out to install cut-rate engines from Ford, because Ford had sold him the buses. The company promised to point anybody who wanted to buy school buses in his direction. Unloading a football field full of buses without engines proved no easy task. The buses were rusting more quickly than John could sell them, and whatever profit he'd hoped for was being overwhelmed by his carrying charges. In the end he came out more or less even. That year the market for school buses was hot in Israel, so most of his inventory ended up in Tel Aviv.

John's most extravagant deal involved five PBY flying boats he bought from the Navy. The PBY was an enormous amphibious plane designed to land on water as well as land. The cockpit was so high up that the pilot and crew had to use a ladder to reach it. The interior was the size of a California living room. John figured he would sell the planes to customers who flew regularly to places like South America, or to Canada on fishing trips. He imagined their landing on calm lakes on lovely summer days. He informed Wayne he'd come up with a terrific deal. Each plane cost the government $750,000 to manufacture; he'd bought all five for $100,000. Wayne thought John was out of his mind.

"Who are you going to sell them to? What do you do with them until you sell them? How much will that cost, and what if you can't sell them? How do you junk them? What about insurance?"

John said all he had to do was locate an airport where he could land and park his behemoths. This proved more difficult than he'd imagined. Few civilian airports liked the idea of Navy PBYs looming over their control towers. PBYs are not beautiful to behold. They exhibit the aerodynamic savoir faire of bumble bees and appear completely incapable of flight. After running up an enormous phone bill, John finally talked an airport in Walnut Ridge, Arkansas, into accepting his flying monstrosities.

Now the planes had to be flown across the country from Seattle, where the steady rain had been rusting them out for months. The pilots he hired phoned back to say the planes were all grounded. They needed repairs. John flew out to Seattle and jawboned some Navy mechanics into doing the work. Then he extricated his pilots from the local bars and watched the PBYs warm up for takeoff like fat climbers setting themselves to run up a hill.

The first in line didn't make it off. The next two got all the way to Arkansas. There they squatted hideously on the runway and proceeded to eat up his overhead. The fourth crash-landed in a corn field in Iowa. Luckily, the pilot was not hurt. John kept hustling and over time unloaded them at break-even prices. The last sale involved him in a lawsuit. A buyer from New York sued him for breach of contract. The contract consisted of a phone conversation in which John had said, "Sure, you can have it if you want it." John won the suit, but it was expensive.

Meanwhile, the farmer who owned the corn field where the plane had crash-landed sent John a whopping bill "for watching over the wreckage." The farmer claimed he'd watched over it twenty-four hours a day for six months, and he charged by the hour. Dragged back into court, John won again. But it took time and it cost more money.

John assessed the situation and himself. He reasoned this way: "I'm not the dumbest man in the world. So if I bought these planes, there must be someone else who would too. What I've got to do is find him and make the deal."

Wayne had said he was crazy to buy big floppy surplus planes already obsolete. But when he's seized by an idea, John doesn't understand, "no." His comprehension extends only to "yes." He sold the last PBY to a book publisher who fixed the plane up like the Taj Mahal and used it to go fishing. This episode would have driven some men mad with anxiety, but John figured that he'd come out more or less even and the profit was in the experience.

13
Politics and Birds of Passage

Sometime in the summer of 1952, United States Senator John Williams showed up in John's office and pressed the businessman to run for lieutenant governor of Delaware on the Republican ticket. The senator told him that "everyone knew him and wanted him to run."

John believes that Williams was looking for a someone so new to politics that he'd had no chance yet to make enemies. When John said it might be interesting, the Senator dialed the *News Journal* and handed the phone over. "Tell them the good news," he said.

John's Southern accent and old boy country style went down well in rural Delaware. From the news accounts of the day, the issues that divided candidates are almost impossible to make out. The babble of charges and countercharges leaves an impression that the Democrats were using the Highways Department (now DelDOT) to grant special favors to cronies. The Highways Department was routinely accused of corrupt practices under the Democrats. It's worth recalling that in 1912 Coleman V. du Pont used his own money to start Highway 13 that would run eventually from Wilmington to Delaware's southern border, despite the objections of Sussex and Kent County farmers who would get the most use from the road. They feared higher taxes. Coleman spent $5 million before passing the highway problem on to the state. Du Pont family members or employees of the DuPont Company chaired the Highway Department for a generation, and Delaware spent twice as much per capita on its roadways as neighboring states.

Little is made of this in news accounts of the day, and the blissful ignorance that prevailed among Delaware's electorate is understandable. A young woman, representing the Active Young Republicans, Inc., is quoted at length in the *Wilmington Morning News*. In a report remarkable for its tortured grammar, she reports that young people are flocking to the conservative party. "We are having a hard time raising our children by the principles of morality and honesty by which we were raised," she says. "On the one hand, if we teach them respect for government they must think it is proper to be immoral and dishonest. On the other, if we teach them to be clean and honest, we necessarily teach them disrespect for their present government."

While the Democrats were charged with encouraging inflation and dishonesty, the Republicans were routinely described as "money grubbing." Posters printed by the Democrats assert that "the next Four Years will be the Most Important in U.S. and World History." Unfortunately, they don't say why.

Adlai Stevenson, the Democratic presidential nominee, was roundly defeated by Dwight D. Eisenhower. Eisenhower carried Delaware, and riding on his enormous popularity, Republicans found themselves in office for the first time in twenty years.

John recalls trying to do something about the "separate but equal schools that didn't have gymnasiums or auditoriums with literacy not much better than we have now (1999)." He suggested the schools might well be integrated in stages, starting with the youngest children. "But there was so much emotion involved, the subject could hardly be raised anywhere." He remembers the state budget at the time was about $79 million. Today it runs over one billion.

Presiding over the state senate and conducting the business of his office, John found the time for running his business cut in half. His auto dealerships languished. He canceled all leasing to the state, which significantly reduced his profit margin. On the other hand, being an elected representative brought him into contact with the socially prominent and powerful. He was no longer just a car salesman from downstate. Bankers with genial expressions rose to greet him in the Hotel du Pont. Senators in Washington included him at dinner. Those in positions of power have always loved a man who can make money.

John had always made political contributions, even when he couldn't afford them. With his instinctive sense for the way power works, he knew even when he was very young that business and government are codependents. It takes oil and vinegar to make a good salad, and it takes good government and efficient business to spring loose a modern economy. Though relations between these institutions is sometimes hostile, their mutual dependence is vital.

John loved the political life. He had shot from the bottom to the top and he was meeting the kings of creation for the first time.

Though his business still staggered along under considerable debt, the boomlet created by the Korean War had lifted his leasing business out of disaster. But his first wife, Kitty, believes politics ruined their marriage. She'd expected to live a normal existence with a home and four children. She'd thought her husband would be with her on weekends. Yet how much time had they actually spent together before? Even when he'd been home, John immersed himself in correspondence courses. He'd spent years studying late at night to make up for the education he'd never got. To Kitty it seemed excessive, to say the least.

His entry into politics was the last straw. She could not go on living with a man who evidently wanted to crowd nine lives into one. John's immersion in public life while simultaneously keeping his leasing business afloat meant he had no time for Kitty at all. Kitty recalls attending rallies and fund raisers and standing on platforms while speeches blew away in the wind. John, for his part, recalls her attending only one of his public appearances. Their different memories of the experience says it all. In 1958, when she heard he really was running for the office of governor in Delaware, Kitty asked for a divorce.

"I was absolutely not going to spend the rest of my life as a politician's wife. No way."

It was a friendly divorce to say the least, in part perhaps because he was too busy to fight with. There's a photograph of her with three of her kids holding a sign that touts John's bid for governor in 1959. They would remain friends for life with less in common each year as he ascended in a cloud of financial success to sit, eventually, on the right hand of Richard Nixon.

While he was lieutenant governor, Kitty had done her best to keep up. For her the high point was a visit to Hawaii. She says she had the idea of inviting all the soldiers from Delaware stationed there to dinner at their hotel. They also visited two young African Americans in the airbase hospital. "And you talk about boys that cried! They were just sort of forgotten by their parents and everyone. And they just couldn't get over that someone cared enough to visit them."

Kitty says that politics is hell on spouses. Had he become governor, had she stayed with him, "I know in all probability I would have become an alcoholic, or drug user. Look at what happens [to other wives]. The President's wife. . . . Having to put up with the life of a celebrity—I couldn't take it. I would have become a liability to him. Not an asset."

Attracted like a magnet to the particular possibilities offered by success in the United States, John flung himself headlong into the mix. Inevitably, he would become the creator of corporations, the human seed from which these institutions emanate. The Constitution has almost nothing to say on the subject of corporations. The American corporate system with its antidemocratic structure is described there as a "person," but not a "citizen." The state may abridge its "privileges or immunities." The entrepreneur, to succeed, must set up a strict chain of command not unlike that on board a ship. But the more complicated the ship, the more his subordinates are involved in the decision-making process. John Rollins arrived on the scene when the modern company was morphing into something very different from its Industrial Revolution precursor. The adversarial nature of workers' organizations (formalized by the Wagner Act of 1935) bans "collaboration" between workers and employers. In 1992, the National Labor Relations Board, enforcer of the act, found (in its *Electromation* decision) that a company had violated the law by setting up "a bilateral process involving employee-initiated proposals." Defining "conditions of work," the NLRB has included such things as "job descriptions, workloads, scheduling, changes in machinery, discipline, hiring and promotion" as well as "rewards for efficiency." While management may dictate these matters, it may not include non-management employees in the decision-making process. The NLRB extracts the worker from decision making and makes him an instrument of management. Service industries do not work well, if at all, organized in this dated industrial form. A new form of worker solidarity is necessary for the most advanced companies—those involved in creating intellectual properties such as computer software or genetic engineering.

John's approach from the very beginning was that he and his workers were "all in this together." He and his brother were always inclined to give low wages and extremely high incentive bonus pay. If the business succeeds, then everyone shares in that success. Those who want a normal eight-hour day and no hassle will not survive in such superheated work environments. Dorothy Harrison, John's first secretary, didn't mind the long hours because of the lively and upbeat atmosphere John generated. She recalls that his shows of bad temper vanished as quickly as they flared up. "He was most always easy to be around. And I never did ever see him fire anyone."

Dorothy Harrison says he was "generous to a fault." She recalls John's saving a man from bankruptcy at a time when he was not doing so well himself. "I remember him saying, 'This won't do. I guess I'm gonna have to give that son-of-a-bitch something.' And he did." Then she adds as an afterthought, "I have always said that Mr. Rollins was a very selfish man in that he could not give of himself. But he'd give you whatever you asked for. A hundred dollars, he'd give you a hundred dollars. But there was something in there that he had to keep inside himself."

Jeffrey, his fifth son (by his second wife, Linda Prickett) remarks, "The thing he hated most in the world was firing anyone. He'd do anything to avoid it."

14
Mr. Henry Tippie

Within a five-year period (1946–1951), the Rollins brothers had generated so much business for themselves that they were losing track of what was going out and coming in. With two radio stations and four auto dealerships, and John spotting new possibilities every time he opened a newspaper, their business was spiraling out of control.

No really first-rate accountant had ever put out a shingle in the town of Rehoboth, Delaware, where the brothers rented offices in the Moore Building, a U-shaped structure a block or two up from beach. Leafing through the *Journal of Accounting*, they spotted a work-wanted notice from someone in Omaha, Nebraska. His name was Henry Tippie.

A young man in his twenties, Henry Tippie had placed an ad in the *Journal*, because the company he'd been working for had self-destructed. He'd never visited east of the Mississippi and thought a trip to foreign parts might be interesting. In later years, he recalled that it required strong light and a good atlas to locate tiny Rehoboth Beach on the map.

Born in 1927, on an Iowa farm near Belle Plaine, a small town east of Des Moines, Henry's childhood was similar to countless other farm boys, including the Rollins brothers. He too was educated at a school where six grades occupied one room. "I'd read from these so called Big Little Books," he recalls.

> They cost a nickel or ten cents. I still have all my country school books. Now they tell me they're worth twenty-five dollars apiece. I never throw anything away so I've got them all. In fact our country school still has an annual get-together. It's the first Sunday after the 4th of July. The schoolhouse no longer exists. There's a corn field where it used to be. But believe it or not, my teacher from that country school is still alive. She's ninety, ninety-two, I think she said the other day. Esther Palmer. She was there a couple of weeks ago. I try to make it every year and she always thinks that I'm one of her prize students. I don't know why.

Esther Palmer taught six subjects to students in eight grades simultaneously. Most of those students are now grandparents.

Henry's father raised corn and hay, and owned twenty-seven cows. Henry learned how to milk when he was five and just strong enough to grip a cow's teat. Like the Rollins boys, he rose before dawn every morning to deliver milk, winter and summer. This routine began when he was four years old. He still knows the family names associated with every house on his father's route, though those people are long gone and their children grown and scattered.

Henry's mother wanted him to escape the farm. She sensed the future no longer lay in the land. But like most people whose survival depends on work that demands constant attention and very little reflection, the Tippies were slaves to the immediate. You didn't waste time dreaming up some alternate life for yourself.

World War II gave Henry his break. Like most kids of his generation, he developed a passion for airplanes. The newsreels were full of B-29s releasing long streams of bombs over Germany, and he longed to pilot one of those bombers himself. But he'd been born a moment too late. Seventeen years old in the last year of the war, he set himself against his father who wanted him to stay on the farm. But his mother viewed military service as his one chance to escape. Overcoming the objections of his father, she signed him into the Army Air Force. She was a quiet woman who seldom spoke, but she had the iron will of someone who had grown up with hardship. Years later when she was in her eighties, he went to visit and found her on top of a ladder cleaning out the gutters of her house.

Henry had been a wretched student, bored and restless, but he got high test scores on the flight test the Army gave him and was placed in a special flight program. However, the war was winding down. His program was canceled around the time the *Enola Gay* dropped its bomb on Hiroshima. All the same, Henry's mother had calculated correctly. Henry had met young men his age who came from worlds he had scarcely imagined. They had fathers who practiced law or medicine or worked in the sciences. They discussed the colleges they expected to attend, the futures they planned. "All of this was far from my background. I'd never heard of these things," he says.

Although Henry loved reading, he'd never been much good at school. It was the world that drew him, not learning for its own sake. His indifference had flamed into eager ambition when he realized that high test scores might make him a pilot. Now the Army Air Force proposed to ship its most promising young candidates to college to earn a degree before they entered flight school. The dwindling war stranded Henry once again in the classroom. Desperately, he volunteered to become a tail gunner. But tail gunners had gone out of fashion. They handed him the GI Bill instead, a free college degree if he wanted it.

Bowing to the inevitable, he decided on accounting. It was practical, a skill he could sell. Because universities were obliged to admit everyone on the GI Bill, Henry's wretched high school record was ignored. But he was, by then, "a completely different person . . . all business. I knew I was going to go through university at the fastest pace possible. So I stayed enrolled for twenty-four consecutive months. I lined up every course I was required to take. I arranged it with all my course work in the morning and my afternoons free [to study]. I figured afternoons were quiet, no distractions."

He took advanced accounting courses at the same time as he took their prerequisites. His favorite class was Western Civilization, taught by a German expatriate who fled Heidelberg when the Nazis seized power. What impressed Henry was the professor's grasp of the past and how this gave him the power to predict the future. According to Henry, "Everything he said would happen in the Mideast has happened."

Henry found himself in the job market in 1949. The economy had slumped. He mailed two hundred letters of inquiry to firms everywhere and received not one reply. To look for work, he was reduced to making the ride into Chicago at night, on a double-decker cattle truck.

The journey east from Des Moines took all night. The enormous trucks were loaded with animals on their way to slaughter, redolent with the ammonia stench of fresh manure. Dressed in his old army field jacket and hefting a cardboard suitcase, he'd pull into the vast stockyards around dawn and take the bus downtown. There he washed and changed into his suit at the Northwestern Station. Having transformed himself into a more or less respectable applicant for a white-collar job, he set out on his tedious rounds around eight-thirty. As laconic as he is honest, Henry had neither means nor inclination to present himself as more than he was, and this proved a poor way to make a good impression.

"Every office had a dozen or more people trying to get interviews. I never got to first base." Giving up on Chicago, Henry took the bus to Denver and tried there. He drew another blank. He needed a year of work as an apprentice accountant before they'd let him take the exam for his license. What he wanted desperately was to escape Des Moines and get into some larger life. But life apparently had no place for him. In the end, Des Moines was the only place he could find work.

His first job was at a small, badly organized firm. He boarded in a single room with another man, and took home $135 a month. When he couldn't cover his expenses, he moved into the YMCA for a dollar a day. By sharing a room and volunteering for all the out-of-town jobs, which paid for meals and laundry, he could just about make ends meet.

Having passed the CPA test at year's end, he found work in Omaha. He was still on the Great Plains, but at least Nebraska wasn't Iowa. The company was owned by two brothers who manufactured and sold disposable cardboard doors for railway cars that transported wheat. Henry fit in nicely. With an annual salary of $9,100 he felt satisfied with life for the first time.

The brothers worked beautifully together, but where there is harmony, discord will appear—in this case the wife of a man who decided that she hated his brother. Henry, given more to practical matters than the analysis of mental conditions, never did understood why a hard-working man should become the target for so much spite. The lady's endless nagging apparently speeded on the heart attack that soon carried off her poor husband. She buried him, and the company disintegrated. Henry was busy cleaning up the debris when the Rollins brothers' letter popped up. They were answering the ad he'd placed in January of 1952.

Departing Washington D.C. at 6:30 in the morning, Henry arrived in Rehoboth Beach at about 10:30. He wore an enormous fur coat with a high collar and his trousers were short at the ankle. With his open, farm boy's face and concentrated, direct gaze, he had the appearance of a very young cleric from the country. There was something new-hatched about him, but he had the toughness of someone raised on a farm short on machinery.

When he clambered off the bus, nothing he saw raised his hopes much. Snow was falling on a provincial street that halted abruptly at a seaside esplanade. Unenthusiastic waves slopped over a pale beach. He'd discovered only that Rehoboth was "one hundred miles from anyplace." Somehow, his trip to the fabled East had terminated in just another hick town.

The only eatery open was the Robert E. Lee Restaurant. While he fortified himself with a hamburger, a woman seated nearby turned to him and said, "Pardon me, sir, but you're not from around here, are you?"

Three blocks up from the beach, he found Wayne and John in the Moore Building. That he'd showed up when he said he would, that he'd actually found Rehoboth, that he'd showed up at all, considerably impressed the brothers. Henry says, "Well, I'd been taught in the accounting business that you don't bother a client with a lot of questions. You get a time established and you present yourself. And because I never had a car, I was used to riding buses and streetcars and trains. I just factored in the complications."

"A typical farmboy," says Dorothy Harrison, recalling her first impression of young Henry. "I liked him from the very first. He needed some polishing, and Mr. Rollins saw that he got it. When he first came in, I can remember—this isn't nice to say—but his pants were too short and he had on white socks. But he kept Mr. Rollins on an even keel as far as finances were concerned."

Henry had worked with two brothers on his last job, a partnership ruined by the wife of one of them. He observed the Rollins boys made a good team and their wives appeared to be just fine. With his broad face and wide smile, John was "outgoing, he had an outside, sales nature." Wayne, more watchful, more withdrawn, looked like someone who did "the inside work, very conservative."

John didn't know it then, but meeting Henry Tippie was a little like meeting the part of himself that was missing. And maybe the same thing could be said for Henry. John was the creative whirlwind, the man who woke up every morning with a new idea, but had neither time nor inclination to balance his checkbook. He thrived in what looked to Henry like complete chaos. Henry wanted everything to balance out. He wanted a cosmos where energy and the way it is expended add up to ideal order, clearly demonstrable in black ink. Ethics for him were an absolute. Henry had the disposition (and kindly nature) of an excellent prelate.

The brothers didn't exactly welcome him with open arms. But they liked what they saw. Henry, as he recalls, was holed up in some motel. They took him to dinner at the local country club where they told him what he could expect. Wayne tested his seriousness by suggesting that Henry accept a pay cut from his previous salary. Demanding that new people take a cut was an item of faith with Wayne. If a new employee wouldn't take less, he was more than likely blind to the quality of the people making the offer.

Henry, sniffing potential in the wind, went along with the cut. Even more to the point, he'd just made a very long trip, he was dog tired, and these two had him at a considerable disadvantage. Nevertheless, there was something about the Rollins brothers that whispered "opportunity." Forty-two years later he called Wayne's unkind cut "the best $15 investment I ever made in my life."

What Henry uncovered when he first looked at John's records was total chaos. In fact, there were no records. The car-leasing business had only been underway for a year and already equipment was missing. One car was gone for a year, until Henry ran it down in the shadowy back room of some body shop. The less said about John's bookkeeping the better. It took months to match the company's figures to whatever was going on out there, but bring order Henry did.

The range and intensity of John's business activity, let alone his running for political office, looks even more astonishing when Henry describes how poorly the brothers were doing at the time. Looking over their books in 1953, Henry was impressed only by their potential. "If you threw it all into a sack," Rollins Broadcasting was bringing in about $100,000 a year. "So on paper you weren't looking at much, even though it looks impressive—well! three radio stations on the air.

"As for the auto agencies, there was one at Lewes losing money. One at Radford breaking even. A Lincoln-Mercury at Roanoke, not doing well. The Lincoln's style was no good. Everything was wrong at Newport News." John, Henry observes, had opened his first Ford agency when selling a car was no harder than rolling a ball down a pool table. "Because everyone needed a car in '45. All you needed was an order taker. The operation was demand driven." By the early fifties, Ford dealerships were doing "very poorly, and the Lincoln-Mercury wasn't worth a dog almost anyplace."

As for the leasing business, he couldn't see much future in it. The concept, much less the business, was in its infancy. There were about one hundred cars parked on a lot, with a good number unaccounted for. So, in Henry's view, all Wayne and John really had was potential. What they didn't have was a firm connection to, and control over, the enterprises they were hammering together.

When Henry joined the brothers on the second floor of the Moore Building in Rehoboth Beach, the place had no air conditioning. The offices were divided by wallboard partitioning, and seven or eight people ran the entire operation, which included a manufacturing group that lost money faster than the brothers could throw dollars at it.

Now the three men began to function as three forces, each one driving as well as balancing the other two. Roughly speaking, this triumvirate curiously parallels the larger triumvirate that drives the nation at large. Wayne might be viewed as the genius of business, Henry as the civilizing force of government, and John as the creative power that brings the dead to life. In any case, they operated as a system of checks and balances. The success of their collective creation depended on that.

To make matters still more satisfactory for Henry, he soon met a young woman with an angelic nature—a college student working in Rehoboth for the summer. As soon as he was able to prove to Patricia that he was not as gruff as he seemed at first, they were married.

15
High Interest and Tremendous Luck

The secret of John's success is a knot not easy to unravel. His faith in business has been vindicated by how well it works for him. It's worth recalling that around 1300 the law in France forbade merchants to come near the rulers. They were not allowed to sell inside manor walls. Farmers set up their markets on crossroads, as they were welcome nowhere else. Eventually these markets became the towns of Europe. Even there only the Jews were allowed to lend money.

By 1950, money was a sign of godliness, and *usura* was the backbone of commerce. Businesspeople were transforming themselves into a new royalty. The ability to make money earned a respect similar to that spiritual redemption received a few centuries earlier. Exhibiting self-abnegation reminiscent of a medieval monk, John worked days that began before sunrise and ended after nightfall. Back then he'd had more exposure to the Old Testament than to modern accounting procedures, but with his genius for learning as he worked, he set up a system of loans, liens, and financial levers that kept the banks happy and his creditors on hold.

John's leasing business was an evolutionary leap, and he knew it would fail unless he sold big companies on the idea. In the early fifties he convinced Monsanto Chemical and Lane Wells to sign on. He worked closely with Peterson, Howell, and Heather of Baltimore, and State Mutual of Boston providing new cars, full maintenance, and selling those coming off lease.

The contract he wrote for the banks gave them blanket security. In effect, they owned everything. They handled all the money and approved the credit of the companies he leased to. The banks also took care of much paperwork, the accounting, the collecting. John remarks that, "People will pay to a bank long before they pay back to an individual or a company."

John's contract with the little Farmers' Bank in Wilmington turned into the most profitable it had ever enjoyed. The bottom line was

John's chutzpa and hustle. He was a man in a frenzy, a character out of Rabelais—all appetite, ready to snap up any deal that came his way. Wayne remembers John once saying that "he wanted to buy everything. He really did want to buy everything, and he never did think about what it cost or anything like that. I'd ask him, 'Where are you going to get the money?' And he'd say that [kind of thinking] would just ruin his deal." Wayne made it his job to try and curb his Pantagruelian brother. "He got us into things that I never would have gotten into," Wayne says, "But he contributed a lot." (Wayne is not given to overstatement. It was John, of course, who flung Wayne into the mainstream of American business and made him aware he could swim with the big fish.)

In 1946, John was a little white cloud on the Delaware horizon, no bigger than a banker's thumb. By 1952 he was running for lieutenant governor. Winning, he gained outline and color. Operating half a dozen Ford dealerships in three states, he was welcome in bankers' offices. His shrewd, sunny nature and high energy inspired trust. Familiarity will always breed a better line of credit, and no one is more welcome in those panelled offices than a man who is generating pots of money and not just talking about it.

Henry Tippie says the company managed to secure a $500,000 line at Farmers' Bank in Delaware in 1953, the year following John's ascension to political office. One-half million dollars is hardly chickenfeed, but John spent it in a flash, acquiring more vehicles to lease. Half of Farmers' Bank was owned by the state, and John the politician was now a familiar figure to the head man at the Wilmington office, William Peyton. Peyton put him in touch with Perry Baldwin, who set up the loan.

Henry recalls that John kept running over the limit by fifty or sixty thousand dollars, until Perry Baldwin said maybe what they needed was a bigger loan than Farmers' was really able to handle. He suggested State Mutual, an insurance company in Massachusetts, where he knew the vice president.

John and Henry Tippie flew to Massachusetts. There was something delicious about two farm boys walking into that marble arena of power and prestige, being offered coffee in china cups with saucers. Wayne recalls a similar business trip down South in their Bonanza in the early fifties. They were on their way to close a radio deal, all suited up and ready to make a strong impression. They landed at Roanoke airport for a pit stop. The washroom was equipped with pay toilets and John said that was unconscionable, demanding money for a call of nature. So he proceeded to climb over the top of the stall.

"Now you've got to climb back over again," said Wayne. "And here we make a special stop, and you're all dressed in your best suit and setting up to make some million dollar deal, and you won't even pay a nickel to go to the toilet."

"Hell, who cares about the money?" John said. "It's the principle of the thing. The question is what would a man do if he came here and didn't have a nickel? That's what I'm doing."

Though Henry Tippie felt their situation was fragile, it never seemed to worry John much. No matter the car leasing operation kept running out of funds and they were overdrawn on their Delaware loan (that half-million dollar line of credit). "We couldn't even pay people," Henry recalls, "and so John and I went up to Massachusetts to meet with Dick Wilson who was the second vice president at State Mutual."

They asked for half a million. Wilson said there was a problem. His bank only made loans of a million; and never to family-held businesses—that is, privately owned businesses that lacked shareholders.

"We didn't bat an eyelash," Henry recalls. "We said we could use the million. We said we'd go public. I think we would have done anything to get that money.

"Wilson came down to Rehoboth, just to make sure we existed. The loan went through and John wrote a check for $1,000 to incorporate. Only we didn't have enough in the bank to cover the check." As luck had it, the check took a week "to get across the street and clear." By then the loan had come through and they used that money to make their check good.

So now they had one million dollars to work with, though Jim Crum would have said all they'd done was sink themselves in debt up to their eyeballs. But in this new and forgiving age, debt was the harbinger of future wealth.

Perhaps the bankers at State Mutual observed in John the real thing, just as a musician knows the difference between a great performer and someone who's just hitting the notes. Operating on a fine instinct, and bound by Henry to the pristine logic of a balance sheet, John was making music.

A modern company goes into orbit only after it taps into a mass market. All politics, it's wisely said, is local. But business today strains to become global. It must franchise itself, or create a device (product and logo) that becomes universally desirable. Through such devices, power is drawn away from other institutions, especially government, and takes on corporate form. John instinctively processed money, merchandising, politics and technology to create a system. By the early fifties, he had assembled the parts that would go into his economic engine. But he had yet to connect with a mass market. That began when he convinced firms like Monsanto to lease.

John was in the first wave of businessmen who moved into auto-truck leasing. The pioneer always ventures into a wasteland. No infrastructure exists out there. The traps are legion and everything has to be scotched together from scratch. He knew he needed office outlets at every airport and railway, clerks trained to keep the customer happy. But getting all of this would take money he still didn't have. He'd begun renting and leasing cars at the Los Angeles airport. The vehicles were delivered by young women dressed in designer outfits and called the "Rollins Girls." News soon got back to Delaware that the Rollins Girls were using his agency to sell themselves. John fired the entire entourage and closed down the Los Angeles office.

Henry saw bankruptcy looming. His gloomy prediction, even his numbers didn't temper John's optimism. Grandfather John F. used to say—if you don't give up, then you don't give up. And even on his worst days, John knew he would never give up. He bought a full-page ad in the *Modern Industry Review* and attached a coupon offering terrific deals on car and truck leasing.

"So we're under a lot of pressure," Henry recounts. "A lot of pressure. And John and I go to California—for some reason he had it in mind to go out to Hollywood." They took with them the handful of coupons that California firms had mailed back. They phoned to announce their presence in L.A. And then they stumbled onto one of those pieces of incredible luck that happen only to the well-prepared.

One of their coupons had been signed by the dispatcher at Lane Wells, an oil field outfit. John and Henry showed up to make their pitch. A senior vice president liked what he heard. "And right there," Henry says, "we signed up the biggest lease [Rollins Leasing] had ever had in its history. About 300 automobiles and 200 trucks. And at that date we couldn't have paid for ONE new vehicle."

They gave Lane Wells the best rates—meaning they gave Lane Wells everything but the kitchen sink. "And we figured the vehicles we leased to them would be in terrible shape, coming back from those oil fields. But they had their own garage and mechanics. So we didn't have to furnish a thing. That had a lot to do with this company going forward. And we did very well after that. Very well."

With real money gushing in at last, they bought more equipment. In no time they had 3,000 vehicles. Suddenly they were visible on the national scene, their company listed on the American Exchange. On Labor Day, 1956, they moved from Rehoboth to Wilmington, renting offices in three separate parts of town. It was John's last year as lieutenant governor. This marked the moment when Kitty decided to make her break from John. She never moved with him to Wilmington. The children did. They visited Kitty weekends. It was an extremely rational divorce, a dull divorce as divorces go, lacking in all the traditional fireworks and poisonous oversupply of adrenalin, a divorce that seems to have been very easy on the children.

Henry Adams coolly calculated at the end of the nineteenth century that, given the exponential increase of power the West was able to generate, the total must reach infinity around midcentury. If we allow the hydrogen bomb as infinity, Adams was dead on. Like two wild horses out of control with our planet in tow, business and technology are pulling after them a world ever more dynamic, ever less stable. Like each of us, the businessman is forced to run to stay in place. It's a world to which John has found himself well-adapted.

Henry remembers a highly recommended CEO who walked off the job one Friday lunch hour in 1959 at their leasing operations office without even clearing off his desk. Henry went over to see what was going on and uncovered a complete mess—bad contracts, misfigured rates, low morale. The West Coast offices were completely out of communication with the East Coast offices. "Coordination was nonexistent," he says. "I went out into the field, asked what their problems are. How can we be of help? You find out everything under the sun. You've maybe got licensing problems, permit problems, they don't get deliveries of the stuff they've got on order. You find that maybe they've got stuff going on out there you don't need from the expense standpoint, personnel, it's a multitude of things.

"It takes different people to implement the things that you want to do. I can have the best plan in the world but if I don't have anybody out here to execute it . . . you're dead without the team approach."

John has always tended to hire people because he liked them. (His first partner in business, Dory Bryan, was hardly a roaring success.) More than once Henry has come in to fire people who weren't working out. He says flatly, "The attitude [toward accountants] is they can't run a damn thing. And that's probably right most of the time." The accountant's way of thinking is necessarily conservative, focused on what exists, not on what can be created. The accountant is always doubtful. John likes to call Henry, "Doctor No."

Henry shut down offices that weren't producing income. He "downsized" and "repositioned the company." He might be compared to a surgeon who cuts into the anesthetized patient and removes what's no longer functioning. In any case, the leasing operation not only survived but leaped into vibrant health. Over the years it has been the solid, long-term performer, the cash cow that was always there.

16
An End to Politics

If the Republican party is the party of rich old men, as the Democrats charge, then John is a most peculiar Republican. He has always been hostile to any hint of class privilege. He plumps always for individual initiative. With his background, he naturally identifies with the poor. Like most businessmen, he believes the American system is designed for individual initiative. Nevertheless, he has become increasingly dependent on team effort and what government regulation can do. He's always been hostile to collectives, suspicious of unions. These views led more or less directly to his political defeat in 1960.

Bad feeling prevailed at the Republican state convention in the final days of August in 1959. The age of air conditioning lay in the future. The Dover Armory, where the Republicans convened that August, sweltered in the tropical heat of a Delaware summer. John found himself pitted against the incumbent Lieutenant Governor David P. Buckson. (John's term had ended in 1956.)

Buckson, a harness racing driver and land speculator, had spent much of his life around horses. Buckson knew that if Senator Williams backed John, he could not win and this made him bitter. Buckson accused one of John's strongest supporters, Roy Willits, of being a "liar," saying that Willits had pretended the personal loyalty he felt for John somehow represented the organization. By "organization," he meant the powerful Republican State Chairman, Ellwood Leach, who had promised not to take sides, and Senator Williams.

Buckson and Willits got into a shouting match in the Armory corridor. According to the September 30th *Morning News,* innuendo blossomed into insult, Willits grew red in the face and balled up his fists. "I'm 65 years old," he cried, "but I still can take care of you!" Onlookers had to grab both men to stop them from attacking each other.

When it came to the party vote, John won. Apparently, word had descended from on high. The delegates fell into line. John kept himself well apart from all the shouting and pushing. Once nominated, he went on the stump and condemned the local Democrats in a style that did nothing to hide his own background. "Now, I used to have to slop the hogs," he told the crowd. "And when you're trying to pour slop in that trough, the trouble is you can't get that hog's head out of the trough. But that's what I'm setting out to do in this state. Get the Democrats' head out of the money trough." Whenever he mounted a platform in the black neighborhoods of Wilmington, the crowd would shout, "Tell us about the pigs, Uncle John!"

His platform included "promises to get rid of the racial bars in hotels, restaurants, and other public places." He pledged to have the state finances reorganized, tax forms simplified, audit expenses reduced. He pledged to clean up the Delaware River—an early indication of the environmental concern that would later obsess him.

Wayne's regard for politicians was very low. He regarded the whole business of wooing crowds with deep suspicion. He disliked empty promises, flattering words, and he viewed John's love of politics as an expensive addiction. He thought John much too outspoken to make a career in politics and considered his brother's fascination with running for office a bizarre hobby—like the King of Prussia playing the flute.

But John was excited by the crowds, fascinated by the spectacle, and entertained by the hypocrisy that attends power. What better place to rub shoulders with every possible human type, from the losers clawing feebly in the mud as they slide to the bottom to the brilliant talkers rising grandly on the column of their own hot air.

Wayne apparently didn't realize how much John's political association played a part in his business success. At any rate, he says almost nothing about it. But John's politicking had allowed him to meet most influential folk in Delaware and Washington early in his business career. A whole generation of the ambitious, the well-placed and the well-meaning were jostling, elbowing, and ascending together. Wayne and Russell Peterson (then a du Pont executive), were John's campaign managers. Peterson was also his speech writer and would himself be elected governor a few years later. John's running mate, the candidate for lieutenant governor, was William V. Roth, later Delaware's Republican senator and chairman of the U.S. Senate Finance Committee.

In Delaware, party divisions are vague at best. The du Ponts controlled the state for so many decades that the party system became more shadow than substance. John raised untold millions for the Republican Party over the years, and claims his adherence is absolute. But he belongs less to a political party than to the party of free will. Restless and too radical in his contradictions, he really has no label. He likes to describe himself as "a fiscal conservative but a social liberal." But to get something accomplished in the contentious world, it made sense for him to stick with a party friendly to business. As one of the creators of the first hazardous waste companies in the United States, he would depend entirely on government regulation to make it work. And that regulation would be put in place by a Republican president, only to be undermined later by a Republican Congress. Nothing is simple or easy.

Wayne was right that John was not born to hedge the truth for the sake of votes. Business is the only field broad enough to absorb so much energy. A reporter's description of John, published in the September *Wilmington Morning News* during the Chicago convention in 1960, indicates the kind of impression he made in those days.

> During today's luncheon, Rollins was fairly bubbling with joy. He smiled broadly, shook hands and bounced about the room chatting with everyone. It was almost a celebration of his victory and there were no negative comments when delegates . . . were asked if Rollins had sewn up the gubernatorial slot. "You've got to give Rollins credit," one delegate observed. "He had only one purpose in coming out here, and he accomplished it. The man gets what he goes after. . . . He's a born winner and who could ask for anything more on our ticket in November?"

1960 was the year that Jack Kennedy won by a handful of votes from Chicago. In Delaware, John lost by a handful.

Wayne blamed himself for John's loss in the 1960 campaign. He was, he says, more of a hindrance than a help. A hot issue back then was the "right to work" amendment and Wayne was all for it. Understandably, the unions were violently opposed. When a group of union officials appeared in the campaign office one afternoon, demanding to know John's view on the issue, Wayne said they should ask the candidate. The union men insisted on hearing Wayne's view. He was John's manager, wasn't he?

Wayne replied, "Well, I feel so strongly about the right of anyone to work that I certainly wouldn't compromise my views just to be governor." He later wished he'd said, "I'm not the one who's running." But the cat was out of the bag. The union men were angered. And the words were no sooner out of Wayne's mouth than John walked into the office. The union folk immediately shot Wayne's statement back at John and asked if that was his view too.

Wayne recalls that John hardly paused. "I feel exactly the same way as my brother," he said. He must have known, at that moment, that he was writing off the union vote.

Wayne and John were "exploited" in their youth, but both regarded their worst days as a very good thing in the long run. The way to a better life lay through inner strength, experience, and unrelenting effort. They rose from the lowest possible kinds of work to become chairmen of the board in their own companies with no feeling of class betrayal.

John assumes that, while the class system will never evaporate, it's still fundamentally wrong and should be attacked. As machines are created that do both physical and mental work, so the worker functions less like a cipher on an assembly line and more like a free agent. As for the newly designated underclass, it's no class at all. Like creatures marooned on an island by some geological disaster, the underclass is cut off and abandoned. Disconnected from learning, denied technical skills, it's the measure of America's failure. John has remarked that business, indifferent to everything but business, is complicit, to that extent at least, in the existence of the underclass. The only way it can change their status is by generating work.

John sees charity as a personal matter. The corporation is not a charity. His future experiments in Jamaica, the bequests he would make to hospitals, his scholarships to needy students—all of these good works are funded by John and Michele personally. Public companies are beholden to their stockholders, and stockholders, as a group, value profit only.

John recalls he lost the 1960 election by some 6,400 votes. For what it was worth, he'd received more votes than any other governor elected before that time. And it was this thin margin of loss that convinced Wayne the failure was his. That hasty reply to the union leaders had undone John. "Perfectly timed to get him beaten," he said.

He remarks that a victory for John in 1960 would have been "very costly." Some years later, when John said he was thinking about running for the U.S. Senate, Wayne tried to talk him out of it.

"I don't think it's in your nature to be the senator from a small state like Delaware," he quotes himself as saying. "First of all, everyone knows every move you make. Also, you like to spend time in Jamaica. I can just see the headlines: ROLLINS SPENDS MORE TIME OUT

OF THE COUNTRY THAN IN. And when the news people ask you what you think, you'll tell them! So you better decide," Wayne admonished his brother, "whether you want to live your life in a glass case, because it's not my impression you're going to shape your personal views to political ends."

John must have reflected on Wayne's objections. When he next saw his brother, he banged his fist on the desk, and declared he *was* going to run. But Wayne's skepticism troubled him. He felt a little like a man with a family to support who goes off to write poetry.

A chance incident turned John around. One day he parked in a loading zone in order to make a pickup, and a man he knew slightly stopped and began to berate him, saying, "If you're going to run for the Senate, you'd better respect the laws and not park like that."

To which John retorted, "Well, I've just decided I'm not going to run. In fact, I've just made that decision this instant. Now what are you going to do about it?"

Wayne remembers that John phoned him and cried, "To hell with this Senate nonsense! If I can't even park my car where I want before I get into the campaign, I can just imagine what it will be like afterwards."

17
Child Development

Around 1960 John began courting Linda Kuechler Anderson. He married her in September of 1961. A music lover who had studied piano at the Julliard, Linda had grown up in St. Louis, Missouri, and she could not have been more different from the easygoing Kitty. Tall, svelte, and dark haired, she had the kind of beauty that caused male heads to swivel like startled deer when she walked into a restaurant. While her new husband had been formed deep in the American grain, Linda's imagination was formed by things more European. Linda loved the grand gesture, and with a husband who attached no strings to her expense account, she was soon organizing lunches and swimming parties to raise funds for the Pennsylvania Chamber Symphony of Philadelphia. In 1966 she excited comment from the *Philadelphia Bulletin* (August 14) by flying in Douglas J. Cooper and his wife by rented helicopter from Bryn Athyn to Walnut Green.

It was Linda who introduced Kitty's children to Europe's alternate reality. Flights to the Mozart Festival in Salzburg became an annual event, and Cathy recalls these trips with pleasure. John Jr. says his life was changed by attending a performance of Bizet's *Carmen*.

John stepped in to curb Linda a trifle when she decided to build a horse stable on the grounds of their home at Walnut Green. She'd made an appointment with an architect, but when that gentleman arrived he discovered John there instead. The *Wall Street Journal* in September of 1973 recounts John saying, "Thanks for coming out, sir, but I don't want any horses around here. I've spent most of my life trying to get away from horse manure."

John is long a supporter of the arts, though country music is more to his taste than Beethoven. He collects English paintings from the last century and admires Andrew Wyeth. Like Wayne, John is a fan of London theater, and he supported Linda's attempt to set herself up as a benefactor of the arts. Wayne's wife, Grace, recalls that when she first met Linda she thought she was a beauty. Even more astonishing was the younger woman's power of self-assertion. Linda never made any bones about what she wanted. Grace herself paints pictures but she's far too modest to put them out on display.

Around 1970, John and Wayne took Grace and Linda on a world tour. They flew first to Hawaii, then to Hong Kong. Grace recalls that Linda "carried an attaché case full of drugs." (She means pharmaceuticals.) Linda was not about to circumnavigate the globe unarmed against who knew what bacteria? "She had pumped me so full of drugs for my stomach upset," Grace says, "that we went all the way through India and I never did know a thing."

In Hong Kong, Grace flummoxed Wayne by polishing off the most exotic foods imaginable. "I ate all kinds—those hundred year old eggs and bird's nest soup." Grace remembers how Wayne was restless, usually in a hurry. She told him, "Now if you're going to spend all that money for transportation, why can't you allow enough time to enjoy things?"

In Beirut bombs were exploding somewhere in the city, and in Egypt, an old Arab guided them up to the top of a pyramid, dragging Grace by the hand. She was sure he'd never had a bath in his life, all silty and covered with dust as if he'd been dredged from the bottom of the Nile. "And Wayne Rollins was dying laughing. He just thought that was the funniest thing that ever was. I went back to the hotel and I scrubbed until I thought there wasn't going to be any skin left on my hands."

When she and Linda visited the Cairo Museum to see the King Tut exhibit, they were told the institution was closed for cleaning because some Syrian head of state would be visiting. Grace says, "And [Linda] had enough brass, she could get you in anywhere. We were the only two American women in that place. No one was around us. [The guard] let us roam around. I was scared to death. All they had to do was say we'd broken in. I didn't enjoy it. I'm sure she gave that guard some money."

Linda recalls that the Cairo Museum was to have been the high point of the trip, and when she was told to go away, she was so disappointed she burst into tears. A guide took pity and let them in. She says she's sent him a card every Christmas ever since.

Like two of Mark Twain's American tourists in *Innocents Abroad*, Wayne and John were taken aback by Linda's appetite for fine art. For Linda, culture was her great love. Later in life she became obsessed with turning a story about Annie, the white witch of Jamaica, into a film. She spent years raising money for it. When she traveled, she wanted to immerse herself in the past, and insisted on seeing every mosque, temple, and museum while Wayne and John poked fun. Linda asked why they'd bothered to come so far if they weren't going to visit all the monuments they possibly could? Wayne said he was worried about her putting on the slippers provided by the mosques to visitors. "Don't you know lepers use those things?" According to John, Linda then disinfected all her shoes to be on the safe side.

John's marriage to Linda would last over a decade and produce two sons, Theodore and Jeffrey. John's breakup with her early in the seventies coincided precisely with his worst financial crisis. Articles were appearing every week in the local paper, and everyone assumed John's "empire" was going under. Linda's spending was severely curtailed. She bailed out in September, 1975. As soon as her divorce from John was final, she married William Prickett (the lawyer who'd attacked John's attempt to bring cable television to Delaware in court). Prickett was an art lover who'd once dressed up as Beethoven to receive an arts committee asking him for support. According to one of the people who was there, Prickett remained "in character" for the entire visit.

John's daughter, Cathy, by then a graduate of the University of North Carolina, was more disturbed by her father's divorce from Linda than she'd been by the earlier separation from Kitty, her real mother. Cathy had moved with her brother, Patrick, to live in her father's house. Cathy and Linda were close. The divorce left her in an emotional no-man's-land. Her father felt twice betrayed. His second wife had left him just when his financial crisis was at its most acute to marry the lawyer who'd attacked him repeatedly in court.

Patrick went on to graduate from Washington & Lee University, married his wife Faye, and worked in his father's companies before starting up his own business in Texas. Cathy worked in the Nixon White House where she met Dan Searby, an advance man responsible for the president's family when they travelled. Cathy moved out to California with Dan and went to work for a staffing firm. She soon took over the firm and, for seven years running, made it the top office in a franchise with 600 offices. John admits to being astonished by his daughter's success. "If I'd known how able she was I would have put her into some business of my own," he says ruefully.

To escape the storm of his parents' divorce, Linda's eldest son, Ted, chose boarding school. He graduated from The Citadel, earned an MBA from Duke, and later worked briefly for his father, managing the construction of a hotel in Delaware before going on to start a business of his own in North Carolina.

Jeff, Linda's youngest, went off to Holderness boarding school where he graduated first in his class. He emerged from Duke magna cum laude with an MBA and came back to Wilmington to start working his way up in Rollins Environmental Services.

Wayne and Grace's two boys reflect the different eras of their birth. Randall arrived in the depths of the Depression (1932); Gary at the start of a new age of prosperity (1944). Randall, his nature reflecting the tough thirties when he was a child, seemed bent on making life tough for himself. Gary, by contrast, was affectionate, patient, and easygoing. Randall is gimlet-eyed, suspicious, and learns the hard way. His father sent him off to the Georgia Military Academy. But after giving the place a brief perusal, he decided it was not for him and returned home. His mother was dismayed. His father put Randall to work building fences at the Cherokee Valley farm. Randall had in mind to better his father's business record. "He had it figured he was going to surpass what John and I had done," Wayne says. "He had a pinball deal, then a recreation place, and a filling station in Lewes." Unfortunely, the man Randall hired to run his gas station embezzled all the money.

"He got out there and he weathered it. He never came running back to me for help. He wasn't a prodigal son, but he had some of those characteristics. He learned that when he was pissing in his boot the warm feeling wasn't necessarily good."

Gary, with his even, pleasant temperament, was not inclined to test himself against superhuman ideals, but he had his own way of getting what he wanted. Once, when Grace refused to let him go out with some of his high school friends, she recalls how he sat down in a rocking chair and rocked. She ignored him. But he sat there silently rocking for so long that Grace finally lost all patience and told him to get out of the house and go waste his time any way he liked.

Gary tended to have good luck. As a teenager, he was thrown out of a Volkswagen car travelling at high speed. The driver lost control, a door flew open, and Gary went flying out. "I don't know how far he was thrown," says Wayne. "But it was right alongside this rock wall. The car threw him out with such force that his watch flew off his arm over the wall, and his shoes were ripped off. He kept rolling and it burned his clothes off of him. He got some scratches and bruises and burns, but he didn't have a bone broken. The least deviation would have thrown him into that rock wall. Just rolling over and over and over beside it, he must have gone over a hundred feet. So you know they were speeding."

During the fifties, Gary spent certain summers at Catoosa Springs where Claudia lived. "Grandmother," Gary says, "was a very religious person. Can't wait to Sunday. Can't wait to prayer meeting. Can't wait to revivals. Some of those revivals got to be pretty powerful. I can remember going to Smith Chapel. Relatives would come up crying. And you're giving yourself to Jesus or whatever. As a fairly young person that had not had a dose of this regularly—I can remember that I used to dread it . . . because I didn't understand a whole lot about what was going on. All of the hollering and crying.

"As I got older, whenever all the commotion started, I'd duck out the back door. By that time we were teenagers. And we'd just kinda fade to the back of the church and let the adults go through all of that."

Wayne worried more about the future of his grandchildren than his sons. He knew very well how money eats like acid into the souls of those who inherit it. The American ethos is populist to its core, and inherited money is often hidden. Money can't buy much moral status in a society where the only respectable activity is *making* money. "It means a lot of responsibility to use [money] wisely, and certainly a lot of responsibility to try to handle it in some way not to spoil these grandchildren. And to tell you the truth, I don't believe I can do it," Wayne says. "I believe it's a bigger job than I can do. So I guess what I have to do is resign myself to doing the best I can and hoping that [the money] spoils as few [of the children] as possible, recognizing that there'll be some of them that it will."

James, John's second-born, grew up handsome and humorous, seemingly incapable of rancor or bitterness. A natural athlete, he showed signs of having been gifted by the gods. If so, the gods decided they wanted him back. Around 1960 John noticed that fifteen-year-old James was having trouble catching a baseball—the first indication of the brain tumor that would kill him eleven years later. John and Kitty had to learn how to suffer their son's long decline.

John spent years going from one physician to the next, hoping for a cure. Ignoring his deteriorating body, Jimmie married Deirdre Taylor, and started up a business in California. Their daughter, Jamie, who was born four months before her father died at twenty-seven (1971), went on to Duke and then earned a law degree from Georgetown University.

Joe Seymour, John's chauffeur of some forty years, had a boy with an identical medical history, though the tumor presented earlier in the child's life. Joe recalls that "Mr. Rollins stayed right with us and did all he could for my boy." Young Joey died when he was twenty-three.

Time is mysteriously configured so that bad events never arrive solo but in droves. In the summer before Jimmie died, Wayne and Grace lost Rita, their oldest granddaughter—Randall and Peggy's first child. She was killed by a bolt of lightning during a July storm at Catoosa Springs. Rita was spending the day with Claudia, her great-grandmother. Late in the afternoon she made a phone call from Claudia's bedroom to a friend as the storm approached. "At six o'-clock we called her several times," Wayne says.

> She didn't come. So I went looking for her. And she was in the bedroom, where the phone was. Evidently she had been lying flat on her back on the floor like kids will, talking on the phone, and that lightning—there was no lightning arrestor on the phone—that lightning bolt came in on that phone and that's what killed her. And I found her there on the floor.
>
> I thought maybe we could revive her, but there wasn't any way. The doctor said that she was killed instantly. I felt responsibility. Grace and I both did. . . . As I look back I don't know how we could have done anything. But you've got to blame something. I think it was more of a blow to Grace even than it was to me.

Roman in his stoicism, Wayne avoids the language of grief and speaks instead of his "responsibility." Yet according to Grace, Wayne always cried easily. It's John who locks in grief. Relatives describe him as impassive at his mother's funeral. Yet he says he still finds himself thinking about her almost every day.

The local phone company was responsible for Rita's death. The owner was a high school friend of Wayne's. Some technician had installed the line without a lightning rod. "The lightning arrestor should have been on there. It was just neglected. I guess [the owner's] lawyer told him not to say or do anything. And it hurt me some—the fact that he didn't come and express sympathy. He never did tell me anything. A lot of people told me I ought to sue the telephone company. My thinking was that I couldn't bring Rita back and I didn't want to put the family through anything that revived or rehashed the thing."

The long line of John's life has often spiraled back around to revisit the past, always from a higher vantage. People are more significant to him than places. Unlike his brother, he didn't go back to the hills where he was born. But Wayne did. It was Wayne who refurbished his parents' house and made it a monument to the family's achievement. John is more attached to memories of his mother, grandfather and grandmother than the fields where they labored.

John regarded his brother's wife as a sister when she came to live in his father's clapboard house in 1931, and he regards her that way today. He hangs onto his friendship with Kitty, his first wife. Yet his ability to metamorphose and change with the times is essentially modern. His nature, to some extent, has an ability to adapt that compares to the technology that identifies our era. Form is determined by function. He swears by what works best.

It took John a lifetime to find a woman as well-suited to the American century as himself. He met her in Michele Metrinko in January, 1976. Michele's family is Ukrainian. Her father, ninety years old in 1999, still held a seat on the New York Stock Exchange. Michele married John in 1977. A lawyer and state-of-the-art version of the American woman, Michele is ambitious, optimistic, crackling with energy.

Michele earned her law degree after graduating from the School of Foreign Service at Georgetown University. Not content with that, she picked up a master's degree in tax law while working at the Securities and Exchange Commission. She ended her career in government as the first woman to become an associate solicitor for conservation and wildlife in the U.S. Department of the Interior.

While an undergraduate, "wanting to travel, wanting to win everything," Michele spotted an ad in the paper announcing the Miss New York finals for the Miss USA Pageant. Qualified to enter because her parents lived in New York, she talked herself into a shot at the title. She says she'd rather have made her mark at the Olympics, but she was more an Aphrodite than a Diana. She dyed a pair of shoes, bought a bathing suit and "dragged my whole family" to the contest.

"There were 125 of us. The air conditioning was freezing. Finally mother (not known for mincing words) said, 'Just lose! And let's get out of here. Your dad has to get up in the morning.' But Michele shivered her way across the stage and got second prize, Miss New York City. This qualified her for a shot at the Miss USA contest in Huntington, West Virginia.

She knew very well that American pageants are just "a business," but she was looking for connections, willing to take chances. Michele instinctively grasped the way American commerce transforms private lives, perhaps because her father sat on the stock exchange. As they placed the crown on her head, she recalls thinking, "I guess this thing isn't fixed after all."

Adding "Miss USA" to her resume made a difference. Getting interviews became surprisingly easy. "Because the wonderful male population is always curious enough to want to *look*. Your *title* makes doors open more easily. Which is not a bad thing when there are a hundred applicants for every job. Even the professors at a law school are going to remember the beauty queen they interviewed. But then you have to work harder to prove you're serious and intelligent, that you aren't just trading on the title."

When John first met her, in 1975, she was working for the Department of the Interior in Washington D.C. Michele's suitor (as everyone was quick to point out) was older than her mother. They told her he was in financial hot water, skirting bankruptcy. His second wife had just left him to marry his most enthusiastic enemy.

"About the time Michele and I started going out together everyone thought I was going to bite the dust," John recalls. "That's what all the rumors were. I was in the Eurodollar mess to begin with. And then Michele came along. She got word I was going broke. This bunch in Wilmington used to tell Michele's dad the same thing. But she helped me. I sold everything and tried to hang onto my [Rollins] stock which dropped from 42 to 4."

Michele was informed by just about everyone that she was making a terrible mistake. The man she was marrying was sixty years old, divorced, and going broke. She was young, blonde, beautiful, and apparently had lost her mind. John remarks that Michele's "main problem" is she can't say no to a good cause. Whatever it was that Michele saw in John eluded the perception of those who knew her best. Money appeared to be the obvious answer. But, as everyone constantly reminded her, he was as good as bankrupt. She had only to read the newspaper for confirmation.

Michele, with her overpowering desire to make the most out of life, was not burdened by a fragile sensibility. She was prepared to give the world back as good as it gave. She had no doubt John would rise from his own ashes and fly like the phoenix. "He doesn't equivocate," Michele says. "If he doesn't feel a thing is right, he'll say it." His teenage daughter, Monique, puts it even more succinctly: "He's got a great B.S. meter."

Michele married him in 1977. Life had sketched them both in bold outlines; energy was drawn to energy. By his late fifties, John had accomplished more than a dozen other entrepreneurs and, if she came on board when he was entangled in the worst crisis of his career, perhaps the danger attracted her, providing her a field where her own energy could operate.

Between 1978 and 1982, they had four children whose names all begin with the letter M. Michele's third-born, Michael, arrived within a few hours of Cathy's daughter, Katie, in California, making John a father and grandfather on the same day. Michele had intended to produce eight offspring, but quit with four "to get organized." While she was bearing children, she was recruited onto innumerable boards. Aside from the Beebe Hospital board, she's worked primarily in education, sitting on the boards of St. Edmond's Academy, Goldey Beacom College, the Ursuline Academy, the Centreville School in Delaware, Cabrini College in Radnor, PA, and her own School of Foreign Service, Georgetown University in Washington D.C.

Through her influence, certainly, John has set aside more time for the children of his late years. The children of Kitty, his first wife, recall that he was seldom home. Linda's two boys say the same thing. The four youngest children have seen more of him. Television is regarded with hostility by Michele. She was super-mom, driving her children all over northern Delaware for lessons in skating, riding, music, art. Monique, interested in painting from the age of six, was driven out to Hockessin to study. When she found her mother too demanding, her father would talk her through it. She quotes him saying, "Life is what you make it, so why not be happy and have a good time? Ninety per cent of the things we worry about never happen."

Their oldest girl, Michele, says that her parents never seemed to get their signals mixed. It was impossible to play one off against the other. While other adolescents sometimes appeared embarrassed by their parents ("I never know what they're gonna say!"), young Michele never felt that way. Maybe it was that her father came from an earlier time when parents had few questions about their own role. Home from college at nineteen, she decided she was now grown up, an independent person. She ignored their eleven o'clock curfew. When she did wander in, her mother was practically apoplectic. She could see in both parents' faces how much she'd frightened them. It's never pleasant to learn that with freedom comes responsibility.

Young Michele shocked her mother when she quit college at the end of her third year to become a cosmetologist. Her mother felt strongly that the young woman should get a degree first. It was John who said young Michele should do whatever work she felt was important to her. "'Success comes from doing work that makes a person happy,' he said. It's hard to argue with that."

Monique recalls her father often making breakfast for the family. "Country fried steak, great gravy and grits, or corned beef hash and eggs. All through high school, he'd wake us up and make breakfast during the time mom was with my grandmother at the hospital. He used to say, 'The worst thing is having two teen age girls. I'm just a dishrag in their hands.'"

To keep up his energy during long, afternoon meetings, John took to the doctor's suggestion that he try tomatoes and peanut butter. As Monique tells it, John invented a sandwich that combined both elements. He once prepared a tomato and peanut butter sandwich for one of her boyfriends, who dutifully ate the exotic object without comment, much to the childrens' amusement.

When she was trying to make her school basketball team, John hung around the concrete pad where she practiced at home, giving her pointers. He'd been a member of a team that went from tiny Co-hutta High to the state championship playoffs and came in second. "He said being the best has nothing to do with being number one. Being best comes from doing best. When my grades were not that great, instead of grounding me like most of my friends' parents, he'd sit down and help me with my homework, until I understood. He told me never to be afraid of failure."

18
Airheads and Airwaves

John is an entrepreneur in more than one sense. He started his hazardous waste company (Rollins Environmental Services) with a new technology imported from England. He has organized the construction of hotels, a racetrack, a giant shopping mall. He has taken over some failing enterprises and made over every aspect of the business until it came back to life.

Nowadays we pin the label *entrepreneur* on anyone with something to sell—a corner grocer, Paloma Picasso using her father's name to flog cosmetics, the manager of a franchise selling T-shirts or chicken wings. Even a man selling a Hillary Clinton "dismemberment doll" at the 1996 Republican convention is ironically described by Garry Wills: "For twenty dollars you could buy a rag-doll Hillary with arms and legs made to tear off and throw on the floor. The *entrepreneur* demonstrated with furious rendings; then he pulled the head off. . . ."

Neither this definition by example nor Webster's description of an entrepreneur as "one who organizes, operates, and assumes the risk in a business venture in expectation of gaining the profit" is adequate. In the last century the word "undertaker" was used, but that word now has a special application. The French have as many cheeses as there are days in the year and a name for each; the Arabs have an entire vocabulary to designate different grades of sand. Yet we have only one word to describe perhaps the most enigmatic and various figure in a culture that is saturated by commerce. And that word we haven't even bothered to translate from the French.

John, true to his nature, kept adding more companies to his retinue. A few failed and were put on the block or sank into oblivion. "Wayne had so much common sense," John says. "I'd get off on a lot of half-assed things and I'd lose my behind sometimes." Memorable among the failures was the manufacturing group he installed in a deconsecrated church in Lewes.

Two engineers approached him in 1951 with a proposition he

thought might work. They wanted to fabricate cable harnesses designed to hook up the Ford auto electrical system more efficiently. Their invention included a switch that automatically caused headlights to dim by sensing oncoming headlights. John did a lot of business with the people at Ford who expressed interest. So he put the engineers to work; they began to ship their gadgets out. But the cables kept coming back by return mail with labels that said "Defective" plastered all over them. John had faith the cable systems would work as soon as the inventors ironed out a few bugs.

Wayne was more doubtful, but Wayne was always doubtful. When Henry Tippie joined them from Omaha, the electronics division was still trying to make the cables function. Henry glanced over the balance sheet and, with his accountant's eye, figured the whole business for a disaster. He informed John that these engineers were eating him alive. That's when John began calling Henry "Dr. No." Losing money bothered him less because he loved a challenge, especially one that involved some new technology. He was sure the gadgets were a good idea. All the engineers needed was time.

Wayne's doubts deepened when he learned that one of the engineers was spending his evenings with a married woman. The gentleman had been flushed from the depths of the woman's bed in downtown Lewes by her husband. The way Wayne tells it, this Romeo jumped, pale and naked, from a second story window into a rose bush. The bush broke his fall, but the thorns did him considerable epidermal damage. He was observed by good Christian women running through the streets, garbed only in dribbles of blood. The somnambulant town of Lewes had already been disturbed by the Rollinses' hectic activity. Now there were reports of naked employees running through the night.

Setting aside the painful plunge into the rose bush and the bad public relations that resulted, the engineers were costing John over $100,000 annually. Wayne recalls the losses went as high as $300,000 one year. Weary of listening to Wayne's and Henry's complaints about all the money they were losing, John decided to buy Wayne out and set up a meeting. Wayne recalls it was on a Monday at eleven o'clock in the morning. He says their conversation ran something like this:

"Hell," said John. "I still think it's got a good profit potential. I'll buy it from you."

"Oh, I won't do that, John," said Wayne. "I'll just give you my half."

John was taken aback by Wayne's uncharacteristic behavior. "You wouldn't do that, would you?"

"Get the papers for my signature," Wayne said. "You can have it."

John kept the engineers on for another year. By then the outfit was losing such vast sums of money that he was forced to admit Wayne and Henry were right. He told the engineers to close the place down and to tell the workers to find jobs elsewhere.

Now the townspeople of Lewes rose up to object. Editorials were printed smiting him in the daily paper. He was portrayed as a cold-blooded capitalist throwing good people out of work, a menace to prosperity and community. Affected by this outcry and hoping to win back the affection of the community, he told the engineers they would have one last chance. They put their machinists back to work, and lost another $100,000. John decided to look for someone foolish enough to buy the business.

Eventually an engineer from Baltimore appeared who thought he could make the idea work. He bought the church with its nave full of machinery and apparently he knew what he was doing, because the business was soon operating at a profit. But thereafter, John avoided manufacturing and stuck with service companies.

Wayne hated intuitive leaps. Cautious by nature, he appeared shy, reticent, the consummate Southern gentleman. But occasionally from the shadows a warrior would materialize. When a school bully began taking his son Randall's allowance and using the boy as a punching bag for his own entertainment, Wayne advised Randall to pick up a rock the size of a fist and use it. Randall did.

These were folk whose grandparents were frontier people. The tough and steely will of those original settlers was still part of Wayne's, and John's, makeup. With his mind for detail, Wayne, over time, worked out a business approach that Ben Franklin would have found congenial. To his way of thinking, moral improvement led directly to material advancement. But whatever you gain by immoral means you will lose in the long run, along with your own soul.

Wayne was loathe to depart from the old ways. He was reluctant to take Rollins Broadcasting public. But by 1960 he had no other choice. He was simply too successful to stick in the small time. He had to come to terms with Wall Street and serious money. He realized this on the day he struck a deal with a mortician from Montgomery, Alabama. He'd gone there to buy a television station. They negotiated in the lobby of a hotel and he recalls how the undertaker interrupted their conversation from time to time to wave at people passing through. "Now there goes Mrs. Roy whose mother and husband I buried. That's Mrs. Noonan! She's the only one left now. Her boy and the father were taken out on the interstate. Took a lot of fixing." He identified everyone by the deaths of kith and kin.

The mortician agreed to take Wayne's offer. But Wayne's banker in Delaware refused to lend him the $2 million he needed unless he signed over everything he owned as collateral, including his house. Moreover, Grace would have to cosign. This last point incensed Wayne, who regarded having to drag his wife into his business deals as a personal affront.

"Well, either you fit the pattern, or you don't get the money," the banker said. "If your company was public this wouldn't be necessary."

The suggestion that he had to "fit the pattern" did not sit well with Wayne. But he had to tell the mortician that he couldn't handle the loan, and the station immediately sold to another buyer for $250,000 more than Wayne would have paid. Wayne reckoned he'd just taken an overnight loss of a quarter-million dollars.

John regarded getting on the New York Stock Exchange as a sign of success. He and Henry Tippie incorporated Rollins Leasing in 1954. Like it or not, Wayne had to acknowledge he was in the big time and had to take the broadcasting company public. He foresaw the red tape, government regulation, shareholders trying to sue; he hated losing control. A public business is regarded by cold-fish shareholders as a money machine. The entire process of putting a company on the New York Stock Exchange felt like taking those coins from Grandma Emma's petticoat where they were warm and safe and handing them over to a bank teller. The company would no longer be theirs. It would expand and merge with the abstract world of money.

Few companies hang onto their names and their single product like Coca-Cola and McDonald's. Corporate success more often imitates the progress of a Disney, which began life as a trouserless mouse and today has investments in outer space. Service industries, like the Rollinses, are an intermediate step on the path from heavy industry (steel, rail, autos) to intellectual property (software, information, entertainment). What Rollins Broadcasting offered for sale was airwaves. And it's worth noting once again that curious attenuation that has worked its way through the living body of technology. The Industrial Revolution began with behemoth machines, locomotives that weighed tons, ships like floating cities. Today we have the silicon chip able to contain more complex information than any one of those ships. Development of the machine has moved from giantism toward the vanishing point, from the blacksmith's forge to a dance of electrons. Stamping out the body parts of a truck and bolting them together can all be accomplished by machines in thrall to electrical impulses. Anyone with a modem is free to flit around in hyperspace where ideas are far more expensive than goods.

To get Rollins Broadcasting hooked into the market, Henry Tippie and Wayne went down to Wall Street. Wayne felt like a country boy on his first visit to the city.

> I thought I'll go up to New York and I'll go down to Wall Street. And I didn't know what the address was or anything. But I thought, I'll go and I'll talk to them about going public. And so I get this cab driver and he takes me down there. And he wants to know where I want to go and I said, "Wall Street."
>
> So he pulls right up in front of this building. Number One Wall Street. I went in. And it was a rainy day and bad weather. And all the partners were in the office that day. There were big desks scattered around. They were all there, located in one big room.
>
> I went in and Calder [a partner in Manheim's firm] introduced me to Frank Manheim, and Frank Manheim said, "Why don't you have lunch with us today?" Over the salad, Manheim, a wizened gentleman with foxy eyes, said, "You only grossed eight million last year. Now we don't touch any company under twenty-five million. How big do you expect to grow?"

Wayne said a hundred million. It seemed like a nice, safe figure. "And just how do you expect to do that?" asked Manheim who was apparently willing to be convinced.

Wayne said it was a sure thing. He was reaching a new audience that was eager for everything he brought them. He mentioned Nat King Cole and Jesse Owens, the Olympic star who was among his commentators. Aretha Franklin. His stations were among the first of their kind.

"Minorities?" said Manheim. "These are minority stations? These are Negro stations?"

"I'd rather have a black station in the black, than a white station in the red."

"Strange, coming from a Southerner," said Manheim.

"Well, now you know how I feel about it," said Wayne. "But everything we've bought we've had to turn around. Every station was losing money. We turned it around because we know our business."

"Well," Manheim said. "I'm going to recommend to the partners that we make an exception in your case."

That is the conversation more or less as Wayne recalls it. Manheim passed Wayne and Henry along to a smaller outfit called Eberstadt. Henry took the company through the necessary accounting hoops. Rollins Broadcasting went public in 1960. Shares of the stock worth $1,000 that year would have been worth over $160,000 in 1992.

By the early sixties Wayne and John were flying around the United States picking up companies like kids in a candy store. Wayne began to buy billboard companies because FCC regulations limited broadcast ownership to seven stations.

Why billboards? Wayne's figuring went something like this: A billboard (in the fifties) cost $350. It rented for $60 a month. So it took about half a year to cover its cost. A house that rented for $60 back then cost $3,000. Covering the house cost took fifty months, not including interest and upkeep.

"[Another] reason we got into Outdoor, a billboard company, and television was so we could continue to expand the business. If you want to attract good people, you've got to offer them opportunity. If you don't expand, there's no chance for the guy below to move up. Remember, my formula was to employ people at a lower salary than their former job. What I gave [in return] was a chance to get ahead, to keep moving up. Expansion is the key to the whole concept."

Wayne picked up General Outdoor, then Gallahan Advertising Systems, in the late fifties. After going public in 1961, Wayne went the whole hog and bought Tribble Outdoor for $3 million. Wayne negotiated with Helen Tribble Mays, daughter of the founder.

Helen Tribble and her sister had become bitter enemies. Fights over family money had reached such a pitch the two women could no longer stand the sight of each other. The sister refused to enter the same room. So the deal with Wayne took place with Helen Tribble Mays present and her sister listening through an open door from the adjacent room.

Only after Helen had signed and disappeared did the younger woman come in to add her signature. These sisters' passionate hatred recalls the greed and lust for power that set families to poisoning and stabbing each other in Renaissance Italy or the English court. And perhaps the Tribble sisters' hatred affected even the weather, because Wayne had no sooner signed the agreement than a violent storm came whirling across Texas and blew down most of his newly acquired billboards. Billboards were not insurable, so he had to put them all back up at his own expense. In effect, he bought them twice. During that same period, he bought KDAY in Los Angeles and WRAP in West Virginia. By 1962, those twice-bought billboards were producing twenty-five percent of his revenue. The executive who manages a company's billboards borrows his approach from mathematics. What and how much he wants the public to see is calculated with a definite precision. A 100 percent "showing" refers to an image so often reproduced in a region that everyone there must pass by it. "Outdoor is fun to create with," says a Rollins manager. "You can go with a 100 [percent] showing and back off to 50 or 75. You can manipulate the intensity."

This sort of talk sets a lot of teeth on edge. The commercialization of public space runs headlong into the issue of the public good. Billboards and advertisements in general have seduced artistic talent into the arms of commerce. Some of the most advanced critics (who appear the most reactionary from another perspective) regard the ad as a genuine American art form, an offshoot of pop culture. The photographer Walker Evans held to this view. "When you photograph billboards, do you do it out of a sense of disdain or derision for them?" a student at the University of Michigan asked Evans, in 1971.

"Well, I love them," he replied.

The shots of Atlanta posters that Evans took in the thirties are nostalgic evocations of how evanescent time has become in America. Seeing Evans's photographs of posters advertising Carole Lombard in *Love Before Breakfast,* Robert Donat in *The Count of Monte Cristo,* or the Ritz Brothers in *Kentucky Moonshine,* the viewer is reminded of how brief is success and fame. In fifteen years who will remember or care about the faces that excite the public now? Something essential about the nature of time in the United States is fixed in these photographs of a commercial art that was never created to preserve anything.

What, finally, did the Rollins brothers accomplish in the field of broadcasting? Wayne, to begin with, invented a way to run stations that otherwise would not have survived. Both brothers were enthusiastic about high rates of incentive pay. When Wayne's son, Randall, came to work for his father, the young man worked for less than anyone else. His objections were ignored. One day he would inherit what Wayne had created, but his father believed that unless he suffered it would mean nothing to him. Whatever came easy was, in Wayne's opinion, absolutely worthless.

What comes over the airwaves only appears to come easy. But it's paid for by the commercial. In the United States the commercial is like death and taxes, unavoidable. Very few American broadcasters have found means to exist without it. The Christian stations and Lewis Hill's Pacifica Radio (in the Bay Area, Los Angeles, and New York) begged money from listeners to stay on the air. Now public radio has been reduced to this expedient.

The most high-minded and excellent radio in America was provided by Pacifica out of grubby studios run by amateur executives and armies of volunteers. Pacifica was the first to set up "marathons," which beat the drum for contributions from listeners. While Christian listeners paid for religion, Pacifica's listeners paid for civilization in the form of European music, political commentary, world literature, and philosophy. Hill believed that exposure to high culture (in the person of those who actually created it) might lead to a culturally richer, more rewarding American society. Organized as a cooperative, the station became a sort of academic circus of the air with commentators guaranteed to infuriate listeners of one sort of another.

Many of the most outspoken African American leaders broadcast by Pacifica were heard first over the Rollins stations—Jesse Jackson, James Baldwin, Martin Luther King, Ralph Abernathy, Malcolm X. The same holds true for black music. (Remarking on Reverend Jackson, Wayne said, "Jesse started at WBEE as an announcer first. Then he saw there was more money being a preacher. So he got him a congregation that paid for his program.")

The first black station that had been established in the twenties under African American ownership was WERD in Atlanta. Wayne now extended that resource to millions of new listeners with WJWL Georgetown, KATZ St. Louis, WNJR New York City, KDAY Los Angeles, WBEE Chicago, WRAP Norfolk, and WBEE Indianapolis.

Wayne also ran the first radio and TV educational network. His philosophy of broadcasting might have been invented by Ben Franklin: to do the right thing, fill a real need. Your reward will be the public good and hard cash. The expansion of Wayne's network was certainly practical. Twenty million African Americans were putting billions every year into the economy. The revenue growth of Rollins Broadcasting beat the industry average by forty percent. By 1964, Wayne was described in the *Wall Street Journal* as a high-profile broadcaster, known for increasing his audience and bringing down advertising rates. Wayne credited the success of his program content to his program director, Ralph Lanphear.

Establishing the means to explore the programming interests of the black community while staffing their stations with black talent, the Rollinses made their company both profitable and socially progressive. Having embarked on broadcasting during a period of major change and upheaval in black communities across the nation, Rollins Broadcasting became an important player in the social advance of African Americans.

19
Making History

By 1964, the Rollinses' miracle year, Wayne was supervising a string of ten radio stations (five of them African American) and three television stations. He'd managed to situate himself in the three largest markets in the U.S. (Chicago, New York, and Los Angeles where KDAY went over to black broadcasting a few days after he bought it). The revenues from these outlets amounted to about a million dollars in 1960, with an after-tax profit of $400,000. In the greater American economy, a flea among shaggy dogs. Public shares went on sale for $8 in September of that year, an excellent value, because the Rollinses were about to orchestrate the first leveraged buyout and increase revenues 369 percent virtually overnight. Their vehicle for this legerdemain was Orkin.

The Orkin Company, founded in 1901 by Otto Orkin, a Latvian rat-catcher, was the largest pest control company in the nation in 1963. Known as Otto the Ratman, the owner immigrated to Pennsylvania around the turn of the century and started selling rat poison in little brown paper packets and employing pest control wagons drawn by horses. In 1925, he moved to Atlanta where the warm weather bred vermin at a rate more consistent with a growing business.

When Wayne met Otto in 1963, the founder's children were in charge: Otto's son, Sanford; Sanford's brother, Billy; and a sister who was married to the company's operations officer, Perry Kay.

George Weymouth, a du Pont family member, first brought Orkin to Wayne's attention. (Weymouth was married to Jean du Pont's daughter, Deo.) He partnered the du Pont firm of Laird, Bissell and Mead, financial brokers and consultants. So Wayne knew Weymouth fairly well. They'd hunted together in Florida. But most of Wayne's contacts with the du Pont clan were made through John. Wayne acknowled that "John is a social animal. You could go to Saudi Arabia, and John would know somebody over there. From the very beginning he was involved with the du Ponts and I met a whole lot of them through him. We'd become good friends with Ned and Carroll Carpenter, and with Ned's brother, Sam Carpenter."

When Wayne travelled with Weymouth to negotiate a newspaper deal in Texas, the last thing on his mind was pest control. The newspaper deal looked good by Friday of that week. Wayne was sure he could make a deal. But on Monday the seller said he'd changed his mind over the weekend. He'd suddenly realized the paper was his life. Sell it and all he'd have left was money.

On the long flight home, Weymouth suggested they take a look at Orkin in Atlanta. "I'd had enough experience to know that to get these brokers to keep showing you [the best prospects] you've got to help them [look good]. Now George had been very patient about our deal falling through. So I said, 'Well, you pick a time, I'll go down there.'"

Weymouth said Orkin was in great shape. But the price was fourteen times Wayne's net worth. It would be like moving from a house worth $150 thousand to one worth over $2 million. That was an order of expansion no sane businessman would contemplate without some fear and trembling.

It was in the early sixties that Wayne realized he really was rich.

> I guess the first time that I ever felt rich was when I could call up on the phone and borrow a million dollars. Because I remembered a time when I couldn't afford a fifteen dollar breakfast room suite. And then being able to phone and borrow a million dollars! . . . At the time we had three radio stations, and I thought I could stop right there because I was making more money than I'd ever spend. But more money than I could spend wouldn't be the same as what either of my sons would spend. Because it's just like a person not eating a whole lot, and their stomach draws up. When you go all those years weighing everything that you spend, always thinking, 'Is this the economical thing to do,' you believe that wanting a thing is never enough reason to spend for it. You need value returned. Unless there's real necessity.

Henry Tippie went with Wayne and John to Atlanta, if only to prove to the Orkin people that Weymouth was still beating the bush for potential buyers. The entire Orkin clan had assembled in the office. The older brother, Sanford, was president. Billy was the plump one. "I don't know just what Billy's job was," Wayne says. "He collected these S&H green stamps. Everyone said Billy worked from T to T,—Tuesday to Thursday. He didn't deny it." John was given the job of steering Billy and George away from the negotiation conducted by

Wayne and Henry with Perry Kay. Perry Kay was the linchpin, the man in charge. His temperament was not exactly life-affirming. Short, sandy-haired, abrasive, he wielded heavy sarcasm like a scimitar. Maybe his situation at Orkin had frazzled his nerves. He'd been saddled with all the serious decisions while Billy clipped coupons, Sanford goofed off, and his own wife (Otto's daughter) controlled the money.

At the first meeting, Otto came in with his youngish wife. Perry Kay was installed like a diminutive Caesar behind his desk. In his vague, gentle way, Otto said he was surprised that Perry Kay had gone out and got himself yet another new car when he'd just bought one a few months before.

"The ashtray got full," said Kay nasally.

Old Otto shook his head, muttering, "Traded in 'cause the ashtray's full? I never heard of such a thing! Just because the ashtray was full?"

According to Wayne, a salesman walked into the office at some point and happened to lay his attaché case on Kay's desk. Kay exploded. "Get that goddamned thing off my desk!" he screamed. "That desk cost more than the house you live in!" Visibly shaken, the salesman quickly retreated.

The Orkin lawyer, Alan Post, was no less histrionic, but his was the controlled emotion of a consummate actor. When the Rollinses handed him their offer, he went pale and collapsed in a chair. He had difficulty speaking, feebly sputtering that it was an insult. How dare they name such an insignificant figure in the presence of the Orkins? Did they have any idea whom they were dealing with? Wayne suggested they talk about it. Post walked out of the office frothing, red in the face. He came back sallow, in deep sorrow. Wayne describes how Post would "stand up on the desk and shout. Then he'd get down on his knees. He'd cry, 'Oh, my Lord, this will ruin us. We can't do a thing like this! You're trying to ruin us!'"

There were at least a dozen items in the contract that set Post off. The one that appeared to affect him most deeply was the "offset on undisclosed expenses." He collapsed and sat there with his head between his knees sobbing. "He had a big fit," Wayne says. "He said they'd never agree to that. They just never would agree to it. He said it would ruin them. He never did say why it would ruin them. He just said he'd never agree to let them do such a thing." And the Orkins all piped up like birds on a wire: "We can't do anything Allen doesn't agree on. We don't know a thing about any of this.

"At ten o'clock that night I wouldn't have given a nickel for our chance of closing that next morning. We had all these items undecided. But we go in the next morning, we sign the deal, and he never does bring up one of them. Just as smooth as can be."

Their deal made financial history. It shook up Wall Street and started a trend. The Harvard Business School would declare the Rollins-Orkin deal a classic case study in leveraging a buyout. The Rollins brothers and Henry Tippie had changed the conventional perception of how a company can grow. The pattern they set established the principle of the leveraged buyout for the foreseeable future.

Henry says, "We were a small company, a very small company—we had like 4.5 million net worth. We were able to go out there and make an acquisition for 62.4 [million], and limit our exposure to 10 million and put up no money at all. No one had ever done that before."

Aside from warrants on Rollins Broadcasting stock, according to *The Investment Dealers Digest* (Nov. 22, 1965), there were loans from Chase Manhattan and Equitable Life Assurance Society ($10 million at 5 and 1/4 percent); and Prudential Insurance Company (40 million at 5 and 3/4 percent) plus stock options. The additional $10 million came in the form of a subordinated debenture issue from the Orkin family with "the remaining monies coming from the Orkin treasury." In short, the Rollins brothers borrowed some of the money they needed from the Orkins themselves. Little wonder Allen Post beat his head on the desk and howled.

The Rollinses and Henry Tippie had come up with a way to make the leveraged buyout look easy. But hadn't they also made the Orkin family richer by many millions while placing themselves under a staggering burden of debt? In the hyperworld of high finance, enormous debt is often the occasion for great rejoicing. No sooner had they gone millions into debt, Henry recalls, than the Rollins Broadcasting stock took off like a rocket.

"We'd gone public at $8 a share (1961). In 1964, we'd got up to $12 a share. Our discussions with the Orkins started about Memorial Day of May that year. The letter of intent was signed mid-June. I think the stock was about $15 to $17 a share. When we closed [with Orkin] the 2nd of September, the stock was at $50 a share. The following April the stock was at $153 a share."

How is it that when a company shoulders a mountain of debt its stock goes straight up? "Well," Henry says, "you have the earnings coming in now from Orkin, minus interest payments. The investor can see Rollins Broadcasting's record. Growth is accelerating. Orkin's earnings are added to each share."

Investors can see that the company is being run by people who know what they're doing. But the clincher is the sudden increase of income with no increase of shares. You can't stuff a giant into a jump-suit designed for a midget. This abrupt influx of new money into Rollins lighted up eyes all over Wall Street, and the mountain of debt, everyone assumed (correctly as it turned out), would be swallowed by growth, expansion, inventive business.

A small army of speculators who possessed not a vestige of the Rollins brothers' and Henry's business savvy now understood how to wiggle their way into big money. Through the eighties, the leveraged buyout became the favorite magic trick around Wall Street. Just speak to your banker, rub Aladdin's leverage lamp, and come out rich. Once in, of course, someone has to make the acquired company grow. Many companies were taken over by people who had no genius for business, occasionally by barracudas in human form who swallowed the guts of perfectly good organizations and swam away leaving a trail of blood in the water.

Both Rollins brothers would go on buying and selling companies, spinning off subsidiaries that outgrew themselves and nesting divisions within parent companies. Wayne felt his role was like that of a parent responsible for the welfare of both the companies he'd founded and those he bought. Even so, his great love remained farming, husbanding the land.

He knew as much about farming and the cattle business as he did about the corporate world, but he would probably have found it un-natural to turn his interest in farming into agribusiness. Though he would one day own some fifty square miles (over 70,000 acres) in various states on some very attractive terrain, he knew ranching was going against the modern grain. As he might have put it, you could make a living for your family but not really contribute to society. A real contribution is derived only from excess, whether it is material, artistic, or spiritual.

Improving on nature was Wayne's excuse for spending so much of his spare time on one ranch or another. He sold land only to buy better land, if he sold at all. Wayne never lost his Faustian impulse to take raw wilderness, forest and swamp, and transform them into a delight for the eye. "In my mind I can see what it'll be after I've finished with it. You look at it and you think, 'Now I can do something that will make it complete, make it beautiful.' Isn't that what valuable is? The character of the land."

There was Catoosa Springs in the forties; then Cherokee on the border below Chattanooga, and Mountain Cove south of Ringgold where he preserved acres of dogwood because every spring he was overcome by the sight of their pale airy blossoms. At Blue Cypress Ranch in Florida, he reclaimed swamp area in a wilderness of alligators, rattlesnakes, and wild boar. Employing a Ringgold man, Harold V. Williams, to work these holdings, he converted hundreds, then thousands, of acres into farmland with irrigation canals, access roads, lakes stocked with fish. He had solar power panels installed in fencing.

For generations the fields around Ringgold had remained in the same hands until he started buying some of them. Suddenly people realized that raw acreage might be more than just scrub and furz. "Nobody had wanted it and then everybody wanted it." One can call the transition a decline from innocence to greed, or a passage from ignorance to economic awareness. There is a curious link between appropriation and art. You can't make over what is not yours.

"Never get married to a car or a business," Wayne says. But he would never say the same about land. Love of land was the bit of his past he held fast to. John didn't feel the same way at all. But then the entrepreneur is often distant from nature, taken over entirely by his genius. Mozart would travel across Europe with the shades on his carriage drawn down. The creative gift is often a kind of curtain, a form of blindness.

In any event, by the time the brothers bought Orkin, they had travelled light years away from the old "cash in hand" philosophy of Jim Crum. Like space travelers looking back at the earth from hundreds of miles out in space, they had to strain their eyes to make out little Catoosa County, let alone the single candle lighting the Bible from which their mother once read to them.

Wayne never wanted to sell Catoosa Springs and Mountain Cove. He loved his parents' deserted and deteriorating farmhouse down valley from Smith Chapel that he and John had refurbished. Even the outhouse was famously preserved—the only outhouse remaining in Georgia.

Having bought Orkin, Wayne sensed he had arrived where he needed to be. From 1964 on he could practice his business the way a pianist plays his best rehearsed pieces, doing what he does brilliantly and feeling no real compulsion to go into the unknown. He picked up Arwell, Inc., a company that opened access to the Midwest with offices in thirty-four states and earnings of $4 million. This put him into food plants, grain, and sanitation inspection. He got controlling interest in Dettelbach Pesticide Corporation. He bought L. P. Martin, a building maintenance company, for $2 million cash.

As for Orkin's founder, old Otto quickly declined into senility. According to Randall, his children had him certified "incompetent." They took over his business affairs. His wife was outraged by their offer to her of a paltry $5 million. The lady had the ferocious tenacity often observed in the younger wives of rich old men. Objecting that it was a fraction of the money his children owed him, she dragged Otto's offspring into court.

The case bumped wearily along for years. Lawyers sopped up the money Otto had left. His wife sold their mansion to pay their legal fees. She moved her decayed husband into a tiny apartment in a nondescript neighborhood. She was countersued by the younger Orkins. Criminal charges for "mishandling" Orkin's corporate funds were laid against her. The court dismissed them. Meanwhile, plump Billy was tried and imprisoned for hiring someone to murder his wife. As in everything else he set his mind to, Billy flopped in this enterprise.

Now flat broke, Otto's wife applied to the government for welfare. The couple were classified as "needy" by the state. Otto's wife was reported picking up government surplus food—powdered milk and dried beans. She sold her wedding ring for $200. Estranged from his children, Otto died in poverty.

20
Old Money and a New Age

Before John and Wayne bustled onto the scene, Delaware was du Pont country. No politician can flourish without close ties to the sources of money, and historically in Delaware that has meant one du Pont or another. The family no longer controls the state's destiny, but its influence is still felt. During his lifetime, Henry Belin du Pont was probably the most influential person in the family, the last du Pont to wield so much direct power. It was Henry B. who went head-to-head with the Rollins brothers.

When the first du Pont, Pierre Samuel, arrived in 1800 with his two sons, he didn't perceive America as it was—the old and the new all jumbled together into a provincial stew. To his mind, America was a blank page where he might inscribe a new and improved Europe. He dreamed of creating "Pontiana," a state run on scientific principles where the only source of wealth, the only object of taxation, would be land. But the Industrial Revolution was rapidly making land too feeble to compete with technology as a source of power.

That consummate materialist, Sir Francis Bacon (1561–1626), had said the compass and gunpowder changed history. The du Pont family provided his proof. Where old Pierre Samuel saw Delaware as a potential Eden with its laws in tune with nature, his son, Eleuthère Irénée du Pont de Nemours, saw an excellent site for the manufacture of gunpowder. The Brandywine River was ideally sloped for building mills. Wilmington had a good harbor. Irénée had been trained at the French king's gunpowder works run by the pioneer chemist Lavoisier (later guillotined by the Jacobins). President Jefferson was an enthusiastic advocate of American gunpowder and put Irénée in touch with Philadelphia bankers.

Pierre Samuel returned to France, but came back to Delaware in 1815 when Napoleon put a price on his head. The old man died two years later helping to put out a charcoal fire that threatened the powder factory. The DuPont establishment was blown up a few months

John and Wayne at work in flight, 1967. The differences in their natures and their pleasure in each other's company is evident. (*Rollins Family Photo Collection*)

John presents the Horatio Alger Award to Wayne, 1986. Because their mother had read the Alger stories to them when they were children, this evening had special significance. (*Rollins Family Photo Collection*)

President Richard Nixon arrives by helicopter at Walnut Green and John moves him along, past Congressman Pete du Pont, Senator Robert Dole, and Senator William Roth. (*Courtesy of the Wilmington News Journal*)

Senator Gerald Ford presents John with the Golden Plate award in 1972. At the time, John was a key figure in Republican Party fund-raising efforts. (*Republican National Committee*)

John and his wife, Michele Metrinko Rollins, at the White House with President Ronald Reagan. (*Courtesy of the White House*)

John and President George Bush. (*Republican National Committee*)

Wayne with his two sons Randall and Gary, as they appeared in their company's 1986 annual report. (*Rollins Family Photo Collection*)

Wayne and Grace Rollins on their 50th wedding anniversary, 1981. (*Rollins Family Photo Collection*)

Dedication of The John W. Rollins Pavilion at Emory University Hospital. *Left to right:* Mary Ann Seavey, Michael Metrinko, Marc Rollins, Monique Rollins, Michele Rollins, John W. Rollins, and Dr. Paul Seavey, former head of Internal Medicine at Emory. (*Courtesy of Ann Borden, Emory Photo Services*)

John W. Rollins Sr. and his family, 1996. The children (left to right) are Michael, Monique, young Michele, and Marc. (*Courtesy of Eric Crossan*)

John on his 83rd birthday with his extended family including in-laws and grandchildren. *Back Row, L to R:* Patrick (Kitty's son); his wife, Faye; their children Rachel and Charlie. Katie (Cathy's daughter); Dan Searby, Cathy (Kitty's daughter); and Ted (Linda's son). *Second Row, L to R:* John Jr. (Kitty's eldest son), his daughter Fontayne; Sean Flynn, married to Jamie Rollins (daughter of Jimmy, deceased son of Kitty) with Jeff's daughter Morgan in her lap; Jeff (Linda's son) and wife Kim with children, William and Kaitlyn on their laps. *Front Row, L to R:* John Rollins III (son of Diana); Diana (married to John W. Rollins Jr.); Michele and John; young Michele, Monique, and Michael (children of Michele.) *(Courtesy of Ulla and Dieter Kohn)*

later in March of 1818, killing one-third of the workers—a recurring event in the history of the powder mill. Irénée's wife, Sophia, was injured so badly she never recovered. Irénée escaped death that day because he was in Philadelphia trying to borrow more money to keep his company going.

In fact, DuPont's founder never emerged from debt during his lifetime. At his death, he owed the bankers the modern equivalent of millions. Eventually the du Ponts were fortunate enough to inherit the most devastating wars in human history. During the First World War, Pierre Samuel II charged European nations twice the going rate for a pound of explosives, demanding half the money up front in order to expand his plant to fill the orders requested.

George Bernard Shaw's character, Sir Andrew Undershaft, the millionaire munitions manufacturer in *Major Barbara,* bears so close a resemblance to various du Ponts (especially the great Pierre Samuel II) that Shaw could well have had Delaware in mind when he wrote his play. Undershaft's workers live in a handsome factory town with free housing, free schooling, free medical care—all paid for by the world's insatiable appetite for death. Like Sir Andrew, Irénée du Pont had supplied every one of his workers with a house, rent free, a garden, and a cow pasture. Like Sir Andrew, various du Ponts built Delaware's highways, schools, much public housing, and a world-famous children's hospital, among many other good works.

In the United States, the attitude toward the rich is often confused by envy and desire, a conflicted state of mind to say the least. The press harshly disapproved of the du Pont family for their immense wealth and for how they earned it, as if the family had created war for its own benefit. It's equally possible to argue that DuPont powder defeated Hitler and saved the free world from fascism. In any case, Pierre Samuel du Pont II switched his company into chemical production a generation before war, blown out of all proportion by atom technology, ceased to be a serious instrument of national policy. It's worth recalling, too, that the DuPont Company was the prime contractor in the fabrication of the atom and hydrogen bombs at the behest of the government, and for no profit.

Various Pierres, Samuels, Lammots and Henrys belonging to the du Pont circle have been criticized for running Delaware like a family farm. The authors of *The Company State* angrily describe the du Ponts' power in detail. James Phelan and Robert Pozen would like to see an oligarchy of businessmen behave democratically. But corporate existence is determined by hierarchy and the du Ponts were an effective, if reclusive, family. Average in everything but their industry, organization, and income, their products were vital in placing the American empire in orbit. Their power and influence appears greater than that of ancient kings. But while they might have turned little Delaware into a another Florence, they tended to hunker down modestly out of sight.

With the declining European system absorbed in destroying itself, the DuPont Company sold it the means at a time when manufacturing was still the slave of political power. After World War II, the American system began to change the nature of political power. With the global market the effective field of combat, corporate heads assumed the guise of shadow statesmen and generals in their boardrooms. Sales campaigns replaced battle campaigns. Nations dumped not bombs but steel and computer chips.

Pierre Samuel II switched his company into chemicals because he understood that diversification was the future. The du Ponts must have been tired of being portrayed as evil incarnate for giving the world what it demanded. But soon evil popped up in a new guise— as pollution.

John Rollins set himself against this new threat when he founded the hazardous waste disposal industry in the United States. He aimed a direct attack on the poisonous by-products of technology but, as we'll discover in a later chapter, he found that trying to beat the devil for a profit was harder work than he'd bargained for.

The Rollins brothers often followed paths the du Ponts had taken earlier. Irénée ran for the House of Representatives and lost in 1828. John ran for governor of the state and lost in 1960. Both families had close relations with national politicians. Irénée was made Director of the Bank of the United States. John became a charter member of the Senatorial Trust, the President's Advisory Council on Management Improvement, and was made head of the President's Dinner Committee. In that job he raised considerable sums of money for Richard Nixon's political campaigns. "Over the years," he says, "I guess I've personally known half of the United States senators, or more, and nine of our presidents."

The du Ponts give millions through their system of foundations, and many of the major institutions and private schools in Delaware are their beneficiaries. According to Phelan and Pozen's mordant report, "DuPont foundations seem deliberately to conspire to give to organizations the du Ponts control, thus assuring that the charitable subgovernment is monolithic and isolated, beyond the purview of the public." Thus an inevitability is labeled "conspiracy." What powerful family ever put social equality before personal control? An individual might do this, seldom a family.

It may be true that the results of the du Pont family's control of Delaware had produced a society brilliant in chemical science but otherwise conservative, safe, friendly, but banal. It can also be argued that the du Ponts, like other fabulously wealthy American families, are unbelievably benign when compared to some of the great houses in history. Enormous power and wealth are seldom associated with the kind of reclusive passivity the du Ponts exhibit. Burkehardt tells us that Ferrante of Naples "liked to have his opponents near him, either alive in well-guarded prisons, or dead and embalmed, dressed in the costume which they wore in their lifetime." Lorenzo de Medici murdered Duke Allessandro in 1537, and then praised himself in public, describing "tyrannicide as an act of the highest merit."

Henry B. du Pont rose only to praise business monopolies. He wrote in the *Wilmington Morning News* (the paper he controlled) in 1968: "Monopoly papers, by and large, feel a far greater obligation to print the news objectively and to give space in their columns to opposing points of view." This may be reactionary nonsense, but it's a far cry from keeping the corpses of your dead enemies around in fashionable costumes.

Old Money in Delaware shivered apprehensively when John Rollins purchased his Norman-style estate at Walnut Green, located in the heart of du Pont country. The former owner was overheard at a cocktail party remarking that she couldn't, for the life of her, recall the name of the man she'd sold it to.

John installed himself there with his children, Cathy and Patrick, who attended Tower Hill—a local private school founded by du Ponts. Unlike the reclusive du Ponts, John was aggressively gregarious. "Uncle John, the working man's friend," in a previous incarnation, he was to be severely tested by vitriolic critics armed with lawyers.

The Rollins brothers naturally met and did business with numbers of the du Pont extended family on their way up. It was George Weymouth who had pointed Wayne in the direction of Orkin in Atlanta. The brilliant buyout the brothers orchestrated there turned the Rollins name into a supernova on Wall Street. John was godfather to one of Edward du Pont's children. He also met the Carpenters, the Lairds, the Copelands—all names related to du Pont originals. "When people talk about the du Ponts," John says, "they have to remember there are something like 3,600 of them." (George A. "Frolic" Weymouth puts the number at 2,800.)

Robert R. M. Carpenter, Jr., whom John describes as "one of my closest friends," was a DuPont Company director for thirty-four years. Carpenter was a gritty presence on the board of the News Journal Company. He once objected gruffly to an editorial that praised some of Kennedy's Supreme Court appointments: "Why should we devote space to one who is an enemy of private enterprise and the capitalistic system?"

By the time John could afford a mansion of his own, generations had passed since a du Pont had heard the heart-stopping roar of dynamite blasting apart a powder shed over the Brandywine, and a century since the last family member spat sulphur from his teeth and sat down to lunch with his workmen.

Henry Belin du Pont sat at the heads of innumerable boards and committees—director at DuPont, Wilmington Trust, Atlantic Aviation, various state commissions, museum foundations, the list is long indeed. As the family multiplied and dispersed and the vast du Pont fortune trickled down to the heirs, to Henry B. fell the task of protecting his family's interests. He had much to do with holding companies, banks, beautifying Wilmington, and maintaining the status quo. The enormous company itself had passed through the hands of bitterly feuding family members into the hands of corporate managers.

It's fair to say that Henry B. was not pleased by the Rollins brothers' rise. The presence of strangers bustling about in his city set his teeth on edge. John, elected Chairman of the Airport Commission in the early sixties, objected to Henry B.'s decision to lease hangar space at the airport for furniture warehousing. He argued the space was much better employed as an air freight center. Returning from a business trip, he was informed that his plane would not be given space in any hangar on the airport. His position as chairman of the commission was cut out from under him. Henry B. wanted there to be no question about who called the shots in Delaware.

21
Developments in Delaware

Wayne moved Rollins Broadcasting into the second floor of a building on French Street in Wilmington in 1958. The office was two blocks from the railway station. These offices were located on a fault line between the prosperous city and poor neighborhoods to the southeast. The building was described by Earl Geiger, the Orkin operations officer who saw it in 1964, as "kind of junky." From the window of his building downtown, Wayne looked out across a condemned neighborhood. Decaying houses, a century old, were scheduled for destruction.

Wayne and John had always been passionate (the best word) about raising the tone of whatever part of the world they inhabited. The corporate headquarters they built years later in Wilmington and Atlanta reveal that Wayne was the more conventional, settling for a square, corporate style that didn't call attention to itself. By contrast, John's fluted fifteen-story building can be seen for miles. Recall, they were children in the depleted world of the Depression where paint was as rare as maple syrup, and they buried their food in the earth to preserve it.

The brothers made plans to revamp the entire neighborhood around Wayne's French Street offices. On the Christiana River side was the railway station; on the city side an ancient slum took up several blocks. These houses were mostly deserted, their roofs decayed, the lots filling up with rubbish. They made plans, as well, to pick up a franchise for transmitting cable television. During the sixties, cable TV loomed over broadcasting as the coming thing. But these plans ran into immediate opposition. Wayne was dismayed by the hostility he ran into in Delaware. The Rollins bid was bruited about as a sign of the New Vulgarity threatening a patrician past. Nothing promotes a feeling of security and well-being like the timeworn routines of Old Money.

John Rollins had already pricked Henry B. to fury by describing the great man's furniture-in-the-hangar plan as fiscally self-defeating. Now every suggestion the Rollinses brought forth was opposed, every permit they filed for, rejected. According to Phelan and Posner in their book, *The Company State,* a well situated businesman (who preferred his name not be used) reported that Henry B. could call a meeting of businessmen and family members at the Hotel du Pont and, over a lunch of cold cuts, raise half a million dollars for a neighborhood improvement program in half an hour. Henry B. was chairman of Christiana Securities (the holding company set up to direct du Pont family investments), he controlled the Wilmington Trust Company, the Hotel du Pont, and the News Journal Company. He sat on innumerable committees. But this last great du Pont lacked the gift for creating a new business and making it thrive. Henry B. exemplified Old Money with all its largesse, its *noblesse oblige,* its divine right to decide what will surive and what will not.

The Rollins brothers were not alone in raising the ire of Henry B. In the summer of 1964, Creed Black, the executive editor of the *News Journal* resigned, charging that "a member of the DuPont Company's public relations department, who had spent his career supervising the company's employee publications," had been sent over to run news and editorial policy. In his letter of resignation, Black wrote, "I, for one, need no further evidence that the ownership wants the *Morning News* and the *Evening Journal* operated as house organs instead of newspapers." Henry B. retorted, "Mr. Black seems to have the curious idea that the owners of the papers should have little to say concerning the policies of the papers. With this we cannot agree."

Sam Shipley, then head of State Development, recalls a meeting in Governor Charles Terry's office with Henry B. du Pont in the sixties. They were discussing how best to use federal money awarded the University of Delaware for a new Marine Studies Department. The grant had come through Vice President Hubert Humphrey. As a onetime Humphrey staffer, Shipley was brought in on the discussion.

"Henry du Pont was there, I don't know why exactly," Shipley recalls. "And he said, 'Well, let's wrap this up quickly. What I suggest we do, Governor, we go to my hotel and have a meeting where it's less public.' The governor turned to me and said, 'Well, Sam, should we have the press involved in this issue or not?'

"I said, 'I would. Because the White House is going to make it public.' And Henry du Pont said in the strongest tone, 'No. I disagree. We'll do it without the press. Except for my paper.' When he said *his* paper and *his* hotel, I thought that was a good indication of the authoritarian flavor of that time."

Rollins Broadcasting ran into major trouble when the Rollins brothers requested a permit to bolt a sidearm to an existing radio tower. They needed the antenna to test their cablevision signal. Other radio towers had gone up that same year and were granted permits as a matter of course. The Rollins permit was denied while a steady dribble of slighting criticism found its way into the *Morning News*. Denied the right to fasten their antenna to an existing tower, John suggested placing it adjacent to an auto wrecking yard in an industrial section of the city. This too was denied on grounds that it would devalue the neighborhood.

As they wouldn't let him put up his antenna in the worst part of town, John intemperately raised a square metal frame for the antenna on his own property in chateau country. This was Henry B.'s corner of the state and the interloper had no permit, so he was apparently asking for a fight. Photographs of the tower near Pyles Ford Road were printed in the *Morning News* of November, 1966. The attorney representing Crawford H. Greenwalt, the CEO of the DuPont Company, and Bruce Bredin (married to Octavia du Pont) described the tower as "a monstrosity." Charles F. Richards, one of Delaware's most brilliant and effective lawyers, represented a group of homeowners and called the tower a "Trojan Horse." Richards suggested that this object would be only the first in a veritable invasion of cycsores. Henry B. du Pont's remarks in court are befittingly restrained. "This proposal will contribute nothing to the welfare of property owners in the area," he said quietly.

Hotheaded John, by raising the antenna over the homes of his enemies, had flung himself naked into their camp and they prepared to make a meal of him. His frustration had gotten the better of him. Because they hadn't let him put up his tower up among the poor, he'd raised it over the heads of the rich. The Rollins engineer, Russell Chambers, told the court the company was interested only in testing its signal in order to build a twelve-channel TV system in New Castle County. But lawyer Charles Richards chased him to ground; Chambers had to admit the tower was completely illegal. No permit had been issued.

Charles Richards said he was appalled by the "light-hearted way" the Rollins attorney "tossed off a criminal violation of the zoning code." "Corporate arrogance," he called it. The bucolic past was being trampled wherever insatiable commerce charged into view. However, the era of patrician power was passing, and the Rollins brothers, love them or hate them, belonged to the future.

John's offices were situated at the Devon on Pennsylvania Avenue, and so were the offices of his dentist, Dr. Herbert Casalena. John sent everyone who worked in his office to Dr. Casalena for their dental work and, according to Dr. Casalena, he paid all their bills too. Another of Dr. Casalena's patients was a Mr. John Flaherty who had been approached by the Rollins company. John wanted to buy Flaherty's prime land further up Pennsylvania Avenue. According to Dr. Casalena, Flaherty fulminated that "He'd rather give his land away for nothing than sell it to that John Rollins." And Dr. Casalena recalls that Flaherty did precisely that—making a gift of the land to the University of Delaware.

John Rollins, in the eyes of Old Money, was a barbarian at the gate. Yet zoning changes of every conceivable kind were being granted all over northern Delaware. Anonymous corporations with abstract names and offices in Minneapolis or Chicago were rapidly moving into the state and buying land. Builders churned up hilly fields along Routes 2 and 202, erecting strip malls, residential acres and apartment complexes. In September of 1961, there were eight major rezoning petitions in the elite Brandywine Hundred region. The "development" of the state was proceeding with the spectacular velocity that modern construction alone makes possible. Entire neighborhoods could be thrown up in weeks and surrounded by instant landscaping. The Rollins broadcasting tower was a convenient icon for the unease people felt about the future. And while faceless corporations were as hard to identify as the Holy Ghost, John Rollins was near at hand and all too human.

In court, lawyers called Rollins' cable plans "a frankly commercial venture, not in the public interest . . . created strictly for private profit." The lawyers' suggestion that broadcasting in America is driven by some motive more elevated than profit is amusing, if not hilarious. Cable television is big business in one of its most seductive guises. But remove profit and what becomes of technology and its manifest destiny? Without the prospect of profit, cable would melt away like many thousands of other inventions that have failed to find a market.

A passionate member of John's loyal opposition was the Wilmington lawyer, William Prickett Jr. Mr. Prickett viewed the Rollins brothers as paradigms of vulgar capitalism. He fought them tooth and nail in court, and out. John to this day remains somewhat nonplussed by the burning passion of Prickett's attack. And as in any good soap opera, it was this same William Prickett who later married Linda, John's then wife—after acting as her legal counsel during her divorce proceedings.

The legally battered Rollins brothers eventually won the right to raise an antenna in Delaware and were promptly attacked on another front. Wayne had applied to the Federal Communications Commission for a license to broadcast programming from Delaware's single television outlet. Rollins Broadcasting was the largest independent network with offices in New York and Chicago. The station they intended to buy, WVUE in Wilmington, was losing money. Wayne always bought stations that were losing money. The Rollins record for saving dying stations was impeccable. This time the brothers wanted a station that would represent their home state "with a particular emphasis on local and regional events," according to the *Evening Journal* of September, 1958.

The FCC dawdled for two years before it got around to a first hearing in March of 1961. (It's worth recalling that John had run for governor of the state in 1960. He was by no means unknown.) Hearings dragged on until January of 1962. Wayne called them "meaningless, and exceedingly costly to taxpayers." Charges of "malpractice" leveled against WAMS, the Rollins radio station in Delaware, by a local civic group were thrown out as soon as a judge examined them.

Those opposed to Rollins Broadcasting claimed the state could be saved from crass commercialism by turning its only TV outlet over to educational television. But Philadelphia's educational television station already served Wilmington with a strong signal that cable would make doubly redundant. The FCC was persuaded by those with better contacts in Washington than the Rollins enjoyed that Wilmington's station should become an adjunct of Philadelphia. Delaware wound up with the same signal from Philadelphia that it already had.

Aside from denying Rollins Broadcasting the shot at a station in their home state, the FCC denied the state a television outlet that might have helped Delaware with its long-term identity crisis. "Dela where?" is the standing joke. The benefits of being small imply enormous potential of the kind exemplified by ancient Athens or the Venetian republic. But Delaware's powers-that-be had insured the little state would remain a silent nation of chemists, lawyers, and bankers. By opposing a television station controlled at home, they shelved a powerful potential for self-expression. The hermetic kingdom remained sealed off.

Could Rollins Broadcasting's fare have been more vulgar, worse than the programming that burbled night and day from the major networks? In 1964, national publications like *Television Magazine* described Rollins Broadcasting as "the most talked-about, fastest-moving television-associated stock on the market—eclipsed only by the stir created by CBS's purchase of the New York Yankees." If their stock was that good, they must have been doing something right. For one thing, Wayne had tapped into one of the most vital and expressive strains of American culture—the African American voice.

The struggle over the Wilmington station between the new men and the dead hand of the past offers a snapshot of how bitter the struggle had become. The ancient establishment encouraged advanced technology but opposed its consequences, declaring its expression raucous and vulgar. But growth is generally raucous and vulgar (as our youth culture attests). Forces like the Rollins brothers who generate new money are crucial to the nation's future, but the establishment wanted them to do their bustling about as far away as possible. Rollins Broadcasting ran one cable franchise in New Castle County, two in Philadelphia and one in Rhode Island. The complexities involved and the expertise that a rapidly evolving technology demanded appeared more than they'd bargained for, so they got out of the cable business.

Unlike John who was so often mangled in the press, Wayne had a quiet genius for looking good in print. He was reticent, wily, self-deprecating, and ironical—traits journalists feel at home with. John's Falstaffian persona belied his sure instinct, his accurate eye. Articles about Wayne almost always report rising revenues, broadcasting towers raised (in Norfolk, Plattsburgh, New York City), brilliant maneuvers, solid gains. John has always enjoyed contention and appears to enjoy a good laugh even when it's at his own expense. He can be outlandishly spontaneous and is constitutionally unable to take himself seriously. For years the media took him seriously only when he was in trouble.

Even so, it was Wayne who decided to leave Delaware when their most ambitious plan for redesigning a derilect neighborhood downtown was thwarted. Wayne's disappearance would prove excellent for him, but a bad thing for the city.

Wilmington is a small metropolis that, like many American towns along the eastern corridor, has neighborhoods both charming and shabby—depending on whither you wander. Back in the nineteenth century, the du Ponts paid America's premiere landscape architect, Frederick Law Olmsted, to design the spectacular park that runs along the Brandywine River downtown. This strip of bucolic green that today travels through downtown Wilmington, passes beneath the thunder of Interstate–95, and terminates beyond the Delaware Art Museum in Rockford Park, is a green gem set off by a medieval-looking stone water tower.

The catastrophic collapse of esthetic judgment that afflicted American architecture after the Second World War affected Wilmington too. By the middle of the twentieth century, a new technology and old-fashioned greed had been translated into grotesque apartment blocks and enormous wafer-constructions that resembled monoliths raised in honor of Moloch. Wilmington razed over a thousand housing units to construct the section of interstate highway, I–95, that connects the city to Philadelphia, to the north, and Baltimore, to the south. Wilmington's former city planner, Peter Larsen, once remarked that Wilmington uses sixty percent of its land space for transportation—the same ratio as Los Angeles. The Poplar Street project and downtown renewal scheme removed another thousand housing units. Even as the planners were putting through the interstate and vaguely pondering a downtown mall, the problems of education, integration, family breakdown, drugs—the entire menu of social poisons afflicting every city in the postindustrial world—grew like a cancer at in the city's heart.

As the learning curve fell, taxes rose. Few saw the vital connection between those statistics. By the middle sixties, downtown Wilmington had become a place to avoid at night. Despair translated itself into violence. Busing to achieve school integration made the town even less attractive to middle-class home buyers. Such was the twilight that existed when Wayne and John Rollins filed their plan at city hall on the last day of 1966. "ROLLINS BIDS TO BUILD CITY CENTER COMPLEX," said the headline. The timing was not good. Only a few weeks earlier Rollins Broadcasting had been in court trying to explain why they had put up a television antenna in du Pont country.

"Many prominent corporate and public officials feel that H.B. du Pont's dislike of Rollins had a major role in the defeat of his proposal, but no one has absolute proof," say James Phelan and Robert Pozen in *The Company State*. Time would make it pretty clear that the rejection of the Rollins proposal for a downtown complex was a rejection of new money and new energy. The old guard, paternalistic, suspicious, slammed the door on its own foot. The rejection of the Rollins proposal to rejuvenate downtown Wilmington was reported in the *Morning News* of March 3, 1967.

Had Henry B. du Pont's grip been relaxed enough to shift the burden of downtown reconstruction to the Rollinses' shoulders, the benefits may well have been substantial. The brothers' blueprint was carefully thought through and more coordinated in its uses than the conventional structures that were subsequently raised willy-nilly in their old neighborhood. But du Pont's control of the Greater Wilmington Development Council (GWDC) was absolute.

GWDC's "in-city mall" idea, brought forward to fill the vacuum left by the Rollinses' rejection, proved a contradiction in terms. The modern mall is essentially a new town out of town, a controlled space for safe shopping defined by free parking. A traditional town is hostile to the car, friendly to the poor who don't have cars. So why plan a "mall" downtown? Henry B. du Pont's complete lack of entrepreneurial vision is laid bare here. Only after his death did the *News Journal,* in July 1971, predict enormous difficulties with the downtown mall idea. But by then GWDC's planners were trapped in a false momentum not of their own creation. The car, the suburbs, the construction of malls elsewhere, made a downtown mall pointless. Had the GWDC thinkers come up with an idea for force-feeding the educational system and upgrading the ghetto, they would have made a real contribution. What they actually constructed lacked coherence or design.

The task of bringing life back into a city like Wilmington is vexed with complications racial and economic, the one growing out of the other. The Rollins brothers were ready and willing to take on the challenge. They may well have been overwhelmed by the chaos that characterized the sixties. Or their plan for rejuvenating a six-and-a-half-block complex in center city may have prevented the violence that followed in 1968. The Rollins brothers proposed to build stores, offices, apartments, and performance spaces along the corridor that divides the downtown corporate complex from the ghetto to the southeast. They envisioned a new neighborhood containing a mix of retail outlets and green spaces that would narrow the racial abyss. Recall that both brothers, each in his own way, had been reaching out to minorities for decades. John had granted many hundreds of scholarships to deserving young people from poor communities. Rollins stations were devoted largely to black culture. With his background of broadcasting to African Americans, Wayne had trained a new generation of black managers and radio "personalities." These were people who knew how to connect with oppressed social groups. It was the black manager of the Newport News station, WRAP, who talked an angry mob out of burning down the building on the day of Martin Luther King's assassination. When riots flared up in Wilmington, few black leaders had ties to both communities.

The Rollins enterprise was a chance to nudge Wilmington toward its postindustrial future some twenty years before it actually took place. Like the MBNA bank that began to transform the city in the nineties, Rollins companies were service oriented, nonpolluting, and rapidly expanding through the nation. Wayne and John were often subjects of articles in the *Wall Street Journal*. Wayne, a businessman routinely commended in media industry publications, a player in the most incredible leveraged buyout in financial history, was not someone a progressive city would normally send packing. But that's what happened.

No Wilmington city officials were at the airport the day Wayne headed back to Georgia in 1967. When asked by the *Evening Journal* that January to comment on Wayne's departure, the mayor, John Babiarz, "expressed the hope that the move might be a temporary one, with a later return to Wilmington." Babiarz had earlier said that the Rollinses didn't get the bid because it was "assumed they didn't really have the money." He did not say who was doing the assuming. Not long after Wayne arrived in Atlanta, he was cited there as the third richest man in the city.

Wayne took with him much more than millions in potential city taxes and hundreds of jobs in construction, maintenance, clerking, and broadcasting. Wilmington needed his talent for problem-solving. The town was sliding, decaying, its poor festering with discontent, and by 1968 it was burning. Many buildings went up in flames after Martin Luther King's assassination. Most of the condemned housing in the area where the Rollins brothers had planned to build was torched in a single night. The fires that burned in Wilmington were like those in a dozen other American cities that night, fueled by an unholy alliance between black rage and a white failure of imagination. The wounds to the city's body and soul are still healing.

Voltaire informs us that the Baron of Thunder-Ten-Tronckh "drove Candide out of the castle by kicking him vigorously on the backside." John Rollins, however, was not to be so dislodged from Delaware. No matter how hard the barons kicked him, he stayed fixed in place and passed on to other adventures and greater prosperity.

As for Wayne, he was hesitant about returning to Georgia where he'd been born poor. He worried it might look somehow like an admission of failure—local boy goes local again. Nor was Claudia happy to see her sons splitting up. She'd laid down the law when they first went into business, "I never want either of you coming to me and talking about the other."

Modern business with its global reach was all very well, but it raised hell with family relations. Claudia maintained that if there was going to be trouble, more than likely it was the women in the family who would start it. "When you get all those daughters-in-law in here, it's going to be a different world," Wayne quotes her saying.

Be that as it may, Atlanta welcomed Wayne. And now that he had a big, comfortable company like Orkin to manage, his detailed, careful approach insured his future. The years of risk were behind him. John's courage and dash were no longer vital to him. New companies he bought would be acquired with great care. He would add vast tracts of land to his holdings and appear at shows where prize bulls were traded. He would buy lands in Florida for quail hunting. He'd turned himself into a lord in the American style, but the Rollins brothers can better be described as Lords of Work. Activity was the domain where they felt most themselves.

In 1984 Wayne restructured the company and shared out a couple of its major subsidiaries to his sons. Gary, the youngest, took over Orkin as chief operating officer and president. Randall was handed RPC Energy Services, the Rollins oil and energy company with 1,800 drilling rigs.

"A farm boy like me who grew up with an outdoor toilet gets real comfortable riding in a jet," he said. "I want to see these boys earn their ride." In 1950, aged thirty-five, he'd managed to save $12,500. By 1976, aged sixty, he was worth about $500 million. He was a power, a source of order, hiring hundreds, generating bequests, grants, increasingly drawn to religion. His wealth would increase, but the drama was over.

For the true entrepreneur, living is pushing commerce to its limit—a limit defined, as a rule, by the technology of the time. The entrepreneur feels alive only when he's riding a wave, when the risk is palpable. A decade after Wayne had settled in smoothly at Orkin, John ran into very rough waters in Jamaica where, for reasons he now admits were irrational, he found himself going under.

22
Romancing Jamaica

John flew to Jamaica for the first time in 1960, after losing his bid to become Delaware's governor. He was recovering from the exhaustion that comes after an unsuccessful political campaign. As soon as he arrived on that Caribbean island, perspective returned. "It was like the world was lifted off my shoulders when I lost." Returning a year later, he fell in love with the island. Jamaica, it seemed to him, had the kind of economic potential that is possible on a tropical isle in an age of jet flight and mass tourism. The Jamaican government of the time was interested in tourism and welcomed his interest.

John had grown accustomed to making the drastic adjustments that ailing concerns demand. The visionary businessman in John always sees how some restructuring here and an infusion of capital there can turn a chihuahua into a greyhound. He courts sober bankers on the one hand, and wild extremes on the other. "A lot of people are brilliant," he remarks, "but they don't follow through. You've got to develop that 'I'm not quitting' attitude." Jamaica would test his patience for decades. But like most long marriages, it began with enchantment.

In the eastern part of the island, mountains lift to a height of 7,000 feet around a promontory called The Peak. The ridges are narrow as the backs of dolphins, the valleys steep between. Cold air from the sea whips up the mountain sides like breezes under a woman's summer dress. The population is multicultural, the majority the descendants of African slaves. The first Spanish settlers arrived in 1510. The indigenous people (the Arawaks) and the native plants (hardwood forests) couldn't withstand the invasion and were soon extinct. The island now supports an imported flora and fauna. The first Africans were brought over in 1517 to replace the original Arawaks, wiped out by European diseases.

The English seized Jamaica from the Spanish in 1655. The Jamaican people threw off colonialism and "free men of colour" were constitutionally recognized in 1830. Slavery was abolished in 1838, universal suffrage granted in 1938. In 1944, the first popular election was held, and the British governor eased out of the cabinet in 1957.

Sugarcane was the agriculture of choice because it does not deplete the soil. The cane was grown on enormous plantations owned by English colonials and worked by Jamaican slaves. "The Jamaicans . . . overcame slavery to establish a tradition of freedom. Jamaica is an entire culture encapsulated in a tiny part of the earth's land mass," John writes in the prologue to a 1973 book of photographs that picture the island. "The fabulous azure sea; the clean, white beaches; the rich soil and lush growth; the foothills rising into lofty peaks" all help to create "a land of enchantment rich in people, legend and legacy."

Exploring the north coast, John came on a ruined mansion set on a long rise staring out to sea. Called Rose Hall after Rosa Ash, the gentle wife of the original builder (George Ash), it had been constructed around 1750. Stripped and abandoned in the early twentieth century, the ruin deteriorated despite various proposals to restore it. Until John appeared, no one had the will or the money.

He bought the ruined walls and about 5,500 acres around it from Sir Francis Kerr-Janet and Sam Bronfman of the Seagram's liquor family. John's architect, Tom Concannon, discovered the original Rose Hall plans yellowing in a Kingston library archive. Guided by these drawings, Cancannon restored the original shell and its interior, floors, and tapestried walls at a cost of $2.5 million.

A photograph of Rose Hall, taken from the air before its restoration, shows a ruin of pale stones overlooking decayed gardens and the sea. A long porch with sculpted balustrades runs across the front of the building, and below that appears a tunnel crossing under the house, a basement that contained the servants' quarters and kitchen. There was also a subbasement that may have been designed as a root cellar. Annie Palmer, the subsequent owner, used it as a prison for her most troublesome slaves. The house was a ruin with gaping holes in the roof where rotting joists were visible.

A photograph after the restoration shows the place scrubbed clean, white limestone walls now chastely pure beneath a dark roof. On the gentle rise below the house, dozens of tables have been laid with white table clothes and flowers in vases. Low stone walls bedecked with orange, crimson and white bougainvillea encircle a round pond full of water lilies.

Concannon describes the ruined mansion, in 1960, as "a gaunt, for-

lorn, rotting pile. . . . The roof gaped open to the rain and the windows were gashes in the limestone walls. The ruin peered at the sea,
its phantom appearance in keeping with its sinister reputation as the
home of Annie Palmer."

John was attracted by Annie's story. Passionate, cruel, and duplici-
tous, she embodies the colonial Caribbean at its worst. Born in 1802,
Annie Patterson's father was Irish, her mother English. The family
sailed to Haiti in 1812. Annie, doted on by her parents, was spoiled
by their servants. This coddled child unfortunately lost both mother
and father in one year to tropical fever. She was left with a nanny who
happened to be a voodoo priestess. By the time Annie sailed for Jamaica she was a beautiful young woman and an accomplished necro-
mancer, skilled in African witchcraft. Raised with all the privileges
granted the European, the oversexed Annie reveled in superstitious
rites and steamy voodoo rituals conjoining blood and sperm, death
and sex. Immersed in a Caribbean world of ghosts and spells, she employed a form of hypnosis that empowered her to evoke images
deeply ingrained in the West Indian people by centuries of superstition. She herself would eventually fade into the ghostly images she
evoked when she was alive. Workers at Rose Hall today admit somewhat sheepishly that they have experienced occasional encounters
with Annie's ghost.

Annie perfected the slaves' trick of hiding her true feelings behind
an agreeable smile. When the Englishman, John Palmer, first saw her,
he was bowled over. She resembled the clever heroine in a Jane
Austen novel. It would never have occurred to the gentleman that
this lovely creature had been up to her elbows in blood rituals. Her
skeleton, buried in a stone casket on the property, is that of a woman
4 foot 11 inches tall, dainty enough to convince any lover that what
she needed most was male protection.

Palmer had arrived on the island in 1818 to take over his uncle's
property and grow sugar cane. Five and a half years into the marriage,
Annie had driven him to drink. She finished him off with arsenic. Her
slaves carried his corpse down to the sea through an underground
passage and buried him on the beach. The grave diggers were then
put to death. Neighbor planters understood that poor John Palmer
was dead from the fever.

Her second husband went insane, probably from the diet of arsenic
she fed him. The slaves who hauled this second corpse through the
passage were also murdered. Husband number three was a greedy
fool who married Annie for her property. She stabbed him in a bed-

room with silk-lined walls overlooking the sea and finished him off by
pouring boiling oil into his ear.

She then took Robert Rutherford, her bookkeeper, to bed. Despite
her beauty and charm—and the fact that she was still in her twenties—Rutherford didn't find Annie easy to love. He began to write
about her in his journal. When one of her housemaids put poison in
her food, Annie had the woman decapitated at Montego Bay and requested the head which she wanted to place on a spike as a warning
to her staff. The grisly object was brought back in a box. Annie could
project images of legendary beasts in the twilight sky to terrify her
slaves into the most abject obedience. One story still told today has
Annie slipping out of her skin so she can make herself invisible to spy
on her slaves. A worker one day discovered her limp skin under a tree
and put hot pepper on the inside. So when Annie returned and put
it on again everyone heard her screaming, "Hey, skin, it's me, Annie!
Stop this pain! Don't you know me?"

Annie was twenty-nine when she was murdered by one of the slaves
she was molesting. Rutherford fell in love with Millicent, a slave, and
Annie set out to destroy her rival. She put a hex on Millicent, who
went mad. Millicent's father, the witch doctor Takoo, was among the
many slaves Annie used for sex. His daughter's murder drove Takoo
to revenge himself on Annie by strangling her to death in her bed.

A Jamaica traveller writing in "The Jamaican Journal" during Annie's lifetime notes: "White women, who are owners of slaves, will, in
general, without any scruple, order their slaves to be flogged; and
some of them will even stand by to see them stripped bare, and punished in the usual disgusting manner."

John's attraction to the Annie legend is influenced by her power
to attract interest to Rose Hall. With white beaches, a blue sea and a
legend to start with, the idea of building a few good hotels came to
mind. But a legend is not so easily domesticated. Annie, apparently,
comes with strings attached. Things unexplained attach themselves
to Annie's bloody reputation. The family who owned the great house
a generation before John bought it, the Fergusons, left when their favorite maid died in a fall from the little balcony where Annie sat to
watch her slaves beaten. For a generation after the Fergusons de-
camped, no one went near the place. The house decayed, like Annie
herself, into a skeleton.

John doesn't have an ounce of superstition in him. But he does
have a touch of Herman Melville's Captain Amaso Delano (in "Benito
Cereno") who boards a derelict Spanish ship where slaves have mu-

tinied. Echoes of Melville's evocation of the galleon—"Her keel
seemed laid, her ribs put together, and she launched, from Ezekiel's
Valley of Dry Bones"—are heard in architect Concannon's description of Rose Hall. Delano's common sense approach is not unlike
John's: "Captain Delano's surprise might have deepened into some
uneasiness had he not been a person of a singularly undistrustful
good nature, not liable, except on extraordinary and repeated incentives, and hardly then, to indulge in personal alarms. . . ."

In his mind's eye, John imagined Rose Hall filled with cheerful visitors, the surrounding coastline developed for hotels and golf
courses, the memory of Annie domesticated for practical commerce.
He meant to employ Annie's bloody history to make something useful for himself, Jamaica, and its people.

North Americans are liable to discount the overwhelming power
of the past. Although he didn't know it at the time, John bought not
only Rose Hall but Jamaica's history too. Our founders employed the
power of reason in a revolutionary attempt to cut us free from the
mad irrationality of history. But anyone who returns to a childhood
home knows that ghosts always lurk there. About his Jamaica venture,
John would say later, "I invested from my heart instead of my head."

To buy Jamaican land and rebuild Rose Hall, John sold stock he
owned in Rollins Inc., the Atlanta company he built with Wayne. That
was in 1960. In 1997, the Jamaica property and Rose Hall were still
draining money from him. His Jamaican enterprise had not made a
profit in thirty-seven years. Had he hung onto the Rollins stock he
used to buy the house and land, he would have put himself ahead by
many millions. But Jamaica has made him irrational too: among his
many business ventures, Jamaica may be the one he regards with the
most personal affection.

For a generation, John bankrolled his Jamaican romance with
money from his other privately held companies—oil wells, three
apartment complexes each worth $7 to $10 million, lands, lumber,
coal. In the seventies, when he found himself in danger of losing his
entire fortune, it appeared little Annie Palmer had him by the throat.
Wayne has remarked that he doesn't entirely comprehend John's
great affection for Jamaica, given the problems that arose there.

"Well, I fell in love there," John explains. Jamaica was both an escape into another reality and a challenge he expected to meet if only
he lived long enough. Its unemployment and poverty seemed to him
unnecessary and wrong. Back in 1961, he'd got it into his head that
he could make a difference in Jamaica. He wanted to uproot what

people like Annie Palmer stood for. He wanted to insert himself in the history of Jamaica as a force for good. Captain Delano indeed.

When John first broached his plans for developing some of the north coast around Montego Bay, Jamaica's prime minister, Hugh Shearer, was enthusiastic. Besides the reconstruction of the Rose Hall Great House, John put up two hotels along the shoreline. The money came in the form of Eurodollars from Chase Manhattan. The Holiday Inn was financed by a $6,250,000 loan from the Bank of Nova Scotia and leased to a subsidiary of Holiday Inns for a twenty-year term. There was also the Intercontinental (later named The Wyndham). Today, John is building a Ritz-Carlton Hotel. Above the coast, winding into the adjacent hills, designer Von Haage is laying out the White Witch Golf Course which promises to be a test worthy of the world's best golfers. These projects are scheduled for completion in 2000.

The government water system was not designed to support such immense projects, so the company has drilled wells; built dams that raised lakes; installed pumps, piping, and cisterns on the hills to supply all the hotels. John believed that his project would inspire other projects of a similar nature. If the north coast of Jamaica becomes *the* Caribbean tourist destination, the economic impact on that impoverished island will be significant. Over $200 million has gone into these projects.

"The Jamaicans . . . overcame slavery to establish a tradition of freedom," John writes in the preface of his book on Rose Hall. "They are a friendly, proud and self-reliant people. With their collaboration we brought into their community facilities to accommodate large conventions, to restore the fabled Great House [Rose Hall] and adjacent landmarks such as Mount Zion Church." Mount Zion Church, dating from the eighteenth century, was on the land John purchased in 1961. Its leaders had apprehensively approached him for a $50,000 grant to shore up their construction plan. He granted $125,000 and threw in a new pipe organ because he thought the congregation sang so well.

John has found the island stonemasons and carpenters to be first-rate. The mechanics, plumbers, and electricians continue to learn on the job. (Prime Minister Michael Manley's utopian scheme, by which numerous small businessmen would use government money to bootstrap their way to independence, failed to take training into account.) The nation's economy is a businessman's first concern, and the last thing a Jamaican wants to worry about. John's solution to the problem of unemployment in Jamaica was to import the economic engine—the "leisure industry" in this case—and plug the Jamaicans into jobs without trying to uproot their way of life.

The North American is trained to live his life as an economic person—someone whose worklife is dedicated to some rational economic end. A life devoted to dreamy philosophy, the fine arts, or other vices of this kind is suspect. A life devoted to simple pleasures and just getting by is unthinkable.

The Jamaican is put off by the rational, commercial imagination. The idea of making a career is an imported idea unredeemed by any ideal of deepening human contact. Selling a chicken should be a social event. Are you really going to wear out your best years turning yourself into a "career?" My friend, you will become not who you are at all. Better to make the marketplace a place where you meet people, where selling is the by-product of social intercourse. Otherwise, you may find what you are selling is your soul.

Bob Fisher, John's man in Jamaica, expresses considerable respect for Jamaican manners and mores. "We [Americans] pay a steep price for our wealth," he says. "Over here I see little six year old girls walking hand-in-hand seven miles to school. They are absolutely safe. We don't have that in the states. I have to ask myself, why?"

In Kingston, of course, life can be dangerous indeed, especially around election time. Whereas North American elections have the character of reformations, the Jamaican election is more like an insurrection. Not only do they throw the rascals out, they replace almost everything the previous bunch achieved. It's politics as iconoclasm.

No accountant on earth, let alone Henry Tippie, would have looked with favor on John's experiments in Jamaica. Eventually, he would be obliged to subdivide much of his land and sell lots to people with money enough to build million-dollar homes. But this didn't occur until after the oil sheiks decided to quadruple oil prices and the economies of the West went haywire and the lending rate went through the roof.

John's business affairs ran into very heavy weather about 1972. In Jamaica, Michael Manley was elected prime minister. Charismatic, tall and silver-haired, with strong opinions and a powerful jaw, Manley allied himself with Fidel Castro and decided to institute socialism. His plan included the expropriation of foreign companies. Jamaican outrage at foreign business concerns on the island was well-founded.

Companies were not paying Jamaica for the raw materials they were taking out. But Manley overspent on public employment and welfare. He had little grasp of global economics. His tenure as prime minister (1972–1980) was too generous to succeed in the bitter world of big money.

Manley did a good job of establishing a bauxite levy that allowed Jamaica to receive its fair share of a business that created few local jobs (about 6,000) and produced a skimpy $25 million a year (1973) for the island. Foreign companies had undervalued the price of ore to keep royalties to a minimum—a clear case of corporate colonialism. Jamaica's revenues went up by a factor of six when Manley's legislation made improper pricing illegal in 1974. But nationalizing the Kaiser and Reynolds mining operations was a mistake. Production fell by a third. Strikes followed. The multinationals cut imports. The International Monetary Fund was pressured by global corporations to put the squeeze on Jamaica. Bauxite and tourism had been Jamaica's best income sources. But tourists, like snowflakes, melt away when there is political unrest.

John knows Jamaica's history and he identifies with the underdog. He has in mind a better life for the people on his side of the island, though the Jamaican desire for self-determination is complicated by violent internecine squabbling and the corrupting influence of big money from outside. The populations on these Caribbean islands, understandably, are easily incited to resentment. The Caribbean islands may be described as a sort of historical roadkill—tiny nations run over by one major power after another.

John didn't make his start in Jamaica as "big money." But from the beginning, he had in mind to create a small economic engine to raise salaries and improve the training of some Jamaicans. (Most Jamaicans seldom get more than a middle school education.) An economic engine must be carefully structured. It demands workers who are well-fed, educated, well-trained, habituated to the concentrated boredom of labor. Evolving a modern workforce from a proud and independent people is no simple task.

Jim Mahoney, vice president of John's privately held companies, relates that John distributed vitamin supplements in the sixties to all the Jamaicans attending school at Mt. Zion. The result has been a new generation taller and stronger—rather like Japanese children after the American victory. John's building programs were set up all around Rose Hall—the Mount Zion Church, the Rhyne Park building program, a town for Jamaicans. After Hurricane Gilbert, John matched government funds to restore the devastated Cornwall Hospital, and he built new houses for squatters who were living on his land. The planned village of Rhyne Park now includes 1200 homes.

Governor John Connally of Texas was for a time his partner in an experiment to raise cattle. The partners hoped to lower the cost of beef which is largely imported. They also experimented with vegetable growing. Some regarded these many projects with suspicion— as part of a sinister plot to pull the wool over Jamaicans' eyes. Plot or not, John Rollins was losing millions.

Extracting its demoralized military from Vietnam in the early seventies, the United States was an injured tiger licking its wounds. For a brief moment, Third World nations rejoiced that socialism was on the ascent and Uncle Sam had feet of clay. The Arab Cartel tripled, quadrupled, sextupled oil prices virtually overnight. Millions of grumpy drivers lined up at gas pumps. Americans felt under siege.

With interest rates climbing from five to eighteen percent, the seventies were the worst possible time to hold mortgages in the millions at variable interest rates. John's new hotels had few occupants and he was loath to sell his assets in order to pay the interest on his Chase Manhattan loan. Meanwhile, the debt compounded.

"That," he says, "is the damndest feeling in the world—when the rate just keeps going up. You're used to five and six percent. Whoever heard of eighteen percent? And you haven't any more income. And you have to sell assets. But you're not liquid. And my stock was low.

"I sold the company planes and closed down the aviation leasing department. That was good for business, because riding coach everywhere put me in such a foul mood I didn't allow anyone to spend money on anything."

Unable to make his payments on the Eurodollar loan, John asked for an extension from Chase Merchant Bankers Jamaica (a subsidiary wholly owned branch of Chase Manhattan Overseas Banking Corporation which, in its turn, was a wholly owned subsidiary of Chase Manhattan, Inc.). Chase Jamaica had done business with John for years. He assumed it should be obvious that he would find means to pay as soon as the interest rate crisis abated. But a convoluted series of maneuvers now took place that would result in the longest civil court case in Delaware history, pitting Rollins against Chase Manhattan in federal district court.

The jury eventually found the sale of John's property to the government "unreasonably cheap and in violation of Chase Jamaica's mortgagee duties." They also found for Rose Hall in another case, tried in Georgia, determining that "Chase Jamaica wrongfully prevented Rose Hall from suing Holiday Inns.

Rose Hall was judged the wronged party by the jury. But then Judge Steel suffered a stroke. A new judge, Murray Schwartz, took Chase Jamaica's appeal and set aside the jury's verdict in an extremely technical brief. The legal war was rejoined. This time Rose Hall was the loser and the struggle would continue for a decade. In the end John would find himself buying back some of his own property from the government. But with the practical man's power to forgive and forget, he regards legal battles as part of the price of doing business. His negotiating team was headed by Don Stansberry and the eventual agreement with the government included repurchasing 3,000 acres along with a plan to put $100 million into Jamican development over the next ten years.

When Michael Manley came back into power in 1989, his understanding of the contemporary economic situation was far better informed. He'd realized that small island states are often subservient to global economic forces the way asteroids are subservient to the gravity of planets. He'd come to believe that workers should become owners in enterprises, and he plumped for education and entrepreneurship at home. In fact, his views were not very different from John's own. But he seemed to have erased their past difficulties from his mind. Meeting John after his 1989 election, he treated him as a friend and ally. "When I told him about them taking my land," John recalls, "he said, 'You mean I've got your land?'

"I said, 'You sure to hell did have.' He said he didn't know—he didn't know what the hell . . . had happened."

Perhaps the prime minister preferred not to remember. As for John, to have arrived with good intentions, and to have acted on those intentions and then find himself portrayed as just another neo-colonialist undermined his enthusiasm at the time. It didn't weaken his resolve. Politicians will always mask their ambition under the guise of "what's good for the people," and Jamaican politicians are no different. As Dostoyevsky once famously remarked, men would rather cut their own throats than place reason before passion. Indeed, what man can abide a voice more reasonable than his own? Most of us remain loyal to the unreason we were raised in, and those raised in chaos are the first to rush to die in support of its agenda.

The legacy of Annie Palmer and her landowning class is present still in Jamaica. Jamaican heroes and heroines are rebels—Paul

Bogle, Nanny, Marcus Garvey. There isn't a Jamaican who doesn't know the singer Bob Marley. To rebel against foreign money affirms the sacred memory of these heroes. The bauxite industry exploited the island. John Rollins, with his service industry approach, represents a more benign economic force from across the ocean. He alone has created more jobs than the entire bauxite extraction industry combined—close to 7,000, versus their 6,000. His original aim, back in the sixties, was to create 10,000 jobs. With the Ritz-Carlton and new golf course functioning, he'll surpass that figure.

Using his Horatio Alger Society connections, John has arranged for many dozens of young Jamaicans to attend Rhinehardt College in Waleska, Georgia. He has made a major contribution to the S.O.S. village where several hundred orphan children are being raised by foster parents in small cottages. Organized into families of nine children, each is headed by a woman who acts as their mother. The idea originated with a couple who began collecting abandoned children and raising them, Dr. Harlan Hastings and his wife, Jennifer.

John even found a way to make his long-time friendship with the country singer, Johnny Cash, pay off for the Jamaicans. Acquainted with Cash and his wife, June Carter Cash, for over thirty-eight years (the families have a tradition of spending New Years together on the island), John suggested the singer perform to raise funds for the S.O.S. program. The money has been used to build foster children's homes on the land John donated.

Despite squabbles with Jamaican officialdom that would have sent most American businessmen home in a huff, John persists in his loyalty to the island. But how can putting up a Ritz-Carlton establishment that caters to the wealthy help a nation in the Third World? Is catering to the rich a practical way to generate a home economy? The poor conditions in Jamaica inspired the idea in the first place. When he arrived in Jamaica in 1960, John had never built a hotel. Tourism struck him as the most practical way to upgrade the poor economy on Jamaica's north coast. He thought it might be possible to create an economic engine powerful enough to raise the local economy to a considerably higher level. Establishing a tourist industry around Montego Bay would bring a constant flow of foreign exchange.

Selling Montego Bay to an indifferent world would take an enormous effort. John believed that only a hotel with international connections might work. He knew that—in order to shed its backwater image—Jamaica must be sold as a virtual paradise to the jet set. Public relations and reservation services would be crucial because the island was cut off, isolated. Consequently, When Michael Manley forced a number of international companies to stop their unfair pricing system in Jamaica and Kaiser (in particular) pulled out, Manley was left with an economy that amounted to little more than a state of nature. At the time, business depended largely on a barter economy while the government tried to create socialism based on the Cuban model. The economy crumbled, and the creation of a tourist trade on these ruins made economic sense.

Unfortunately, a massive modern hotel with all the amenities doesn't attract customers simply because it exists. Its life begins when the hotel is tied into the global economy with its network of jet travel, instant communication, and public relations. The global economy really began when European nations crossed the seas to India, Africa and the Americas to set up shop—the age of discovery. But in an age of mass tourism, the package tour and the internet, virgin beaches exist only in advertising brochures, or in spots that no tourist has the time to discover.

During the years that John's third wife, Michele, was bearing her four children, she joined Vice President Gene Weaver on the Rose Hall project. The Jamaica operation was hemorrhaging millions. John had no sooner doubled the number of hotel rooms to over 2,000 than the tourists vanished. There was political unrest on the island brought on by a worldwide recession. Michele says she saw Jamaica as "an unstructured wild card that could be incredible—or nothing. Depending on, well, a lot of things. Like luck. I was having baby after baby, and no one had time for Jamaica. You lose your business when that happens. With the losses he was experiencing at the time, John couldn't afford to have a $100,000 a year manager running that property. So I began to fly down there every Tuesday. Pregnant as I was, I would take one child and leave one home. Thank God for my mother."

The Jamaica project that Michele took over includes the 1200-home development project, road building, water and electric projects, and all of the supporting facilities. The Rose Hall Great House, at great expense, has been made to look at it did when it was first built. The idea is to give visitors some sense of a vanished world, one more refined and more brutal than our own. Michele says, "People no longer want to just go on the beach [in Jamaica]. They want to get in touch with the culture. They want to feel part of the country they've visited."

John says that until the new Ritz-Carlton hotel is up and running in 2000, the Jamaican operation will continue to incur enormous debts. During most of 1999, John spent his time on the island working to solve the inevitable crises that surfaced: contractors' disputes, technical interfaces between the island and the mainland, workers' training. When he finally opens his palace, the global economy must cooperate. A sharp recession could spell disaster for the tourist industry. John shrugs off the possibility. He plays the part of a latter day Kubla Khan, raising his pleasure dome. He never dwells on a thousand potential catastrophes. He sails past his eightieth year. Time is pressing.

23

Conversation in Jamaica

In August of 1970, John, brother Wayne and some of their children came to the ceremonial ground breaking for the new office building on Route 202, the Concord Pike. Slipping out of the city across I-95, Concord Pike runs north to the Pennsylvania border through a litter of strip malls, phone lines, and shops that sell everything from electronic pianos to dog collars. A block off the highway residential districts fan out, lawns and gardens under maples and dogwood. The general impression is that of an avenue designed by building inspectors whose only architectural requirements are that every building must squat low to the ground and remain as undistinguished as possible.

The transformation of sleepy old Delaware into a paradise of commerce was well underway when the Rollins plan was made public in 1972. But when John produced his plan for a fifteen-story building a howl went up. A lot of people felt that a building so tall would surely destroy Concord Pike's architectural unity. That the neighborhood consisted almost entirely of mismatched strip malls and a phalanx of grotesque signs apparently offended no one. However, all of that aesthetic blight had occurred naturally the way weeds grow. The idea of something so different somehow offended a great many people. The notion of a tower looming over their familiar world of packing-crate constructions set in acres of black asphalt where cars parked violated some arcane sense of status quo. The building's design was in fact far more elegant than the biscuit boxes surrounding it, but that curiously escaped the attention of many people. It was tall and that was awful.

No one knows, or no one will say, how John wangled a permit to put up a fifteen-story building on Concord Pike. Henry Tippie says the council handed John the permit exactly one day before a new law declared buildings over five stories illegal. Many of John's most vocal detractors live in the Brandywine Hundred region, where old money and a new managerial elite rub shoulders. Along Concord Pike, franchise restaurants and outlets selling everything from computers to running shoes have mushroomed overnight. The land John selected backed onto a row of houses facing the DuPont Country Club's golf course. DuPont golfers knocking their way from hole to hole would find their southeast view oppressed by this icon of change.

Completed in 1974, the new building has a penthouse that looks like an afterthought, but the sweeping white vertical lines that rise straight from the ground fifteen stories to the top are in a different league from everything else in a neighborhood where only the stone churches have integrity. The entrance and foyer are laid with white marble, displaying none of the gold costume-jewelry effects that Donald Trump finds so appetizing.

Possibly no one found the new building attractive simply because it was attractive. Indeed, what the Rollins building lacks is the authentic quality of corporate banality displayed, for instance, by its neighbor AstraZeneca next door. Constructed some years later, AstraZeneca's offices hunker down like bunkers designed to withstand a terrorist attack. Narrow windows squint from a series of low, interlinking buildings. Apparently no one complained when plans for this project were unveiled.

Remarking on the Southerner's affection for tall buildings, Wilbur Cash observes in his *Mind of the South,*

> Probably it would mean nothing if I said that the skyscrapers which were going up were going up in towns which, characteristically, had no call for them—in towns where available room was still plentiful, and land prices were still relatively low—for it would merely be said that the Middle West was doing something of the same silly sort. But if I told you that they were often going up in towns (like Tar Heel, Charlotte, and Winston and Greensboro . . .) which had little more use for them than a hog has for a morning coat—in towns where there was no immediate prospect of their being filled?

He adds, "Do you not recognize it for the native gesture of an incurably romantic people, enamored before all else of the magnificent and the spectacular?"

When John lost both his brother and Henry Tippie to Atlanta, he found himself alone for the first time in twenty years. At forty-eight, his success in business had been astonishing. But the economic world, like the sea, is full of unpleasant surprises, even for big fish. And while John was no minnow, he was no General Motors either.

As the Rollins building rose, so did the interest rates. The cost of money was to prove a much greater threat than local opposition. John could live happily branded as a philistine, a capitalist, a Brobdingnagian. Those were only words. But rising interest rates were sticks and stones. And when the real estate market collapsed, he felt the pain.

The building was completed in 1974 when, as Henry Tippie says, "Things are very, very bad. So now," Henry sums up the situation, "you can't rent the space in the building. I mean it's a fifteen-story building and you've got about ten floors of it with no one in them. There are birds flying through here, and there's office space all over Wilmington free back then."

Henry Tippie regards the world of business the way a scrupulous prelate regards the City of God. Business, too, has its absolutes. The laws of business are as firmly fixed as the stars—and he can show you how on a balance sheet. If you can't get more coming in than you have going out, where will you end up? Old-fashioned virtue lies at the heart of Henry's business vision. Contrary to popular perception, the men who run corporations often locate their worst problems along moral fault lines. The most damaging decision is the dishonest one. If you aren't scrupulously honest, then no matter how smart you thought you were, catastrophe will overwhelm you in the end. Henry doesn't regard business as the salvation of the world, but it comes close. Within its own precincts, business doesn't make a mockery of high intelligence and true accomplishment as art and politics are wont to do. No one is secure in those institutions. In business success has a measure. There can be no illusions.

Henry views the sixties as a great flowering of illusions. Like Wayne and John, he'd grown up in a world where the young were forced by hardship into self-sufficiency and self-reliance—a world that didn't understand excuses. As John says, "People don't really care too much about your problems. Maybe a few do, but most people don't want to hear about it." These men were raised in a time when it was still possible to say, "You have only yourself to blame."

Those born over seventy years ago must occasionally find themselves appalled by the era they have brought into existence. They have created such material abundance that it sometimes appears the young are drowning in goods. Anyone who doubts this should watch college students arriving with trailer-loads full of clothes and appliances to begin their studies. And along with abundance has come psychology. What used to be called a moral lapse has been redefined by psychology as an emotional problem. The child is no longer a moral creature with free will but, rather, a sort of floppy disk where parents inadvertently inscibe the errors that will plague the new adult. Given a fine appreciation of just how much we are all helpless victims has made us deeply aware of our profound inadequacy. However, none of this is so in Henry's world, where the best route from a motive to its achievement is an honest line, straight and true.

Henry had moved his family to Austin, Texas, in 1971. As one might expect from a man so practical, his reasons for going to Texas were carefully thought through. Atlanta was in turmoil. School integration had degenerated into social war with the kids as pawns. Henry, on principle, would not place his children in private schools. As he puts it, he was "not from that culture."

Henry had no impulse to over-shelter his kids from a society that only pretended to go easy on kids. "I've watched this [permissiveness] play with too many kids, and half the time they're [in college] for a good time. And I guess I feel I'm from a background where it was a privilege to go. It really meant something to me. And that's how I'm going to look at it. Yeah, I could put them in private schools, but I don't happen to believe in it."

He expected his children would walk out into a world very different but just as tough as the one he faced as a young man. His lack of privilege he regards now as an asset. Why deny the same to his own kids? "The real world is people in the public area. That's where you're going to get the hard knocks. It's not with this small group that's able to go to private schools. Maybe I'm all wet, but that's how I feel about it."

He has no doubt the public schools "have gone backwards." Busing scattered his children all over Atlanta. The youngest had gone to two separate schools in one year, and the oldest was switching schools every year. "So now you're in the shuttle business of picking them up, here, there—the thing's an absolute nightmare."

With an economy thrown into overdrive by the price of OPEC oil, Texas was enjoying a spell of rapid expansion. The state levied no income tax on individuals or corporations. Henry met with the owners of a small television station. The manager was an alcoholic. The company had debts of $600,000. There were cables festooned all over the control room. The windows on the second floor were blacked out with psychedelic posters. "The engineer's idea of lunch was two bottles of beer. I mean the whole thing was unreal. It needed to be cleaned out. Let's put it that way."

After making the station profitable, Henry picked up a building materials business and put together a holding company, called Kingstip. He got it listed on the American Exchange in 1972. He increased its revenue from $10 to $40 million within three years. He had new partners—a father and son. "The son was kind of semi-alcoholic. I have to say the guy was brilliant. Highly articulate. Somebody I always thought had forgotten more than I'll ever know. But liquor ate him up and he died."

Henry was now connected with the Rollins brothers only as a trustee. "I had little to do with John who was rolling with all these other people up there." John missed Henry though. It had been Wayne and Henry's role to keep John from jumping off the cliff of a wild idea. But Jamaica and rising interest rates had blindsided him. "[My accountants] keep telling me we're making money," John told Henry. "But in the meantime we've got no money, and it's only getting worse."

Henry suggested John's people should come to Austin with the books and he'd check them over. John packed a gaggle of his accountants on board the jet and flew them to Texas. "They rolled in," Henry recalls,

> and went down to the Driscoll Hotel. And they asked me to come over there. And they showed me all this creative accounting. And meanwhile they've got a bunch of liquor over there. And I'm thinking, this is a disaster in the making. They've capitalized stuff they ought to [list as] expense so they don't have to face up to it. And all these deferred charges. This place is out of control.
>
> And in early 1974, John's getting under tremendous pressure. . . . And meanwhile Wayne got sucked in with all this demand for collateral. Terrible problems. Bankruptcy a possibility from a personal standpoint. And maybe a company standpoint.

Henry could see ruin staring John in the face. According to John, Wayne came up with $12 million to give him a hand, but refused, still, to loan him his car. "All because I broke the axle of his $50 Ford when I was a kid. He never did get over that."

Like a long-distance runner eating up his own muscle to hang in the race, John sold off whatever he had left. He sold a large portion of his stock in Rollins Inc.—about three-fourths of it. Traders, sniffing blood in the water, made millions by consistently shorting the stock. Its price skidded from $40 to $4, then bumped $2. The new companies he'd acquired were not turning a profit.

Concentrating on his Jamaica problems, John had left his leasing business in other hands. Another drain on his finances was his hazardous waste disposal company, Rollins Environmental. "Everyone wanted me to build those plants, but no one was giving me any business," he says. "To tell the honest truth, the financial organization was in a hell of a mess from the time Henry left until the time he came back. The worst mistake you can make in business is not have the proper financial control. I don't care how good you are at everything else."

Henry began flying to Wilmington on weekends the year before John moved his company into the new building on Concord Pike. For the time being he ensconced his offices in a Holiday Inn. Henry noted that many of the simple and straightforward procedures he'd set up had been discontinued. In their place, a new generation of accountants had installed a whiz-bang melange of occult numerology and tricky set-asides.

In Henry's view, the man in charge of John's leasing outfit looked like a typical business school product—full of theories and excuses. "John had some MBA guy running the thing. I don't know how the hell he got him. Friend of somebody's. Look, there's nothing complicated in business unless you make it complicated."

The company moved its offices from the Holiday Inn to the new building, but things kept getting worse. "John got into a bunch of personal financial problems. And he's got a domestic problem that's getting in." [Referring here to John's divorce from Linda.] "Sometimes I'd come up on a Friday [from Texas] and look around here," Henry recalls. "I walked through here one Saturday with him. And there were expense accounts lying around. I looked at one and showed it to him. Some guy went down to Washington and back and he's got $1,000 in expenses. I mean you can't stay in business with that kind of thing going on."

In early 1974, John found himself coming under "tremendous pressure" as the New York bankers tried to sell his Jamaica property out from under him. John asked Henry to return full-time until he was out of the woods. Henry admits to some hesitation. "It was about this time that some newspaper down in Dover printed a cartoon of John sitting in the street with a begging cup. And I didn't know whether it was saveable or not." Henry was forced to reflect on his own career. "I'd got a lot of experience. Where did I get it? What had that done for me? I'd done well in Austin, and I didn't need this [mess in Wilmington]. But it was a repayment for all he'd done."

The media, sniffing blood, circled in the middle distance looking for sign of weakness. They sensed a Hollywood ending to a classic American business story. Maybe headlines were already being composed in the mind of some editorial writer: "NO SECOND ACTS IN AMERICAN LIVES AS JOHN ROLLINS TAKES THE FALL."

Henry flew to meet with John in Jamaica. After John had laid out the situation, Henry laid down some stiff ground rules. "I was not going to get involved if I'd be second guessed."

Both men knew it was going to be extremely painful. Henry wanted Wayne involved too, since he was involved anyway. The brothers were committed to each other to the death. If John went down Wayne would probably not have gone down with him, but he would have been damaged. The psychological fallout of failure has shredded more than one family. It might not have damaged the love between these two tough, middle-aged brothers, but it could wreak havoc among the more tender-minded young who assumed smooth sailing was a way of life. There would have been furious wives, confused kids, reporters knocking on the door, cameras at the gates.

John's eldest son, John Jr., a recent MBA and new to the company, recalls he had to sell everything he owned, including house and land. His wife, Diana, sold everything in the house—the furniture, coats, jewelry. The only thing she kept was her wedding ring.

"You find out what kind of person you're married to when you go through something like that," says John Jr. "Looking back now, it was the greatest learning experience of my life. But I'd never want to go through it again."

Like those barns in Faulkner's South that appear to burn spontaneously when a man has enemies, John's enterprise was cracking and crumbling. It looked that year as if everyone associated with him would be carried off by the conflagration, while lawyers danced in the street. Having sold his airplanes, his helicopters, and his downstate land in Delaware, he rented out his house and took up residence in Florida where there is no state income tax.

Henry had made it clear he'd come back only if granted plenary powers. The job he had to do "would need fast-on-your-feet decisions on the basis of best information available. That's how I saw it. No sacred cows." John agreed.

Their conversation in Jamaica gave Henry the right to call all the shots. Success or failure depended on him. Henry began by crossing off the directors he wanted to let go. "I felt they were worthless." (Henry never minces words.) A board meeting was held which Henry didn't attend because he was not a member of the board. John told eight of the fifteen board members they were axed. It was a job he hated, but he knew Henry was right.

Applying his cleaver to all that was offensive in his sight, Henry hacked away most of the fat in eighteen months. He fired from top to bottom: vice presidents, janitors, and anyone lollygagging between. "There wasn't anything in this company that didn't have a problem." Rollins International occupied five floors of the new building; when Henry was done, the survivors could easily fit into fewer than three.

And the result? "Today," he says, not without pride, "we've got the best profit margin in the business in truck leasing. Ryder (their top competitor) has said in print we're the Cadillac of the industry. Let me tell you, back then our Eastern division [was so badly organized] it didn't even know the West existed."

Henry visited every regional office. "That's where you find out what's wrong. Not in this damn place!" he says, dismissing fifteen stories of office space with a gesture. He uncovered problems under every stone he kicked—strategy, delivery, service. "Too many people doing nothing. The guy who was president then, I could see he wasn't worth anything."

He brought in John Rollins Jr. and laid out his plan before the young man. He told him to execute it precisely in every detail. John Jr. did so, and Henry allows that he more than proved himself. "I've always said I had to get him reprogrammed. Get him to where he forgot he ever had an MBA. He now has a Ph.D. A Ph.D. in experience. He's a top operator. Because you can have the best plan in the world, but you're dead if there's no one who can make it work."

As for Rollins Environmental, it was "absolutely bankrupt." "I would have locked it up," Henry says. "But I couldn't because it owed so much money—mortgages, collateral, cross-collateral. Rollins in New Jersey was the guarantor on the Deer Park operation in Texas— an absolute pigsty. Bad rates. Giving the customer money to insure his business. You walk through the front gate into mud. It was just a giveaway. Two sets of management. They couldn't run anything. It had to be cleaned out. It took time."

With his eye fixed on the gaping holes in John's bottom line, Henry had small appreciation for John's foresight in developing the hazardous waste industry. He'd got there first, yes, but then he'd run smack into a wall of indifference or outright hostility. He'd fired up his first system back when it was still legal "to dump toxic waste in a ditch." But from Henry's point of view, the New Jersey hazardous waste facility was a dead loss. It "had never made a dime in its history. The plant at Baton Rouge made money mostly from its landfill." But that proved an unholy mess and had to be dug up and buried all over again. It was an initial design, not a technological marvel. This kind of experimentation made Henry impatient, perhaps a little crazy.

When Henry, John, and John Jr. went to speak to the bankers they had to convince them that Rollins International was still a good idea. One of John's previous accountants had worked out a loan schedule to present to a banker. Henry uncovered a $5 million mistake in the document. "Now that is embarrassing," John says. "Having to go back and tell them you need another $5 million!"

They'd worked out two plans, one for $20 million, another for $30 million. Henry recalls one particularly persuasive point they could make: the bankers stood to lose a fortune unless they took the plunge. Continental Illinois National Bank in Chicago had $12 million in loans outstanding. The bankers had two choices, put up more money or lose every cent they'd loaned the Rollinses.

The bankers blinked, blanched, and put up the money. Henry began to draw on the funds as needed, a million at a time. "We cleaned all this garbage out of this place," Henry says drily. "We had numbers instead of hieroglyphics by then. We knew what the hell we were looking at."

An echo of the avenging angel sounds in his voice: he uncovered sin and came with a refiner's fire to burn it out. The light of reason prevailed. The licentious spirit of the sixties flew shrieking back into the sinkhole that spawned it. Damned were the faint of heart—managers who couldn't follow "simple" plans and bankers who grew chickens' feet and ran away squawking havoc.

Recounting all of this, Henry shows emotion only when he recalls the bankers who had faith in them. He reserves a faint contempt for those who lacked fortitude. "Later, they wanted to come back. But even today I won't get on the same elevator with those people. I don't want fair-weather friends. The hell with them."

Years afterward, when Rollins Inc. was doing very well and Continental Bank got into trouble, "[We] sent word that we would not take one dime out of their bank. 'You stayed with us. We're staying with you.'"

John's personal finances (thanks to Jamaica) were awash in red ink. His liabilities were enormous, his assets dwindling. A stock whose worth has fallen to six dollars may climb back up to fifty again. It may also drop to two as Rollins International did. It may vanish entirely. It didn't. They were among the first corporate managers to "down-size" a company in the modern manner. This painful pruning, done without fear or favor, made it possible for John's enterprise to leap back into vibrant life. The winter of his economic life was over.

24
Nixon

John was among the organizers of the Citizens for Eisenhower-Nixon committee in 1952. That was the year Senator John Williams asked him to try for the nomination for Republican lieutenant governor of Delaware. After assuring him he was a shoo-in, the senator picked up the phone and asked him to announce his candidacy to the *Morning News* then and there, before he changed his mind. John had the impression he had no opposition whatever until the next morning when six others announced their candidacy for the same office.

Few names among our presidents are more controversial than Nixon's. Yet few presidents since Franklin Roosevelt have guided into existence more legislation important to the public welfare. He bombed Cambodia, but then extracted the nation like a bad tooth from Vietnam—a task impossible to accomplish without pain on every side. His administration set in motion the affirmative action policies that attempted to improve the status of African Americans. He started a meaningful dialogue with the Soviet Union, and was considered a pariah by powers in his own party for opening relations with China. The Environmental Protection Agency (EPA) was created during his presidency, and then given the legal bite and supplementary laws that made it work.

Arguably, Nixon's presidency accomplished more than either Jimmy Carter's or Ronald Reagan's. Nixon wrote into law the national "War on Cancer" in 1971, and signed a directive to outlaw the development of offensive biological weapons in the United States. Army labs were converted to the exclusive development of protective vaccines and basic research into the control of lethal microorganisms.

In 1960, John supplied the tractor-trailer rigs that converted into platforms for the Eisenhower-Nixon rallies. Television was not yet the overwhelming power it soon became, so candidates were not measured out in sound bites and promoted like toothpaste. The first Republican lieutenant governor elected to office in twenty years in

Delaware, the tireless proprietor of half-a-dozen Ford dealerships, one of the organizers of the Young Presidents Organization (YPO, an international forum where entrepreneurs aged forty or younger could meet), John enjoyed the heady sensation of a man plunged in the maelstrom of public life and swimming to the top.

He would eventually meet many of the world's most influential people. The list of those at the top is finite, and individuals in power come and go quickly. The professional circles that drive the modern world are like small towns—enclaves of biochemists, heart surgeons, theatrical producers, or the CEOs of high-tech companies. When John says that he knows half the senators in Congress, he is only talking about fifty individuals. He's been photographed in the company of enough famous politicians to crowd a caucus room. Influence has a lot to do with money and access to the rooms where the powerful get together. Power derives from performance, and from perception, which is why reputation is so important. Nixon felt the most respect for self-made men, perhaps because he had himself beat his way to the top despite an awkward public persona that would have sunk most politicians.

Nixon got to know John initially as a member of the YPO and a fund-raiser. "I was," he recalls, "vice chairman of the Republican Finance Committee. Then I was chairman of the President's Dinner [Committee] when Nixon was president. And I've always been a charter member of the Senatorial Trust, which exists to encourage direct interchange on issues between senators and other members. And every time they'd have one of these House dinner fundraisers, I'd lend a hand. So I got to know them. But I make it a habit that I never ask for anything pertaining to business."

"I liked him from the start," John says of Nixon. "We always had a good relationship—in the sense that I could be frank and tell him what I didn't like." The question is what did John need, and what did Nixon do about it? Clearly, John could never have started the hazardous waste industry without the legislation written during Nixon's tenure. John was a good ten years ahead of the curve. When he went to London to learn about hazardous waste disposal, there were almost no laws enforcing industrial cleanup in the United States. Then Nixon arrived on the scene. By that time the public had become aware of environmental degradation. So the creation of the Environmental Protection Agency became a hot issue. And just as Ronald Reagan happened to be at the helm when the Soviet Union imploded of its own inertia, so Richard Nixon was president when America decided to clean up its act.

A volatile mix of acute intelligence and sometimes paranoia, Nixon may have felt that John was someone he could relax with a little. Nixon spoke in fits and starts. John's intuitive ability to fill in the gaps went over well because this president (as the Nixon tapes make clear) hated having to explain himself. Easygoing self-assurance settled Nixon down.

John objects strongly to any pejorative description of Richard Nixon whatever. His loyalty remains absolute and he still believes that Nixon, despite the Watergate scandal, was a good president, if not a great one. When Nixon was out of office, John invited him for a visit to Jamaica. The ex-president arrived with a vast entourage of Secret Service men. Michele recalls that she took one look at Nixon in "that dark blue suit he always wore, his uniform," and ran out to buy him a "Ruth Claridge wardrobe of tropical play clothes." She picked out a selection of colors in order to give him a choice. Nixon, she says, was immediately drawn to the slate-gray outfit, setting aside the bright yellow with pineapple motif and crimson red. The slate-gray, so well-suited to his conservative taste, unfortunately came with a Jamaican donkey motif. The donkey, after all, was the logo of the Democratic Party. Even so, he plumped for the slate-gray and donkey be damned. His wife Pat said that as she'd been everwhere and seen most everything, she'd be only too pleased to sit with a book and enjoy a proper vacation. Nixon went out into the island and everywhere he appeared was mobbed by Jamaicans. "We were all somewhat overwhelmed by his popularity over there," Michele recalls.

Having come of age in an era of atomic fear and secret agents, Nixon fashioned his career out of Cold War paranoia. America lived in a state of hysteria over pinkos, commie dupes, and liberal professors. Having stood firm against Communism, Nixon dismayed his conservative cohorts by going to China because the conventional wisdom of the time insisted that Communists were not entirely human. While most American presidents are violently disliked, or even hated by hearsay, John insists that Nixon was liked by those who dealt with him personally. John's Nixon is a high-minded realist who occasionally mistook mosquitoes for wasps, but a man with a singular ability to x-ray through complex situations and to act with decision. What fascinated Nixon most, John says, was political power in all its manifestations. He astonished John by consistently predicting upcoming elections by one or two percentage points.

During Nixon's first term, John was selected for the President's Advisory Council on Management Improvement. James Mahoney, who chaired the Council, had the job of insuring that no one on the list would "embarrass Nixon. I came to the dossier on John Rollins," he says, "and all I could find was an international correspondence course degree! I thought, 'Oh oh. We're going to have trouble with this one.' But he turned out to be the person closest to the president."

The membership of the group says something about the sort of men and women Nixon wanted to hear from. Included were Leatrice E. Gochberg, a mortgage banker from New York, so nervous the first time she met with Mahoney that she spilled a martini all over her chest; Wayne Hoffman, who started the Flying Tiger airline; Gail Melick, who advised against the South American loans that ruined the Continental Bank; and Charles Wyly who left IBM with Ross Perot to set up his own software outfit. The military man was Bernard Schriever, the youngest four-star general in the U.S. Air Force. Schriever, according to Mahoney, was "a brilliant guy. He gave us the ballistic missile. He was the impetus behind the Rand think tank. Most of the think tanks were Schriever's idea." And finally there was businessman Dwayne O. Andreas, one of two Americans allowed to fly his private jet into the Soviet Union.

Democrats were represented by Wayne Thompson, onetime city manager of Richmond, Virginia and Oakland, California, and Rufus Miles, who served three presidents as a top administrator and was Lecturer in Public Affairs and Director of the Mid-Career Program at the Woodrow Wilson School of Public and International Affairs at Princeton University (1966–75). Rufus Miles apparently believed that social heirarchy determined the individual's views, while John Rollins held that liberal social programs must stand on fiscal conservatism, by which he meant the generation of fresh economic activity. Unless social thinking led to economic activity it remained at the level of crisis management.

When Mahoney and Ms. Alma Yoemans set about "enhancing the opportunities for women in government bureaucracy," it was John whom Yoemans selected to present the notion to Nixon. Mahoney quotes Yoemans: "By my reading, John is the only one who is a real friend of the President. All these other guys are acquaintances. John and the President like each other. They talk on a regular basis. And if we can convince John that we have a real opportunity in this country to use women to a fuller degree. . . ." According to Mahoney, Nixon did put pressure on departments to employ women in positions of higher authority.

James Mahoney today works (and lobbies) in Washington for Rollins companies, and he has no doubt John had "a major impact on getting an environmental agency with teeth. I wasn't present [at his conversations with Nixon]. But he advised that politically speaking the timing was right. The American people wanted it." However, John believes that his friendship with Nixon worked against him more often than not. He wanted the same treatment as any other businessmen, but his high profile made him a target for exclusion. EPA officials certainly made no concessions for him just because he had a line to Nixon. In fact, as we shall see, the EPA's regulatory process often short-circuited his attempt to deal with hazardous waste.

Working under the excellent William Ruckelshaus, Maurice Easton, an industrial consultant to the EPA, was enthusiastic about John's experiment in hazardous waste disposal. The agency was also enthusiastic about creating stringent regulations regarding this new industry. Yet twenty years later, when John brought to the agency's attention the very lax standards governing waste disposal at cement kilns, no one wanted to listen.

In the fall of 1971, Richard Nixon created a small sensation in the chateau country of northern Delaware by dropping in on John's estate from the air. With him were Senators Bob Dole, William Roth, Congressman Pete du Pont, and Congressman Tom Evans who recalls acting as liaison. Appointed chairman of the GOP's National President's Dinners Committee, John organized $500-a-plate suppers that November, and communicated with the president. The national mania over communism had by then spawned the "domino theory" that led to Vietnam. The perception of American policy makers was unblemished by any higher complexity. Innocent minds saw communism and capitalism as two gunfighters down at the OK Corral. Highly intelligent men in the State Department fervently insisted the loss of Vietnam would mean the loss of Indochina and then almost everything else. Our fondest Cold War delusion held that all national and cultural complexity would melt in the acid bath of communist ideology. But by the end of the century it was feel-good global capitalism that appeared more likely to achieve that apotheosis.

Demonstrations against the war in Vietnam became a way of life for university students who endured tear gas, police truncheons, jail and even death (at Kent State where students were shot and killed). About a dozen war protesters (Delaware Youth Against War and Fascism) showed up near Walnut Green to inveigh against Nixon. Having achieved the American Dream, the farm boy from Catoosa County had arrived at such a state of grace that he could invite the President to dinner—and then be vilified for it. What could be more American than that?

The sixties was a decade of rumors set in motion by John Kennedy's assassination. Americans didn't report sighting the four beasts of the apocalypse in the sky, but flying saucers were seen everywhere. After President Kennedy's death came the assassinations of Martin Luther King and Bobby Kennedy. With the Vietnam War's progress being measured in body counts and with the confusion about why we were there in the first place, it often seemed the nation was in thrall to some unholy collusion between politicians, Mafiosi, and the CIA. Hundreds of magazine articles and books attempted to establish such connections. Had not the House of Kennedy and Camelot itself been founded on father Joseph's illegal millions? The national habit of indulging every evening in television tales of violence, sex and madness created a rich mulch where conspiracy theories could flower. The national scene resembled Jacobean drama, lacking only a sufficient poetry to lift it out of yellow journalism into art. The media more than matched Richard Nixon's own propensity for perceiving a chimera in every closet.

In keeping with the time, wild rumors about John Rollins circulated locally. Gossip and paranoia invented enormous government contracts that John had supposedly garnered for putting billions of feet of cable wire all over Vietnam. It was whispered that he'd inherited his vast wealth from a father who owned dozens of auto dealerships, that he'd made a fortune disposing of hazardous waste by dribbling it from his tanker trucks across the United States.

Nixon's visit to Walnut Green was an innocuous event. He was scheduled to meet a number of national industrial leaders selected for membership on the Dinner Committee. The President arrived by helicopter and landed on the extensive lawn that surrounds John's home. A single photographer was brought in to record the event. As reporters were not invited, local news focused on the dozen protesters in the road. The high drama of the evening was provided by Tom Evans' little daughter who got her hair caught on a button of Nixon's suitcoat during the photo op. Five-year-old Mary Page and the President spent a few moments intimately entwined as they struggled to free themselves, and their tussle was leaked to the *Morning News*.

Around the time that the Watergate debacle achieved gale force, John was subpoenaed to appear before a grand jury. A number of those people John had worked with were indicted for perjury. An important money raiser, John was naturally of some interest to the prosecution. They wanted to know where all the money had come from. On the day he went to testify, John left his car and driver at the hotel and caught a cab. He asked the driver to drop him off at the back door. Out front a hundred newspeople had assembled on the marble steps with cameras flashing. The media had not thought to send someone around back. Speaking in a commanding voice to the security police, John said, "It's vital that I enter Courtroom Five." Staring into the pale blue eyes of a very large, stern man in a dark suit, the guard quickly passed him through without delay.

As chairman of the President's Dinner Committee, John was reported to have raised $5 million during one campaign year. He was questioned about these funds, but he made a practice of never handling any money himself. "That," he remarks, "is where you always get into trouble." As a fund-raiser for the Republican Party, he'd always insisted that not all the money be siphoned off to Washington. Half should remain in the state to benefit state elections.

The grand jury asked for the names of those contributing to Nixon's campaign and the amounts. "I looked at the situation and I thought, 'My goodness, somebody is really trying to feed me to the wolves.' They had a list and they'd ask if so-and-so had given a million dollars. And I'd say, 'Well, he might have. I can't swear that he did. I didn't see the check. I never handled any money. I don't think you'd be interested in hearsay.'"

About the time that Nixon entered the first term of his presidency, John was already well on his way to creating America's first hazardous waste disposal industry. The idea had occurred to him when he acquired the Matlack fleet of tanker trucks, "a pipeline on wheels." Matlack transported some of the most toxic chemicals ever created, carting the stuff to plants that produced everything from Teflon® to formaldehyde. At that time, no safe method had been devised to get rid of poisonous residual sludge, and hundreds of thousands of tons of chemical excreta were overwhelming major rivers and poisoning aquifers.

John began his search for a practical disposal method in 1967. He travelled to England, where the Purle Brothers, Ltd. had developed an advanced technology for cleaning up the Thames River. Purle had so reduced pollution in the river bisecting London that fish had reappeared in its waters.

Rollins-Purle, Inc. began operating in Logan Township, New Jersey, in 1969. The Environmental Protection Agency was established in 1970, the same year that John's Baton Rouge facility began commercial operation. The Federal Water Pollution Control Act of 1972

was passed that same year that John's Deer Park facility began operation. The environmentally powerful Clean Air Act was implemented
in 1973.

By the time the Watergate story broke, Nixon had locked himself
into a no-holds-barred war with the media and lost. Nixon's departure ended John's close association with the White House, but not before he'd acted as a special ambassador to Mexico and as a delegate
to the World Environmental Conference.

A man with John's talent for raising money will never lack friends
in government. But even after his political demise, Nixon continued
to invite John to his New York apartment on occasion. John recalls
the ex-president loved discussing international politics in great detail, and he liked to go to bed early.

Nixon was able to name every leader of consequence in the United
States, and would do so while flying coast-to-coast as he passed over
their states. He'd catalogue their strengths, weaknesses, and voting
records and predict their chances in upcoming elections. World leaders were of equal interest to him. The president had apparently studied how their characters affected their governments or, conversely,
how political systems affected personal behavior.

All of this was certainly impressive but, in John's opinion, "He was-
n't worth a damn in economics." Absorbed in fighting a Cold War
that looked as if it must last forever, Nixon created enormous anxiety
in the Soviet leadership when he drew China away from Russia. Yet
he never grasped how American business with its materialistic promise had become a far more persuasive force than political idealism.
American enterprise eventually buried the Soviets under an ocean of
consumer goods and Star Wars paraphernalia.

The American people, in their tireless pursuit of happiness, could
conceive of war only as commercial struggle. In 1989, Soviet power
magically transformed former commissars into born-again capitalists
almost overnight. Unfortunately, latter-day capitalism that operates
without powerful legal restraints quickly devolves into rapacious
greed. John Rollins's long love affair with politics is clarified by Russia's situation. He has never been a businessman who sees government as an impediment to business. Good government is crucial to
business success. Like government, a business must work for the public good, or it destroys itself.

25
Refining Fires

In the suburbs of ancient Rome enormous pits were dug and into these *fossae* were dumped the city's offal, including the corpses of beggars, criminals, and other unidentified dead picked up each morning from the streets. Thousands of years later, these sinkholes are still unapproachable. No one can build near them, much less on them.

These ancient pits are nothing compared to the deadly muck modern technology produces. The propensity of economic man to foul the outskirts of his cities and the banks of his rivers constitutes the dark side of scientific technique. Millions of tons of chemicals and heavy metals are spewed daily out into streams and bays. For a time many looked on pollution as a sign of progress. The postindustrial world is reluctantly conceding that progress today must include cleaning up the mess. In the fifties and sixties, the notion of the entire planet as a non-renewable resource blossomed into Ecology. It occurred to John around 1960 that, with the right legislation, getting rid of toxic waste might be turned into an industry.

He had acquired Matlack early in the decade, a trucking line that delivered chemicals all over the states and Canada. His drivers had to deal with liquids that turned into gases or burst into flames on contact with the atmosphere, and gases that exploded unless they were kept under pressure. After these deadly liquids had been delivered, the trucks required cleaning. Nobody wanted to get stuck with the residue. The specter of hazardous waste rose up before John a good decade before it turned into a national nightmare.

In England his partnership with Purle Ltd. was signed in November 1968, the same year Nixon was elected. The president understood the balancing act required to get a Congress to create regulations that would cost the chemical companies millions to implement. Regulation in any form is divisive. It divides management from workers, government from business, parents from children. No one wants to be regulated. Yet the alternative is chaos. Naturally, the companies most responsible for hazardous waste will have the strongest incentive to fight regulation tooth and nail. Among these social infants are some of the most powerful corporations in the world.

What are hazardous materials? Jet fuel, solvents, acetone, automobile paint loaded with cadmium and lead. There are contaminated soils—some irradiated, some poisoned with toluene isocyanate, a monomer that reacts violently with water. The medical offal from research labs contains everything from volatile liquids to diseased blood. About 70,000 chemicals are used in industrial amounts. Perhaps 2,000 of these have been studied for their effect on living things. One woman in eight, we are told, falls victim to breast cancer. Many believe that a tragedy is unfolding. The threat exists below the threshold of human perception and because only the results are visible, their origin is always in doubt.

The toxic materials that the Rollins plants attempt to control are among the worst offenders. By regulation, each must be identified and weighed by the pound to forestall dangerous reactions when they are burned.

John's son, Jeffrey Rollins, has served as sales manager at their plant in New Jersey. "All of the stuff handled here is dangerous," he says. The workers wear impenetrable gloves, hard hats, masks, heavy coveralls. Early in the expansion of this plant several men from an outside construction crew ignored the warning sign and either smoked, or used a cutting-torch, near explosive material. Several were killed in the explosion that resulted. The fires that break down dangerous molecules are fueled by the poisons themselves. The kiln rotates slowly, and Dante's hell is no less carefully designed than these chambered vortices and cylinders. Temperatures swerve violently from 600 to 2400 degrees Fahrenheit. The gas stream is cooled in a tower packed with objects that resemble wiffle balls. Heavy metals are separated from the water stream by a high-impact scrubber, not an easy process.

John had no idea that a technology for burning glop would be so involved. The destruction of highly volatile liquids creates high temperatures; but, like sand particles settling out in a river delta, heavy metals will drop out only in a cool, slowly drifting environment. So these machines imitate the system of nature, circulating earth and water, fire and air.

Dr. Nick Pappas, President of Rollins Environmental (until its recent sale and reorganization), recalls the day that hydrofluoric acid got into the air system of DuPont's Mexican plant. "I forget how many were killed. But everyone in the room was dead. Hydrofluoric acid dissolves your lungs and it does it quickly. I mean it's terrible, terrible stuff. . . ."

Rollins Environmental publishes a great many handsome brochures on recycled paper to describe their services in detail. The most dangerous substances hide behind an abstract facade of scientific terms. From beneath the skin of this bland terminology monsters peep out. The particles that John is trying to get rid of, PCBs and dioxins, are among the most deadly and long-lived poisons ever created. As Nick Pappas says, "It's John's ambition to burn up the nastiest stuff known to man."

Webster's describes a dioxin as "any of several carcinogenic or teratogenic heterocyclic hydrocarbons that occur as impurities in petroleum-derived herbicides." This inscrutable definition carries a heavy freight. A carcinogen is a cancer-causing agent. A carcinogen interrupts the process of life at the cellular level, bringing disruption, disorder, and death. Teratogenic means "causing fetal malformation or monstrosities." It derives from the Greek word for monster, *terat.*

The word "impurities," once unpacked, yields a squadron of ugly terms: "defiled, unchaste or obscene, adulterated." The word "herbicide" consists of a vital first syllable immediately violated by its neighbor. "Herb" conjures up an image of green life; "cide" derives from the Latin *cide,* killer. All of these variations on death are tucked away in that little word "dioxin."

According to Webster's, a PCB is "any one of a family of industrial compounds produced by the chlorination of biphenyl; noted chiefly as an environmental pollutant that accumulates in animal tissue resulting in pathogenic and teratogenic effects." It's worth recalling that "pathogenic" derives from the Greek *pathos,* suffering. This little dip into the dictionary suggests how much death and suffering is hidden away in these terms. Put simply, John enlisted to struggle against death, which appears to come in almost as many forms as life.

Besides these killer chemicals, destroyed daily in the superheated furnaces that Rollins runs, there are heavy metals: lead, barium, mercury, cadmium, arsenic. These substances cannot be destroyed; they must be stabilized and diluted. The effect of heavy metals on the human body is not easy to decipher. They take their time. The whole subject acquires the character of poetry and myth, a story of invisible agents that bring on idiocy, madness, and death. The hazardous waste plant is designed to render benign some of the most awful poisons ever created. Its refining fires are an alchemical mill devised to preserve life.

When Nick Pappas talks about getting middle management to look beyond this quarter's bottom line, he is taking the high road of natural philosophy. His implicit question is this: What has a higher value—money or life? Should we remove poisons from water and air, purify the earth—or go for the bottom line? Having declared for life, John set up his own kind of alchemy. He wouldn't put it in those words, but he has a similar end in mind and the idea of transforming matter to enhance life is what excites him.

In Nick's view, the thing that attracted John to hazardous waste disposal was the difficulty of making it work. "I think this is more his baby than anything else. I think it's because of the great complexity of it. Technically, this is the big leagues." Nick had been introduced to John by Irving Shapiro, the highly regarded (now retired) CEO of DuPont. At that time, John was looking for a manager with special technical knowledge. Nick was an executive vice president at DuPont and John, with his usual intuitive flair, knew he was the man as soon as they met. His first year with Rollins Environmental was by far Nick's easiest.

"After that, the last three years [1992–95] have been the toughest of my professional life. Having to watch the earnings go. Having to let people go. Having to get costs down. In 1991, the first year I was here, we earned in round numbers $50 million pretax. Last year, we lost almost $30 million. I'll be blunt about it. If I had known any of this, I would not have taken this job. I didn't need this job. I didn't need the money. I didn't need any of it, okay?"

In Nick's view there are powers out there, well-organized and well-rehearsed, who are destroying the industry John created. John had other options, other companies. But what of the nation? This was an industry on the side of the angels. John figured he might make money, or he might lose it. But no one could argue that getting rid of poisonous waste wasn't important. If hazardous waste disposal continued to be left to an unregulated Mafia, then society was poisoning itself morally and physically.

"I've never felt in control of my life," John remarked in 1995. "Because if you have five or six companies, sure as hell, one or two of them are going to be down. We recently bought the hazardous waste division from Westinghouse for $125 million. And I'm fighting this thing in Congress—I'm on the phone every morning. I was in Wash-

ington, I guess at 6:30 this morning, arguing with them." Odd to see
a businessman fighting for government regulation. To do so, he pits
himself against companies more powerful than his, companies now
better situated to influence the lawmakers. He has to do a lot of the
arm-twisting himself. Nor is the environment the hot issue it was back
in the seventies and eighties.

Two or three centuries ago John might have been a broad-beamed
merchant in London or Edinburgh whose greatest fear was a ship lost
at sea. Now technical innovation comes with every upgrade in software. New companies are spawned out of thin air by shifts in government regulations. The hazardous waste industry needs both research and regulation to make it fit into the complex system it serves.
It takes a balance of public awareness, corporate compliance and
proper legislation. When he sails out into the winds of politics, the
businessman lays himself open to the public interest—a drafty business where the winds shift as suddenly as the media's attention.

Waste disposal is a more vexed issue than most of us realized in the
sixties. Driving business and driven by business, technology has laid
waste valleys likely to stay that way until a new ice age comes to scrape
clean the face of the continent. A short visit to Butte, Montana, or a
flight over the gold pits of Brazil offer obvious examples. The creation of new deserts is proceeding faster than any other time in history. According to *Harper's Magazine,* the Amazon rain forest supplies
forty percent of the earth's oxygen. It may well vanish in a century or
two. W.T.K. and Mingo of Malaysia and Fortune Timber of Taiwan
have acquired over eight million acres of Brazilian rain forest, with
options to pick up another twenty-two million—that is fifteen percent
of the harvestable rain forest on the planet.

The chemical industry has a voluntary waste-reduction program,
but a company like Formosa Plastics U.S.A., the greatest defecator of
hazardous waste among middle-sized chemical companies, spews out
its tons of poison in Taiwan, where an almost total lack of pollution
control makes business more profitable—at least for the time being.
The ratio of corporate profit to human misery may take another century at least to become obvious.

By starting up the hazardous waste industry, John's plan was to convert what he perceived as a national crisis into a profitable enterprise.
His method was to fasten an economic engine to a potential disaster
and reverse its direction. Waste disposal had been handled most often by unscrupulous types eager to dump substances from crankcase
oil to medical toxins into the nearest available landfill or lake. Large

chemical concerns created "lagoons" where deadly pools seeped into groundwater. Oils, pesticides and nitrate runoff—not to mention methyl mercury and a fine array of heavy metals—ran underground, into lakes and seas. The Mafia made easy money by filling tank trucks with acid waste and making long trips with the drain faucet open, dribbling a thin line of the stuff from Newark to Miami.

Only after Rachel Carson wrote *Silent Spring* did the public start reflecting on the creeping death around them. It might be far off, it might be near, no one really knew. But it was out there. Dumpers had already saturated miles of beach and forest with poisons that would have to be cleaned up at enormous public expense.

In New Jersey during the fifties, the state excavated a deep pit of sandy soil; for twenty years that sand was used to construct freeways. When the contractor no longer needed the sand, he ingeniously sold pit space to dumpers. It took another decade for the abyss to fill up with thousands of barrels of toxic waste, at $5 a barrel. Another twenty years passed, and those barrels began leaking into the groundwater. The pit was declared a superfund site. Rollins was given the contract to clean up the mess at their New Jersey plant. Jeffrey Rollins says the barrels that cost $5 to unload now cost close to $1,000 each to dispose of properly.

The disparity in those figures offers a bleak glimpse of a possible future. Companies that don't process their waste will be sued out of business, leaving taxpayers to pick up the tab. The superfund, with its public money, operates as a giant bailout for companies that saved money a generation ago by dumping.

Yet the government, according to Nick Pappas, is the greatest polluter of all. If the government may still be said to represent the people, then the people are responsible for a chemical dump along the Savannah River that is two-thirds the size of Delaware. A dump in Alpina, Michigan, is of lesser size but equal intensity. Near Hanford, in Washington state, the site of the government's atomic weapons plant, the land will never be habitable again. Plutonium has a half-life measured out in cosmic time. Yet none of the regulations the government passed to create superfund sites in the seventies applied to government sites until 1993.

John paid a high price for getting into the business ten years before anyone else. What looked to him like absolute necessity was the very last thing on the chemical industry's agenda. They didn't want to hear about it. Where he saw a chemical latrine, other people saw a penny earned. The very idea of having to pay good money to make

HANGING THE MOON

something unpleasant disappear was counterintuitive, like rain falling straight up.

John built two plants while the government struggled to pass the regulations that would power up the new industry. Because people didn't want hazardous waste plants near their communities, it took superhuman eloquence to convince people that the greater danger lay in not building the plants.

Industry was no less hostile. "They hate us," Nick Pappas says. "They want us to do it cheaper and cheaper and cheaper, because we don't provide them any profitability, or product quality, or any of those things they want to put their money in. This business is as complex a business as God ever blew breath on, I can tell you."

In the seventies a strange alliance made up of the environmentally concerned New Left and Richard Nixon helped to bring on the heroic age of environmental legislation. 1970: establishment of the EPA and the Clean Air Act. 1972: Clean Water Act. 1976: Resource Conservation and Recovery Act (RCRA) and Toxic Substance Control Act (TSCA). 1980: CERLA which made polluters liable for their own cleanup. This enthusiasm for legislating a clean world continued into the madcap eighties with diminishing enthusiasm. So many rules and regulations were passed that they canceled each other out. Bureaucrats just out of college, and filled with academic zeal, ran headlong into tough old CEOs. They had to learn to talk to each other.

Having passed laws that demanded the breakdown of carbons and hydrocarbons by burning and the cleanup of chemical dumps, the EPA realized there weren't enough incinerators to do the job. Rollins Environmental was out there, soon joined by Westinghouse, Browning Ferris, Laidlaw and others. But the EPA bureaucrats needed much more burning power. By turning to the cement kiln industry, they more than doubled the nation's waste-burning capacity overnight.

"So their idea was," Nick says, "why not take those volatile liquids that are being produced by the chemical industry—waste solvents, and so forth—and put those through cement kilns and let the cement guys burn those in place of fossil fuel." Soon the cement kilns were burning sixty percent of the waste fuels. "The cement guys were capturing more of the market. But in addition to burning liquids, they started burning solids—chlorinated materials and metals."

To do this the kilns needed to mix heavy metals with liquids, and this created "a whole subindustry of blenders who set themselves up to blend cocktails for burning. Now, once they did that, in John's view and my view, they were doing something environmentally unsound." So now the battle between the unregulated cement kilns and the regulated disposal companies was joined. "The cement kiln dust—they have the right by law to put anyplace. So what they're creating in the country today [1996] is a buildup of these heavy metals in cement kiln dust, which they dump in the quarries where they got their limestone in the first place."

The kilns' profits are high. "The tipping fees for clear liquids are from five to fifteen cents a pound. The solid stuff—the nasty stuff—costs anywhere from forty-five cents to a dollar a pound. So the more of the heavy metal they can get mixed into the stuff, the more money they make. That's the driver. Until recently they were selling this stuff as a liming agent to farmers—to change the pH of the soil. Hundreds of millions of pounds. Unbelievable.

"Fundamentally, the United States today [1995] is being treated as a Third World country. Out of the 150 cement kilns operating today, twenty-five of them burn hazardous waste. Old 1920s technology. These are obsolete cement kilns, foreign-owned. When you think about the enormous price society paid to get the lead out of paint and the lead out of gasoline because of its neuro-toxic impact on children—okay, when you think what we paid to do that, and now to take industry lead and cadmium and chromium and arsenic and redistribute it back into society by this process—to my mind it's unthinkable."

Can these European companies burn this stuff back home? "No!" Nick throws up his hands. "In Holland they can't burn hazardous waste in cement kilns at all. The House of Commons debated the issue in the United Kingdom, and they came to precisely the same conclusion. They should burn only clean fuels. These foreign companies were let into the business and our public doesn't know anything about it. There isn't a single cement kiln in the United States that has a permanent permit to do what it does. They're all on so-called 'interim status.' The honor system. Not one of them has gone through public hearings, trial burns, health risk assessments. While we're in the laps of the agencies. We're electronically hooked up to them. They know what our processors are doing day and night. John told me, he said, 'I don't want to run a shithouse. I want you to know, I want to run the best goddamn occupational, health, and safety environmental company in the world.' And I think we've got that right now. It's the best in the world, and that's what John wanted to create."

How long will it take for heavy metals left by the cement kilns to affect human beings? The sixty percent increase in laryngeal cancer among cement workers in Germany within a ten-year period is some indication. (Those are the present statistics.) If a few calves and human babies are born downwind with three legs or two heads, that may prove acceptable to society (figuring in jobs created, and gains to stockholders). Perhaps such arguments today are won only by those with the most eloquent bank account. But time is not on the side of business in this business. The squabble between the hazardous waste industry and the cement kiln people lies on the fault line separating a business world responsible for its poisonous trash from companies that plump for profits their grandchildren will have to pay for dearly.

"I make speeches to chemical manufacturers," Nick says. "These guys have got themselves convinced that what goes through the cement kilns is okay. I tell them I think they're crazy. They're just taking out future liabilities they're going to hate." He rattles off a long list of companies destroyed by this sort of shortsightedness including Dow Corning and DuPont with its fungicide problem which cost the company a billion and a half to settle.

As Nick points out, "Understanding what your future liabilities might be is a very complex thing. And this cement kiln thing—these guys are just asking for it. Middle management in the chemical industry, they've got this thing in place, so now they're defending it. I ask them, 'Why are you guys doing this just to save a few bucks?'"

26

The Hazards of Waste

In the late sixties John applied for a permit to build a hazardous waste plant in Baton Rouge, Louisiana. The city was not wildly enthusiastic about the idea. But the Exxon Chemicals Corporation certainly was. And the city of Baton Rouge was graced with Exxon's looming presence at its center. Exxon was producing seventy-five tons of poisonous sludge every day and desperate to get rid of the stuff. Baton Rouge depended on Exxon, whose offices take up a lot of space downtown. John got his permit.

The hazardous waste industry is not just a new business. It's an alien way of thinking. It's un-American because it openly admits that the byproducts of our "lifestyle" include poison and death. This flies in the teeth of our trademark optimism. Industrial waste is as complex as it is dangerous. It raises a dark vision of a dystopian future in which technology degrades the biosphere and we are all held accountable for a hundred years of glut by floods and tornados.

The permit granted Rollins Environmental by Baton Rouge put their hazardous waste site out on Scenic Highway (so-called) among other industrial plants well north of the city. Directly across Scenic Highway from the new plant crouched the neighborhood of Alsen. This unfortunate community was shoehorned in between factories, the Mississippi River, machine shops, refineries, and warehouses. Barges unloaded yeast, ethyl acrylate, and other unpleasant substances on the river. And not far away stretched Devil's Swamp with its chemical water and bilious earthworms. In addition to a paper mill, an oil company, and a marine services outfit, the area featured a wastewater treatment plant.

The Rollins plant operated through the seventies without much public notice. But Alsen residents were not happy with their new neighbor. The nearest resident lived about seventy yards from the so-called "landfarm" across Scenic Highway. When the wind was blowing from that direction, the smell drove people indoors. Rollins was, in fact, one among a host of odor-producing outfits up and down the industrial corridor. But on days when Rollins' "landfarm" was aerated, the odors from Exxon's waste being turned under put them in a class of their own.

It was Bob Anderson, the environmental reporter for the Baton Rouge *Morning Advocate,* who saw in Rollins a perfect target for environmental concern. The company even had "Environmental" in its title. That Rollins was pioneering a new and difficult technology to deal with environmental hazards is never mentioned in any of the dozens of articles Anderson wrote. In his reports, he turns the Rollins facility into a symbol of environmental menace, a threat to every citizen, titmouse, and badger. The landfarm was closed down during the last months of 1981, eliminating most of the odors. (Anderson in various 1985 articles liked to refer to the nonexistent landfarm and its "odor problems" as if it still existed.)

In the middle eighties, about the time that Anderson's articles began appearing in abundance, a lawyer materialized in the community of Alsen where, it's very likely, no lawyer had ever been seen before. He informed the residents that the best possible thing for their community was a lawsuit. They were willing to listen. They had been suffering from the technology around them for a long time.

Steve Irving, the lawyer, looked younger than his thirty-six years. With his shiny brown hair and a rosebud mouth flowering in a handsome brown beard, he was known for a snappy, in-your-face courtroom style. When interviewed by the media, he adopted a relaxed, friendly-yet-deeply-serious demeanor. Irving believed that inciting the media was important to his work. Nothing feeds on publicity like publicity. A news article profiling him leads off, "You've probably seen him on television." The young lawyer was as ethical as a television personality could be, and he wanted that clearly understood. Nor did he hide his political ambitions, frankly stating that he intended to become the next U.S. state attorney. "I'm a paid troublemaker," he said. "And I love my work."

Back when Irving had worked for the attorney general's office, he had had his own agenda and didn't mind advertising it. His boss gave him six weeks to resign. This prompted Irving to write a letter accusing the attorney general of political patronage. He sent a copy of this letter to a television station and was duly interviewed. The publicity led to a "full-scale investigation" by the Legislative Fiscal Office and his charges were declared without merit. They probably had some merit. Most people who have attempted to work in Louisiana agree that the state has a deeply flawed political apparatus. It's not Russia or Liberia but it's not Massachusetts either. It's also possible that Irving was very impressed by his own moral quality. Moreover, he might well make a career for himself by embarrassing those who lacked his talent for moral discrimination. He'd discovered that a behemoth company can be stopped dead in its tracks by one little lawyer—because inevitably some regulation is broken, some rule bent, and someone in a white collar has known sin.

Rollins Environmental Services had been operating for over a decade before it was singled out as an icon of environmental blight. Irving's problem was his lack of evidence. The Natural Resources Department (NRD) said they needed something specific to hang Rollins with. They needed information "that might indicate the source of pollution." A private well tested near the Rollins plant revealed no contamination. The NRD established a twenty-four-hour environmental hot line for people to use if they smelled anything weird. But with heavy industry belching gases all around Alsen, locating the source of specific noxious fumes was a tricky business.

A hazardous waste disposal plant is a lawyer's paradise. It arouses anxiety. And it operates in a spider's web of convoluted, sometimes contradictory, regulations. A few years earlier, Irving had halted the construction of another hazardous waste facility, Conservation Specialists Inc. (CSI). He had a good case, and proved that CSI didn't have the capital to do all it promised. Irving also stopped I.T. Corporation from building "the world's largest hazardous waste disposal facility" in Ascension Parish by making a loud legal noise over rather minor legal issues (*The Greater Baton Rouge Business Report,* December 1985). Why attack a plant designed for hazardous waste disposal when there were only five such facilities in the entire state of Louisiana? Like many lawyers, Irving was not concerned with the big picture. Careers are not built on a nice consideration of larger issues. Now, like a pit bull going for the ankle of an intruder, Irving set about routing Rollins.

The lawyer knew the American system had generated so many rules that it's difficult to get anything done without breaking a few. It may be that God Himself had to break a few rules to create the universe. And maybe that's why we so often blame Him for everything that fails down here. One thing is clear—it's a great world for lawyers. Irving was soon joined in his struggle by Patricia Norton, state secretary of the Department of Environmental Quality (DEQ). Like Irving, Secretary Norton had been a staff attorney for the attorney general of

Louisiana, a colleague of his before he got himself fired and she found herself elevated to Secretary of the Louisiana DEQ.

Steve Irving understood how to turn the dull stuff of rules and regulations into drama. He knew how to make the evening news. Secretary Norton was also on a roll. Bob Anderson turned her into his Joan of Arc. In a *tour de force* of feel-good reporting, he characterized Rollins as the most heinous environmental hazard in Louisiana. Doing battle against this steaming, stinking dragon was the fair-haired Norton—brave, attractive, courageous in her dedication to Mother Earth.

The people in Alsen understandably wanted Rollins closed down. They wanted all the plants looming over their little houses and fainting gardens closed down. Given half a chance, they would have sold their houses and gone somewhere more fit for human habitation. But for them there was no exit. Alsen had been zoned industrial, and industry was their fate.

The people of Alsen couldn't very well issue an injunction against the industrial revolution, so in February of 1981, Irvin arranged a $2.5 billion class-action suit against Rollins Environmental Services. A month later he filed another suit for $3.6 billion. These arresting figures assured surprisingly little cooperation from the people in Alsen. The suit represented 2,000 citizens but only about twenty of them became active and about fifty attended some meetings. But the hope in their eyes died when a judge required that they press their suits individually, ruling there was no basis for a class action.

By the end of 1981, Rollins had closed its landfarm and was trying to clean up the remains. The decision to aerate Exxon's waste by ploughing it under had been an expensive error in judgment. Rollins had to dig up the earth, then leech and incinerate the residue. The incinerator, however, kept operating, turning the waste from numerous plants around the state into a disposable ash.

John was learning how easily a hazardous waste disposal plant can turn into the site of uproar and hysteria. Anyone who has tried to get rid of a gallon of bad paint, or a few quarts of crankcase oil, has experienced environmental anxiety. Now imagine Exxon in downtown Baton Rouge trying to get rid of seventy-five tons of chemical sludge every working day.

The idea that the Rollins site was there to dispose of Exxon's hazardous waste was never mentioned by Bob Anderson. He neglects to tell his readers in his reports on Rollins that the by-product of almost every high-tech process is usually some deadly poison that must then be disposed of somehow. Just as Jonathan Swift agonized at the thought that his beautiful Celia had to use a toilet, the modern consumer hates to dwell on the foul stuff generated in the guts of the gorgeous technology that makes our lives shiny and bright.

Bob Anderson cast Steve Irving, Patricia Norton, and himself as society's heroes, watchdogs of the public good. He would occasionally fall to writing about himself in a poetic vein—about his love for woodducks and sparkling fish and how big corporations sadden trappers by slurping up entire swamps along with the alligators. His sentiments accord with those of most Americans. But his attacks were short on specifics, and he was given to elegiac run-on sentences: "I've sat in the homes of people living near improperly operated hazardous waste sites smelling with them the stink that has made their lives miserable and prevented them from enjoying the yards and gardens they once cherished."

The Alsen residents were more precise in their complaint about Rollins. Steve Irving asked them to write down the actual dates on which they smelled noxious odors. In the month of July, 1982, they recorded the 8th, 9th and 28th. This is not exactly overwhelming evidence for the total misery claimed by Irving. Nor is it clear that the odor was caused only by Rollins. The reluctance of state environmental officials to fall into lockstep with the pit bull litigator is understandable.

Bob Anderson liked to remind his readers that Rollins had been cited "over 100 times for various violations." He didn't mention that ninety-three of those violations were paperwork infractions—not too surprising in a workforce hired from among the poor and poorly educated. Taking up arms against this sea of bad publicity, the Rollins people decided to convene an "odor panel." John's workers bagged air from various locations around Baton Rouge where odors were particularly pleasant or obnoxious—sewer mains, gas stations, public gardens, public toilets. Individuals were then asked to sniff these air samples to determine which odors were the most offensive. Their response proved that there were places in Baton Rouge that smelled worse than the Rollins disposal site. In fact twenty-one out of twenty-four samples were judged more offensive than the air samples collected at the Rollins perimeter fence.

Rightly distrustful of any company that attempts to police itself, an environmental "control group" established its own "nose patrol." These good souls hung about for hours outside the Rollins Environmental property, sniffing more or less continuously for several days. They reported there were definitely "nuisance odors" drifting over the fence on five of the ten days they employed their noses.

Meanwhile, lawyer Irving was busy in the local neighborhood collecting clients for yet another lawsuit. He found three men in an electrical shop down the road who had all had open-heart surgery. He immediately blamed this on Rollins. These new clients of his were having "serious [health] problems," he told Anderson, "and they are very, very worried." Anderson reported Irving's suspicions and accusations in detail. That Irving himself may have suggested to the workers that bad smells clog up human arteries didn't occur to Anderson. Nor did he look into the fat content of the heart patients' diets. For all he knew they subsisted on a menu of bacon and eggs. Checking out facts wasn't really his style of reporting. Things quickly boiled down to rumor, odor, accusation, and litigation.

In the meantime, some 200,000 gallons of hazardous waste had been left in barrels in Tate Cove because the state refused to give anyone a permit to move it. Rollins proposed to get rid of the stuff in its injecting facility in Iberville. The state accepted the Rollins bid. But by this time every move Rollins made was reported by Anderson as a plot against nature and the people of Louisiana. Like crows departing a dead tree, loud objections flapped into the air as politicians rose to thunder denunciations from the state capital. The *Morning Advocate,* in September of 1982, reports State Senator J. E. Jumonville Jr.— confusing hazardous waste with the trash under his sink—crying, "I don't take sewage from my house and put it in your yard. I handle it in my own." Representative Harry "Soup" Kember harrumphed, "We have been the rectum of the United States long enough!"

Now the state secretary of the Department of Environmental Quality elected to make her move. Following up on a phone call from Irving that alerted her to odors drifting beyond the Rollins perimeter fence, Secretary Norton made a surprise visit one hot August night in 1985. She appeared at the gate around 10 o'clock P.M. with two deputies, and was passed into the compound.

She saw black smoke rising from the stack that she described in her report as "100 percent opacity black smoke being emitted from the incinerator stack for approximately 20 minutes." In the incinerator operating room she questioned the operator closely. In her opinion the worker was operating the unit "in a disorganized and confused manner." She said she herself got a severe headache from the fumes "20 seconds" after she walked in the gate. Nevertheless she stayed on the premises for two hours and made a detailed inspection, going over the grounds in minute detail and carefully detecting "strong odors" from the landfill and the truck washout pit.

What she failed to notice during her questioning of the operator was that he'd fallen from a truck flatbed about the time she had entered through the front gate. This all emerged later when the Rollins attorney, William Broadhurst, questioned the operator. When he first saw smoke and realized the automatic shutoff was malfunctioning, the operator rushed to shut down the incinerator. A misstep sent him sprawling from the truck to the ground. Stunned, he made it back up the stairs "and shut off the malfunctioning incinerator, ran back outside to complete backup shut down operations, then fell a second time hitting his chin on the control room's iron steps." A moment later he ran into Pat Norton who, instead of questioning him, decided he was a victim of "toxic fumes."

Meanwhile, all around Baton Rouge companies were dumping an exotic brew of oils, plastics and chemicals into the waterways and rivers of Louisiana. The Department of Natural Resources fined sixteen other companies for discharging 200 barrels of oil into a canal and great quantities of acid and xylene isomer into the Mississippi. Kansas City Southern Railroad was cited for 107 environmental violations at its rail yards in Baton Rouge and Shreveport.

Rollins had once been fined $500. Anderson mentioned this often. He devoted dozens of column inches to his chosen subject, slashing away and repeating "thick black belching smoke" like a mantra. He was composing a modern saga that featured a headstrong, lovely young secretary of Environmental Quality with flowing hair battling a filthy, belching old smokestack.

Together, the newsman and the secretary began to whip up a little frenzy of their own. National TV picked up the Rollins story. It was aired on ABC's *20/20*. Baton Rouge had made the big time with a cast video enthusiasts knew well: the driving young lawyer who risks his neck white-water rafting on his time off. The courageous and attractive political appointee who jeopardizes her career for the poor and downtrodden. The prize-winning reporter who dogs her every move and learns to love her brash, but sensitive, toughness. The nervous governor, walking on eggs. And the corrupt corporation, awash in hard cash, steering its course directly over the crushed bodies of the little guys.

When Georgia Pacific admitted responsibility for ninety-one vinyl chloride discharges over eight years, Anderson eked out six column inches (*Morning Advocate,* August 20, 1985). The quantity of vinyl chloride released into the waters of Louisiana didn't much occupy his interest. Nor did he quibble about Georgia Pacific's settlement of a $5 million suit for $625,000. He reports instead on the generosity of the settlement, "the largest of its kind in the nation's history." Georgia Pacific is, of course, a Louisiana institution. Rollins Environmental, by comparison, is a negligible factor.

In court, Rollins agreed with the residents of Alsen that its land-farm was a failure. It closed down the field and proposed a $2.1 million settlement. Steve Irving advised his clients to reject it. He confided to Anderson that he could do much better than that for them. He had in mind something over $6 million. This was a million more than the state had sought from the giant Georgia Pacific with its numerous vinyl chloride discharges and 29 cases of failure to meet reporting requirements. (In the end Irving would get nothing.)

Secretary Norton informed John that his Louisiana plant was closed. She said she was going to "take every legal means" to wash that plant out of Baton Rouge forever. And the secretary's popularity soared. Her outer office filled with flowers and balloons. Anderson announced a great victory for the environment. "Thank you. Thank you. Thank you!" began the article he wrote four days after the closure, quoting a note the secretary had received. Letters cited by Anderson described Secretary Norton as "bold" and "courageous."

But along with the flowers came letters to the secretary from companies that now had no idea what to do with their waste. Baton Rouge heavy industry was suddenly saddled with tons of hazardous muck and nowhere to dump it legally. BASF Wyandotte wrote the secretary complaining that "a permanent closing may not serve the interests of the state." Sunbelt Environmental Management wrote, "the already short supply of environmentally sound disposal facilities . . . are so backlogged (not only in your state, but throughout the nation), that we must schedule weeks in advance. . . . The backlog . . . results in generators exceeding their 90-day removal dates and increases the amount of hazardous waste being mixed with their plant refuse and taken to local dumps because they have no place to store it and can't afford the escalating disposal charge." Similar letters arrived from FIW of Illinois, Shell of Texas, and Degussa Corporation. The letters were restrained and furious. None of these corporate howls of pain loosened the secretary's stiff upper lip and not one found its way into Anderson's columns. Instead he reported that Secretary Norton "does not feel the economic impact of [Rollins's] closure is as great as the environmental impact of allowing the site to continue operation." He reported that her fans were describing the secretary as "glorious."

The secretary's staff meanwhile mailed out information packets about Rollins's Baton Rouge site to interested financial brokers. The stock plunged, dropping $150 million overnight. The company retaliated, serving a lawsuit against the secretary, claiming her disinformation had caused the stock drop and a loss of jobs.

The state DEQ cited other firms in October of 1985 that emitted noxious fumes and a polyvinylchloride release of "unknown quantity." The redoubtable Anderson gave these infractions a column inch or two. Even after the Rollins company had been idled, he came up with ingenious ways of keeping the story alive. NORTON CLARIFIES STATEMENT reads one headline, printed with a photograph of the secretary—long hair cascading, a mysterious smile playing about her lips. The "clarification" is a repeat of her initial statement, "We intend to close the facility [permanently]." At the end of the article, Governor Edwin Edwards is quoted as politely hoping, but not by any means demanding, that the secretary will "reconsider her decision." As a former law partner of the Rollins attorney, William Broadhurst, Edwards was skating on thin ice whatever he said.

How much had Rollins in fact damaged the environment of Louisiana? Ten years before Rollins arrived, eleven chemical firms had dumped waste near, or on, a cattle ranch, inundating 545 acres. The farmer later charged that Rollins had poisoned one of his watering spots and twenty cows had died. Rollins arranged to replace the dead cows and had a fence built to confine the herd away from its property. Elsewhere in Louisiana, oils and chemicals were spewing into the waterways, dribbling out of rusting barrels in silent woods. These merited an occasional line in the *Morning Advocate*. Major corporations admitted dumping thousands of gallons of hazardous waste into rivers and canals. These statements received a paragraph or two. Anderson quotes without comment the state attorney general excusing Georgia Pacific's vinyl chloride dump. "Some of the discharges occurred during freezing weather when relief valves froze open," says the obliging official. Would a little heat applied to those relief valves have made them operational during the frozen Louisiana winter? Anderson isn't interested. He mentions neither that BASF Wyandotte in Louisiana was now driving its hazardous waste over a thousand miles to a Rollins facility in New Jersey nor that the people of Louisiana were footing the bill. No suggestions are offered for what Dow, Georgia Pacific, Exxon should do with their tons of hazardous waste. The impression is left that well-written legislation will cause the hazardous muck to evaporate all by itself, like a duck's breath.

John had created a company whose existence was an open admission of the bitter truth: namely, that our economy produces hazardous waste in enormous quantities, and disposing of it is a filthy, difficult, vexing business. It takes more than guidelines and regulations to get rid of the stuff. It demands an advanced technology, a new body of case law, and cooperation rather than endless confrontation between those people who do the job and those who write the regulations.

Secretary Norton wandered briefly into the charnel house of modern technology, and she was appalled. It was like stumbling onto a decomposing whale in the dark. It was huge and dead, and it changed forever the way you thought about your favorite beach. The secretary wanted a pristine, lovely Baton Rouge—not black smoke and chemical stench. She ordered Rollins to smell like a rose and when it didn't, she slapped its face.

She was praised by the Audubon Society for her dedication to "cleaning up the environment." But only Rollins was cleaning up the environment. Everyone else was involved in a shadow play, an intricate game that bore more resemblance to a fiction filmed in Hollywood than the awful truth. In effect, the secretary was hugging a solitary tree while all around her the forest was burning.

The most revealing piece of journalism published in the *Morning Advocate* is a staff photograph snapped by John H. Williams. It shows some twenty residents of Alsen at a town meeting. They are not young. Their clothes are rumpled, the frames of their glasses made of cheap plastic. They look depressed and quietly cynical. They are all African American.

Secretary Norton had once remarked how difficult it was to issue an environmental permit when a company has "500 angry residents who don't want the facility next to them." But if she ever complained to Anderson about a zoning philosophy that isolated the people of Alsen in an industrial "park," he never mentions it. It was safer, easier, more acceptable to complain about Rollins's odor than to step into the roaring furnace of racial politics.

Williams's photo puts things in focus. Rollins Environmental had been located in a neighborhood where the city bureaucracy figured no one would complain. The African American residents were already engulfed by the sounds and smells of heavy industry. As one resident states: "They gave us the plants, Devil's Swamp landfill, the airport, the parish prison, Rollins. They sure wouldn't put Rollins in Sherwood Forest, or Villa Del Rey. We're just a bunch of black people out here and we're tired."

The truth is seldom simple. The Rollins plant was overwhelmed with hazardous waste because America was overwhelmed with hazardous waste. The Rollins plant had indeed emitted black smoke and, before it was closed in 1981, that landfarm was so bad some days that Allied Chemical workers across the Scenic Highway refused to work out-of-doors. The *Morning Advocate* reports one expert witness remarking that while Rollins's landfarm was ninety-five percent "effectively managed," no facility of that type can be operated without odors.

There was much wrong with Rollins's operation, but its role in dealing with hazardous waste was completely lost on the reporter, the secretary, and the lawyer. Baton Rouge needed Rollins more than Rollins Environmental needed Baton Rouge. What the company needed least of all was a residential neighborhood next door to its plant.

Maybe Bob Anderson didn't have to mention the racial composition of Alsen. Maybe that was assumed by his readers from the start. Maybe it was not politically correct to mention race. But in the end race was the underlying factor in the location of those plants.

Bob Anderson wasn't being paid to cut deep or raise welts on the body politic. But he did his job, inadvertently perhaps, when he quoted E. W. Pate, a local resident, who says, "I have gotten sick, and I have seen my mother wake up at night choking." Had Bob Anderson written that Alsen's black residents had themselves been treated for years like some kind of hazardous waste, he would probably have been fired.

John Rollins had been an environmental activist in the most radical sense. Radical because he didn't just agitate about hazardous waste (though he did that too). He created an industry organized to get rid of the stuff. Having imported the technology from overseas, he paid a lot of people a lot of money to improve the system on the job. Ten years later, Steve Irving, Bob Anderson, and Secretary Norton were hard at work making hazardous waste disposal look like hazardous waste creation. It's not fair to say they were more concerned for their own careers than the unhappy citizens of Alsen. But what they earned for themselves is clear: national television exposure while the people of Alsen got nothing, except the right to stay where they were, surrounded by an industrial blight that had been growing up around them since 1945.

In the end, Rollins Environmental was requested to appear at an administrative proceeding, a deputy secretary of the DEQ presiding. Secretary Norton presented her evidence. Lawyers sparred. The judge did not close or fine Rollins, or even issue a warning about black smoke. The DEQ, in a quixotic decree, ordered the company to make some improvements on the Alsen Community Center building. What that had to do with improving the air quality is anyone's guess.

In October, down at the Catfish Town's Pilot House just one day after Rollins had fired its incinerator back up, Bob Anderson was given the Blue Heron Award by Citizens for a Clean Environment and applauded for his "outstanding contribution to environmental awareness."

In 1995 John Jr. said, "Dad's always kept his interest focused on the environmental company. That's always been his baby. I sometimes think truck leasing and Matlack could drop off the ends of the earth; he wouldn't really notice them. He's proud of what we've accomplished. But it's the environmental company that is closest to him. He works day-to-day with them. He started this industry and it's what he cares most about."

Nick Pappas makes the same point: "It's potentially his greatest contribution, his legacy to the future." But being a pioneer in an industry that demands other companies clean up their acts is asking for trouble. By founding his company before the Environmental Protection Agency even existed, John had "positioned" himself well in advance. After the Nixon administration passed the first truly meaningful environmental legislation, the company's profits rose (from $4 million to $33 million in the four years after 1982).

As we've seen, some cement companies sidestepped the stringent regulations governing plants designed entirely to destroy hazardous materials. Companies producing hazardous waste left Rollins in droves to pay the lower fees the cement companies offered. Rollins stock dropped from $15 a share in 1990 to around $2 in 1996. The work force was cut from 2,200 to 1,600 (*The News Journal* December 22, 1996).

In January of 1997, John sold two-thirds of his Rollins Environmental Services stock to Laidlaw Inc. of Canada. His company could no longer sustain the losses. Rollins Environmental disappeared into Laidlaw Environmental Services (with offices in Columbia, South Carolina). It seemed the foreign cement kilns had won the battle.

But nothing in modern business is simple and hazardous waste disposal, as Nick Pappas learned to his dismay, is a devilishly difficult proposition. According to John, Rollins Environmental, after a protracted negotiation, succeeded in combining its burning capacity with Laidlaw's holding facilities to make waste disposal more efficient for both companies. In the meantime, the owners of those outdated cement kilns found that burning heavy metals cuts down on their productive capacity. So they have backed off. Of course the thousands of tons of cadmium and lead they have spread across the landscape will remain.

By 1998, there were fewer than a dozen old-style cement plants still in operation. In 1999, the original Rollins Environmental, now merged into Laidlaw Environmental and Safety Kleen, adopted the Safety Kleen name. The industry that John founded in the United States now treats hazardous waste nationwide and overseas in this corporate guise.

27
The Rule of Chance

John had driven away from his parents' farmhouse in the thirties, promising to provide. By century's end, "providing" was the least of it. The city, the landscape, consciousness itself had been transformed and he was among those who had done the transforming. A young composer moving to Vienna in 1760 entered a discipline exquisitely organized to take advantage of his genius. Mid-century America was no less ready for John's talent. Within half a lifetime, he and his brother listed six of their seven companies on the world's stock exchanges. In a certain sense, John can be compared to the composers of the eighteenth century born at the very moment when the art of music was complex enough to sustain great projects.

When John first leapt into business in the summer of 1945, the postwar atmosphere in America felt like the morning of the world. The average yearly income then was $2,390 and a new home cost under $5,000. A new car cost just over $1,000. Grand Rapids became the first community to fluoridate its water. Jackie Robinson was the first black baseball player to break into a major league.

The Harvard philosopher, George Santayana, described us this way at mid-century: "To the good American many subjects are sacred: sex is sacred, women are sacred, children are sacred, business is sacred, America is sacred, Masonic lodges and college clubs are sacred. This feeling grows out of the good opinion [the American] wishes to have of these things, and serves to maintain it. If he did not regard all these things as sacred he might come to doubt sometimes if they were wholly good."

Santayana implies that, for many Americans, a thing not wholly good may be viewed as wholly bad. This simplistic absolutism provided an inroad for McCarthyism and led, eventually, to the war in Vietnam. During the sixties, the nation suffered a sort of nervous breakdown as all our repressed desires flooded forth. Having defeated fascism, we could assume we were more moral than corrupt old Europe. But now we had to somehow absorb the My Lai massacre, Birmingham's police dogs, the murder of civil rights volunteers in the South, the assassination in Dallas. America saw that its waters were polluted, its schools decaying into battle zones, its public places defaced by graffiti. A thousand social experiments flowered and flopped. Like a living cell attacked by some deadly virus, the family decayed. Many clung to private versions of the sacred, but the social body was lacerated by witch hunts in the fifties, freedom marches in the sixties, recession in the seventies, Wall Street corruption in the eighties.

The seventies might be compared to a bad hangover after the sixties high. During that decade John fended off his worst disasters. These arrived in various guises, mostly of the financial sort, with spiraling interest rates, layoffs, an economy threatened by the Arab oil embargo. At his lowest ebb, his wife, Linda, walked out on him.

Wayne still lived according to the strict code that was as much his identity as the face he shaved every morning. In September of 1976, the *New York Times* reported that Rollins Inc. (based in Atlanta) had openly reported on its quarterly statement a payment of bribes (called "licensing fees") in Mexico. Wayne believed it was right to tell the shareholders that bribing officials in that country was the way business was normally conducted. No bribes, no business.

According to the *Times,* Rollins Inc. reported that it had paid $127,000 over five years for a variety of small services—licenses, people to watch company cars, "whether or not the cars needed watching." The *Wall Street Journal* of September that same year reported that Rollins Inc. "admitted the payments—and said it would be forced to continue them. That bold assertion came at a time when scores of U.S. companies were practically falling over themselves in a rush to confess improper foreign payments and promising to stop them."

Admitting openly that bribery was the only "legitimate way" of doing business in Mexico, Wayne raised a whirlwind of protest. "We thought we were being simon-pure," he comments dryly. Official Mexico flew into a fury. In the forked language of diplomacy, a Mexican bureaucrat asserted that "Rollins' statement [is] absurd and insulting, because companies from around the world do business in Mexico, and certainly all of them don't bribe our officials!"

Well, perhaps not *all!* However, every businessman making deals in Mexico was aware, and the same *New York Times* article reports, that "more than 200 companies . . . [had] admitted making questionable or improper payments, and the SEC has taken nearly two dozen others to court for failure to disclose them." The International Minerals and Chemicals Corporation, for example, reported paying more than $3 million for bribes in five years. It was viewed as a kind of direct lobbying.

With a show of refreshing candor, the Securities and Exchange Commission said it didn't mind bribes as long as they were disclosed. But the Federal Communications Commission objected and spoke vaguely of fines and penalties. The *Wall Street Journal* concludes, "If there's a moral to this story, it's that when in doubt, keep your mouth shut. It appears that by trying to abide by the law *and* his own conscience, Mr. Rollins got his company into a pickle."

Wayne's power and influence had run headlong into his mother's moral instruction. The furor forced Wayne to acknowledge the higher wisdom of hypocrisy. As Machiavelli observed, the quickest route to self-destruction is telling the truth in public. "We made a mistake when we made our disclosure," the *Journal* reports him saying. Rollins Inc. announced it would no longer bribe Mexican officials. As that meant business would no longer be possible in Mexico, Wayne sold off his Mexican affiliate as soon as he could find a buyer.

John's eldest son, John Jr., recalls the seventies as a grim decade, full of anxiety and rumors of impending collapse. Working to save Rollins Leasing from going under, he was depressed by the rain of attacks on his father. "I quit reading this local newspaper [the *News Journal*] years ago. During the '70s there'd be an article every week. They criticized my father, my family, my company. He's a very good man. He doesn't just go out and ruin the small guy. Because he's been the small guy. But the attacks on him have been nonstop ever since I can remember. Enough is enough. I didn't need to be burdened with that bullshit. We have a job to do, do it, keep focused, and keep all this noise out."

John's war with the Internal Revenue Service provided a sort of *dies irae* counterpoint to his other problems. It's worth mentioning here because it fits so neatly into the picture of a life where little has come easily. The entrepreneur's task is to make possible what appeared impossible, to make order where there is confusion. Early in their career John and Wayne once tried to organize their business to pay the lowest possible tax. The experiment failed in a year. John observed then that worrying over taxes takes the focus off doing businesss. Paying taxes is really a sign of success.

During the years that the IRS decided to rake through John's finances with a fine-tooth comb, an endless menu of charges was proferred, amended, withdrawn, reconfigured and massaged by lawyers in thousands of pages of letters, briefs, and legal documentation. There were quibbles over chauffeur's uniforms, lawn sprinklers in Jamaica (were they personal or corporate?), and much bureaucratic brooding over toys and children's underwear given to Jamaican children. Additionally, the IRS alleged that all his expenses associated with horse raising were not deductible, even though John had paid millions to own a track that existed for horse racing. To draw a hard line between John's private life and his business activities is probably impossible, but the IRS made a stab at it. Unfortunately for those trying to keep track of his deductions, John seldom, if ever, makes a trip without involving himself in business. He goes to London on vacation and comes home with plans to set up the first toxic waste disposal system in the United States. He travels to Jamaica to rest after losing his bid for state governor and buys land on the north coast, having decided he will put up hotels.

John's association with Nixon, plus his own financial unravelling in Jamaica, and perhaps even his quarrels with local powers may have played some part in the IRS investigation which began in 1970 (starting with the '67 return). He was more than just a wonderful target of opportunity. He was disapproved of by some very powerful people. Extensive audits for the years 1967–69 turned up no significant adjustments, yet the IRS continued to request time extensions on the three-year statutory time limit to keep these years open.

His tax problems were handled by one of the most reputable CPA firms in Delaware, Price Waterhouse. According to Financial Vice President Eugene Weaver (who was with the Rollins organization from 1970 to 1999), one of John's tax accountants happened to run into a top IRS official at a cocktail party; he complained about the lack of closure on the 1967–70 audit. The official apparently had words with the group leader of the audit team involved. The group leader then decided to show his mettle and go after the Rollins organization in earnest. An investigation was launched whose cost might well have funded a jet fighter or a new government building.

The Rollins case resembles an updated version of the infinitely complex *Jarndyce v. Jarndyce* case in Dickens' *Bleak House*. For over twenty years, *IRS v. Rollins* would work its weary way through the courts like a hedgehog passing through the gut of a boa constrictor.

And like the hedgehog, most of the IRS allegations began slowly to disintegrate.

The IRS case was both highly technical and essentially irrational. When the government charges a rich individual with fraud, the public assumes there cannot be smoke without fire. John Rollins is different from many rich persons because the wealth he creates, as we have seen, generally implies something for the commonwealth too. He lives off a small fraction of what he generates. It's his talent for ordering economic activity that creates possibilities for others, and it's that activity that his wealth fuels. But he is a citizen and the IRS decided to make an example of him.

The IRS appeared to enlist the media on its side by publishing all their charges and attaching dollar amounts. These were duly reported by *The Morning News*. "John Rollins is no stranger to U.S. Tax Court," reads a typical headline for November of 1979 over an article that cites every figure given it by the IRS.

The largest dollar amounts involved stock transfers by John of stock that he owned in Rollins Inc., and Rollins Truck Leasing. He contributed this stock to a pair of companies that were struggling, Dover Downs and Rollins Jamaica. Dover Downs had been insolvent since its inception. John alone had sustained it. At dispute was whose taxable income was involved—John's or the company that had received the stock from John (and sold it to fund continued operation).

It was indeed legal to transfer stock from one corporation to another, as long as the contributing individual owned 80 percent of the voting stock of the company receiving the stock contribution. The IRS claimed that John sold the stock himself and contributed the cash proceeds to Jamaica. In fact, Jamaica had received stock and paid the capital gains tax on the sale—and the IRS had accepted this at the time. After the statute of limitations ran out, they alleged that John had sold the stock himself and contributed cash to Jamaica. Charged with having to pay capital gains twice, John went to tax court seeking an estoppel order from the judge. These are rarely given, but the judge perceived the irrationality of the IRS demand and granted the order. The IRS took the case to court.

Some seven years later, on June 4, 1985, the *News Journal* reports that Judge Francis J. Cantrel of the U.S. Tax Court in Washington expressed himself "highly critical of the IRS, and questioned its motives in dealing with Rollins." By that date, what with interest, late fees and penalties, the putative tax bill had risen to over $20 million. However, the IRS, the judge said, had "violated its duty to be consistent and deal fairly." Acknowledging that his ruling against the IRS was not usual, he said the Rollinses "were misled by [the IRS commissioner's] actions and justifiably relied on them. . . . To allow [the commissioner] to prevail here would lead to an unconscionable settlement." (Webster's defines "unconscionable" as "unscrupulous. Beyond prudence or reason.")

Ruling in favor of John, the judge reduced the deficiency that lawyers were still chewing over. As for the auditors who'd initiated this high-priced boondoggle, they had long since been removed to other offices. John estimates the case cost him over $17 million in fees and expenses. (The tax he actually paid after two decades in the courts amounted to around $2 million.) The government's expenses were far greater of course, but these were quietly swallowed by U.S. taxpayers.

According to Financial Vice President Eugene Weaver, the IRS was inconsistent again when it attempted to disallow "all the expenses of John W. Rollins & Associates, a sole proprietorship that provided management services to John's private companies, partnerships and joint ventures." Again, the IRS wanted to include the management for income received from the companies in John's personal income. Weaver remarks that, "The IRS was taking an inconsistent position. They wanted to tax him on income he paid himself while not permitting him to deduct the expenses incurred in creating the income."

In 1984, the IRS informed John that he would be the government's test case with regard to political contributions. They proposed to tax his contributions just to see if the case would hold up in court. Putting John Rollins before a judge, they hoped, would help clarify the law. In effect, they were forcing John to subsidize the proof of the law's constitutionality. The court threw out the case.

Perhaps the most costly aspect of the Internal Revenue Service's long war with John and his accountants was personal. Judge Cantrel's statement leaves small doubt that old-fashioned malice played a part in this long saga. A government agency does not act "unconscionably." Only the people who work for the agency can do that. John now had more than enough on his plate, what with interest rates skyrocketing, Dover Downs draining him, and Jamaica unraveling. The complexities of his financial situation were more than his second wife could live with, much less comprehend. Seeing what looked like ruin staring her in the face, and with IRS auditors coming and going like ants at a picnic, Linda left. The IRS, however, would not let her off so easily. The Service claimed that the money her husband had given her to run the house was excessive—more than anyone might reasonably need to run such an establishment. (In those days a spouse was held to an annual limit of $3,000; there is no limit today.) The auditors may well have had a point, or may simply been out of their depth in Linda's case, because she was a famously big spender, and it was John's habit to give her pretty much whatever she asked for.

The bad press, the public animosity it raised worked its way down even into the children's world. Linda's second son, Jeffrey, recalls, "I remember the IRS coming after him and putting an auditor in the office building. The local paper got hold of it. I was in middle school. The kids made remarks. I got into fights. The paper had made lists of how the house was staffed and how much was spent. Some guy at school started saying how we never had to work hard for anything. I got really upset and said dad had worked for everything we had, he'd built it all. And this kid just started laughing and said he'd read the paper. He started saying, 'Silver spoon, you never worked, your parents never worked, everything was just given to you.' And to top it, he said, 'Your dad's a crook.' So I just popped him in the face. He was a lot bigger than I was, so I ended up on the bottom. Just an ignorant kid."

John likes to say that success is achieved when you "find a need and fill it." But time and again he has found himself holding the halter of some aging white elephant that, by hook or by crook, he made over into a charging bull. The best example of this legerdemain is provided by two race tracks, both in Delaware. He bought into the Brandywine Raceway because it seemed a good investment. It went bad on him. As for Dover Downs, it was never his aim to own it in the first place. He wound up with nevertheless because an old friend (and onetime political rival), David Buckson, asked him for help in 1967.

Buckson and his father were harness racing drivers in their day. David Buckson was able to raise money he thought sufficient for building a race track in lower Delaware where he planned to bring thoroughbreds and harness racing. Having underestimated both the expense and cost overruns, Buckson's company ran out of money. So Buckson went to John in 1968 and said he needed $250,000 by the very next day, or construction would halt. Locked into the deal with Buckson were people John considered his friends, so John came up with the money they needed. Soon these investors needed more. By the time the track was ready for use, John was in over $12 million. Never loathe to assume that only more will get you more, he plunked down another million for a "super speedway."

He'd been cited some very soothing projection figures. They told him that the gross daily income (the "handle") would be a million. "That's what I thought it would be when I invested in it." But, according to the *Morning News* of May 20, 1979, the average daily handle "hovered around $150,000; average attendance about 2,000."

According to Financial Vice President Gene Weaver, the total never averaged much over $225,000 a day. And the investors soon learned that the owners of the best horses would not race on a track five-eighths of a mile long. Having paid heavily for the construction, the interest and associated costs, John now began losing money steadily and in very large amounts.

In retrospect, the Dover Downs track looks like a luxurious extravagance. Early photographs show open-air seating, a modest building and a very pretty oval track. Its builders appear to have dreamed that customers would spring full grown from the surrounding fields. Once John got his hand in, he continued to build on what was there. At first it looked as if some enterprising but slightly cockeyed Carthaginian had decided to build a Roman Coliseum in the Arabian Desert. Bettors, it's true, are willing to travel great distances, but they never did so in sufficient numbers and the track logged enormous losses. But John continued to work on the plant, the laws that affected its operation, and the nature of the racing events as well. There were other driving forces at work—the state's thirst for revenue and gambling hunger, the unassuageable desire of a great many people to put what they hold at risk. There was also the sheer joy of watching well-trained horses compete. This was not, however, a decisive factor. But over the ages most people have come to Shakespeare not for his poetry, but for the swordplay and sex.

Dover Downs is an hour from Wilmington by car, and considerably more on a race day when traffic is heavy. Those driving from Baltimore and Philadelphia must add about an hour. The city of Wilmington's population is slightly over 70,000; the track had seating for 9,000 in the beginning. The city's income per capita in the early 1990s was about $14,250: European Americans—$21,600; African Americans—$9,000. However, the surrounding suburbs, largely white and affluent, had twice the city's population and were forever expanding.

John spent a lot of time on the phone in the seventies, trying to organize his way out of his $12.5 million Dover boondoggle. When things are not working out, John doesn't hesitate to say as much. In April of 1974, when his fortunes were at their lowest ebb, he was quoted by the *Morning News*, "Hell, everything I've got—except my wife and family—is for sale, I suppose."

The Dover Downs owners' grand plan had been to make their track part of an "area circuit" that embraced the Brandywine Raceway, near Wilmington, and Liberty Bell Raceway in northeast Philadelphia. When the Keystone Racetrack opened in 1969 two miles from Liberty Bell, Liberty Bell asked the Pennsylvania legislature to let it operate weekends, when betting peaked. At the time, only Delaware's facilities were open Sundays, and Delaware's track would garner busloads of racing fans from as far away as New York on Sunday.

When Pennsylvania and Maryland authorized Sunday betting in the early seventies, Delaware felt the pain. The hurt was compounded by the world oil crisis, a stock market recession in 1974, and the closure of the main highway between Wilmington and Dover. Then the bridge over the Chesapeake Canal closed down for repairs. Racing fans were forced to make long detours over winding country roads.

Meadowlands, the most competitive racetrack of all, opened for business in 1976. Meadowlands was positioned geograhically at the center of the most heavily populated area in the central east coast and it delivered a terrific blow to its competition. The best horses and the heaviest bettors flocked there. That same year, Resorts International opened, leading other corporate entities into the gambling business. Harness racing began to look as old-fashioned as jitterbugging. Horse racing in general languished as younger gamesters chose the glittering superficiality of casinos over the pungent and elegant reality of horseflesh.

From the day it opened until 1982, Dover Downs lost an incredible $13 million, despite a series of tax breaks granted by a legislature that didn't want to see this source of revenue dwindle to dot. John was largely responsible for handling Dover's losses. By 1982 the bank was no longer willing to extend the mortgage which had been at default for months. Financial Vice President Gene Weaver negotiated with the bank and convinced them to take a discount on the debt. John took over the entire debt, thus turning himself into both the major shareholder and the main creditor. No one at the time really thought he could turn the Dover invalid into a healthy enterprise. It appeared inconceivable. But, now unencumbered by banks holding mortgages or worried partners running scared, John was free to attempt the impossible.

John's stake in the Brandywine Raceway tended to increase as the track's troubles multiplied. By 1971 he'd established a controlling interest in it. In 1998, his wife, Michele, remarked, "John has on his plate five different projects, any of which most forty-year-old men would consider a life's work." That's pretty much been John's situation most of his life. He likes to push ahead with a series of companies, herding them along in parallel. Those that are diseased get generous infusions from those in good health. The Jamaica project is an example of an invalid that has required transfusions for forty years. The Brandywine Raceway too involved decades of intensive care. John apparently gets some kind of deep satisfaction from taking on businesses that look unsalvageable and then making them succeed. He falls in love with horses, or an island, and then spends half a lifetime turning them into economic engines. The intractable nature of the task appears to be part of its allure. There are easier ways to make money, but they don't often beguile him.

By bankrolling the tracks for almost twenty years, John had been sustaining a sort of mini-welfare system in Delaware. When the fans deserted Delaware, the horse farms moved out. Michele estimates that some 5,000 employees and part-time jobs dribbled away with them, a great loss for so small a state.

The Brandywine Raceway is north of Wilmington on the Pennsylvania border. When John first bought into the track in the early seventies, it was making money. John merged Brandywine into Rollins International (the company that eventually became Rollins Truck Leasing). But the same forces that brought down Dover were affecting Brandywine. Its customers soon grew scarce, drawn away by tracks nearer to home, like Liberty Bell. Affected by the oil and stock market crises, trying to cut costs in order to compete with Liberty Bell, Brandywine closed during the winter months in 1974–75. The company lost $4 million.

In 1976 (when Meadowlands and the casino, Resorts International, opened), Brandywine was spun out of Rollins International. John stayed on as the major shareholder, and those he bought out were doubtless delighted that they'd found someone so foolish. The handwriting was on the wall. As younger people flocked to casino gambling, it appeared obvious that horse racing was losing its appeal. Liberty Bell and Brandywine were engaged in a leviathan struggle to pull in what fans remained. The legislature could pass laws cutting the tax load, but couldn't legislate people back into the stands. By 1983, the Brandywine Raceway was losing over a million dollars annually.

Michele says that "John wanted to keep harness racing alive. He loved the whole horse thing. There were people like Eddie Davis, the most famous harness driver around. Eddie kept his horse farms in

Delaware. But you begin to fall out of love with something that loses $3 million annually. He began talking to the legislators. I guess [the politicians] felt that John could swallow $3 million a year losses [Brandywine and Dover combined]."

Brandywine closed in 1995 after losing between $2 and $3 million annually during its last seven years. Liberty Bell had given up the ghost in 1985 and had become a shopping center. To turn Brandywine from an empty oval into an economic engine, John proposed a fairly obvious solution: tear down the obsolete track and put in an upscale mall. The County Council roundly trounced this idea in 1986. All seven members voted against it. John revised his design. In 1991 he proposed that slot machines at Dover and Brandywine could save harness racing there.

The possibility of slots at the Brandywine track was not well received. The idea of slot machines jingling in chateau country raised a storm of objection. The emotional tone of the opposition was eloquently expressed by columnist Ralph Moyed in the *News Journal* of April, 1988. "If John Rollins thought he could make a go of the Brandywine Raceway by staging gladiator fights on the infield, I wouldn't be particularly bothered. Fights to the death between IRA terrorists and Ulster Protestant irregulars, for instance, might even draw a better class of fans than now attend the harness races." Having looked down his nose at the track's former clientele, Moyed goes on to condemn future pleasure seekers by evoking a mass of unshaved men in dirty raincoats carrying bottles of hooch in brown paper bags: "The target market may be at the very bottom of the economic scale—people who never seem to be able to hold onto anything more than the price of cheap wine."

Moyed scornfully suggests that John should turn for advice on the gambling business to "the unchallenged expert on control of the industry, Nicodemo 'Little Nicky' Scarfo . . . on trial for murder [and who] could end up in the electric chair." Expressing contempt for Delaware legislators, Moyed says that a better use for racetrack real estate would be a pig farm. It "wouldn't stink any more than the auto exhaust of such a complex and would make a lot less noise."

Moyed appears never to have smelled an actual pig farm, but by alluding to John's lowly beginnings, he aptly expresses the elite rage of the plan's opponents. With developers swarming all over northern Delaware, John's presence offered (once again) a convenient lightning rod. He represents the vulgar future that the well-heeled and sensitive fervently wish would happen somewhere else. All the evils of

Delaware's development are attached to his name like cans to a dog's tail. Yet as malls go, the plans for his development, as we shall see, would prove considerably more elegant than anything else going up on that stretch of the Concord Pike, in that corner of the state.

It became clear in the eighties that there was only one way to save horse racing and its culture in Delaware, and that was to compete directly with Atlantic City on its own terms. Thus racetrack owners appealed to the legislature to allow coin-operated slot machines at the tracks. Like virgins in love, the state's politicians pondered how far they dared go. Laws to allow the slots were passed in 1989, but vetoed by the governor.

The state, however, had had its lottery in operation for fifteen years. Harried by careers, high taxes, and the need to afford schools that would give their kids a better chance, the professional classes are generally too busy to spend much time praying over roulette wheels or flinging dice. Gaming is for the bored, optimistic, fatuous celebrities, or the just plain addicted. The casino is like Pandora's box: whatever evils fly out are redeemed by hope. For generations, the poor and lowly were banned from Monte Carlo and Baden-Baden. Such glamorous palaces were reserved for the upper crust. Aristocrats, New Money, and the useless offspring of rich men went there to degenerate in splendor. In the United States gambling was pretty much confined to a gray stretch of desert in the far west. But as the Mafia's grip loosened and the public debt mounted, America's legislators finally understood that a grandmother should have as much right as a duke to lose her money—or win a fortune. A slot machine is less elegant than roulette or *chemin de fer,* but maybe it reflects the American love of technology.

Every attempt at regulating gaming has died quietly in legislative committees. What else could governments do but love an industry that demanded such intense regulation, an industry that could be taxed at every press of a button? The legislators were only following the example of the churches. Bingo in church basements had trained a generation of grandmothers to play the numbers. The church can't very well argue that Bingo is spiritually more uplifting than the slots at Dover Downs. Both raise money for good causes. Science has made chance our god and chance smiles down on gamblers, politicians and worshipers alike. Now that America's casinos had been wrestled away from the Mafia and handed over to corporate America, gambling was to be called "gaming." Governments (city, county, state) have been quietly putting games of chance into their revenue stream for years. By 1996 gaming had become the most popular entertainment for adults. Corporations like ITT and MGM raise marble halls dedicated to the god of chance. Spinning roulette wheels light up eyes in many a chamber of commerce. *Mother Jones* Magazine has figured that this new "industry" is spending $100 million a year to influence state legislatures. Gaming is putting serious money into the pockets of Native Americans who've installed 150 casinos across the country. According to PBS's *Front Line,* the Viejas Indians in California have been putting $1,000 a week into the bank for every man, woman and child in their tribe. The police in gaming states may count on higher salaries. Teachers, highways . . . the list is long.

Generation of revenue aside, the ancient association of gambling with vice is ever present. Pornography is given aid and comfort by free speech; gambling is cosseted by freedom of choice. Walt Disney did a brilliant job of cleaning up the Grimm brothers' blood-spattered world when he scripted *Cinderella,* but not even Disney can make gambling harmless. Like alcohol and tobacco, gambling is addictive to five out of every hundred persons. But no one talks about closing down the distilleries, smokers continue to cough themselves to death, and the buses keep rolling toward Atlantic City—and Dover. Even television is addictive—perhaps the greatest addiction in human history. Yet what politician dares oppose the technology that allows him to enter every living room in America?

So it's no surprise that when Delaware established the lottery in 1974, the legislative soul-searching stopped. The General Assembly allotted a minimum of 45 percent of the gross income as prize money and a minimum of 30 percent to the state's General Fund. In 1996, over 52 percent of the state's gross returns were distributed as prizes, 33.4 percent went into the General Fund, and 11.8 percent went back to business interests.

The odds of winning the "Powerball" jackpot hover around thirteen million to one. A ticket buyer is more likely to be struck by lightning than win the lottery. If poor folk would put those dollars into a bank account each week, they'd be thousands ahead in a very few years. But simple logic and the human condition are natural antagonists. Wayne Rollins once said that he would probably support a state lottery because there was no way to cure the gambling fever. "I guess what I believe is there's going to be a group of people that's going to bet no matter what," he remarked. "It's like Prohibition. It seems to me gamblers always find a way to do it. I don't know if that's enough justification [for the lottery]. But I don't have any hope we'll stop a fellow from gambling whether we have a lottery or not."

John didn't lacerate himself over the moral question because he does not romanticize human nature. He made it clear that Delaware's politicians had a simple choice. They could go on milking his white elephant, or turn him loose to transform the creature into a golden goose. He argued that the slots would raise the kind of cash it takes to bring harness racing and great drivers like Eddie Davis and big money back to Delaware. The state would own and rent the machines to the track.

By the middle nineties, the growing popularity of stock car racing made for another major change. A new NASCAR track was constructed under the supervision of Melvin Joseph. The early wooden bleachers and dirt track have been transformed into a sports palace bearing a certain resemblance to the Pompidou arts center in Paris. The National Association of Stock Car Racing (NASCAR) has been scheduling races on the Dover track since 1969. Starting with seating for 1,000, the "monster mile" audience has steadily expanded. At the Winston Cup Series in September of 1999, 130,000 jovial fans packed the stadium.

The enormous popularity of these races is mind-boggling. They draw bigger crowds than the Superbowl and pour over $40 million annually into the local economy while bringing national media attention to the state. Cars resembling little scarabs, brilliantly decorated with the names of their corporate sponsors, careen around the mile track four hundred times with a continual earsplitting roar. Thousands of fans sit mesmerized and baking in the sun and they love it—the spectacle, the chance that something terrifying may occur at any second, the glorious dissolving of the individual, anxious ego in this enormous, carefree crowd.

With receipts swollen by the popularity of this dangerous and exacting sport, the harness racing purse became big enough to attract the best horses and riders. The Dover Downs have become the Monte Carlo of the region's hoi polloi. Beefed up by NASCAR and gaming, the harness racing purse moved from 89th in the nation to second place in 1999. The best trotters in the world are streaming back onto the track, and locals again supplement their incomes by working at the horse farms, or at the Downs. Newly installed simulcast screens give patrons a synoptic view of races on tracks in other states.

Together with Delaware Park (owned by another operator), Dover Downs became the most profitable operation of its kind in the nation. Delaware bettors generated more net proceeds per machine than any other state, including Nevada. To revive their own race-tracks, other states have been constrained to imitate Delaware's model. Dover Downs Entertainment's CEO, Denis McGlynn, who began as a marketing intern, has worked his way up through the company and has been instrumental in its success, according to John.

In 1996, Dover Downs had an average monthly income of $4,873,808 with an annual gross of $58,485,696. According to the Lottery Office, the proceeds from its slots alone amounted to $13,978,082. The state also gets gaming income from Delaware Park (larger than Dover) and Harrington which started up in August of 1996. Dover Downs was listed on the stock market as Dover Entertainment, Inc.—John's seventh company to go public. Priced at $17 per share, the stock sailed up to $22 its first day out. According to the *News Journal*, John's forty-nine percent stake was worth $139 million. At John's eightieth birthday party celebration at the Hotel du Pont, Michele told assembled guests that gambling that year, 1996, had garnered "$17 million in state taxes." Today's figures for both the stock and the revenues generated are significantly higher.

When NASCAR now comes to the Downs, the surrounding fields take on the appearance of a medieval fair. The landscape around the track fills with campers and bulky RVs. Flags flutter, tips are exchanged, the turf is churned into mud by thousands of enthusiastic fans jammed shoulder-to-shoulder among the vendors of everything from ice cream to earmuffs. The earsplitting rumble and whine of competing stock cars rises from the track and there is an electrifying mix of technology and danger. It's the American equivalent of the bullfight. Indeed, John has led a cash cow into the pastures of Dover, the green fields grow money, and a lot of folk are having a grand time.

Ralph Moyed often condemned John Rollins for giving Delaware what its citizens appear more than willing to pay for. It sometimes seems that for our toilets to flush harmoniously and our computers to behave rationally, we pay with a reduction of spirit. Educational standards are well down from a generation ago. The tortured content of contemporary art, suicides among the young, and violence in the schools all indicate a malaise of the spirit. On the other hand, science and the genius of commerce are enjoying their finest hour. Business drives the system, coordinating the sciences, government, and the banks to provide the comforts and the amusements we now take for granted and criticize, always with good reason. Is all the comfort and convenience bad for us? Indeed, our minds are filled with trivia, but would we trade our superficiality for what we've left behind—grinding physical pain, backbreaking labor, and people with divine rights ordering us around like cattle?

Does the success of a blood sport like racing, or of gaming, point the direction our republic is headed? With social programs cut back, thirty-nine states have decided that gambling is not an affliction but a solution. Sarah Jackson, Delaware's secretary of finance, has written, "The Lottery . . . helps pay for the majority of state services, such as public and higher education, environmental protection, and public safety. In fiscal year '96, the Lottery contributed more than $57.8 million to the General Fund—an increase over last year of more than $14.5 million, 34 percent."

Our "value free" culture, makes room for much that would have been condemned a generation ago. Business has moved into the vacuum created by a spiritually troubled society. Business is itself peculiarly value free. Its highest good is profit, and it exists only to supply what people want, or can be persuaded to want.

Claudia Rollins's grandson, Gary, has a vivid memory of that stern and proper woman refusing to go down into the basement of Wayne's home because there was a pool table there. In her view, pool tables were icons of corruption. The Delaware lottery opened for business in 1976, the year that Claudia died. John's mother inherited her sense of right and wrong from ancient Jerusalem, as did he. Would Claudia have given her blessing to the slots at Dover Downs?

"No," Gary says. "If she was alive, John never would have done it."

John agrees. "I wouldn't be doing it."

It may be that Claudia saw into the human heart with a precision obscured today by information overload. Her beloved Bible has become just another text on the Internet. The therapy industry translates good and evil into "normal" and "abnormal." To distinguish right from wrong we must turn to our accountants.

28
End of the Yellow Brick Road

Around 1945, when Wayne bought his first piece of open land in Georgia, "development" was still an antisocial concept in rural Georgia. The drowsing fields were associated with husbandry and the seasons. Wayne's father-in-law, Jim Crum, hadn't added a square foot of land to his original acreage in forty years, and there was something admirable in that, a certain biblical severity. Making do with what the Lord had provided.

Thirty years passed and land development became part of the great tide that was lifting all boats. But in the last decades of the century, development was again antisocial to a lot of people, few of whom ever read a Bible. When John announced, in 1983, that he was seeking New Castle County Council's permission to construct an upscale mall featuring stores like Neiman Marcus and Nordstrom's on the land once occupied by the Brandywine Raceway, a storm of protest rose up. Leading the attack was the Civic Council of the Brandywine Hundred (CCOBH), an umbrella organization representing perhaps 140 subdivision communities in and around the Brandywine Hundred.

Siding with John were the state's construction workers. The president of Delaware's Building Trades Council said unemployment was running around twenty percent. This controversy raised the issue of Delaware's financial well-being. Should lawmakers be opposed to new industry and to heavy industry in particular? An answer was not easy to sort out. Land use planning was the under aegis of the State Planning Office, established in the early 1960s. H. B. du Pont was the power behind this organization. The office was never enthusiastic about developing heavy industry, bad news for blue-collar workers. However, air and water in Delaware were polluted enough already. According to Delaware's Division of Environmental Control, little New Castle County and its industries put out half the amount emitted by vast metropolitan New York. To turn Delaware's riverside into another northern New Jersey was not a good idea. The battle that ensued over the construction of big oil refineries on the coast is de-scribed by Governor Russell Peterson in his *Rebel with a Conscience.* Construction workers booed his wife, Lillian, when she spoke for the Coastal Zone Act. The issue (jobs versus environment) was vexed, to say the least. According to James Phelan and Robert Pozen, the plan-ning council never sorted out firms "by types [or allocated] sites by advanced planning techniques or strict environmental control stan-dards." They charge that Peterson, a DuPont executive before he en-tered politics, wanted to keep out heavy industry and "attract office complexes." Governor Peterson's understanding of the entire issue is complex and multilayered, part of his experience. His description of the du Ponts focuses on their individuality, and he sees heavy in-dustry and its representatives in government as undiscerning with re-gard to human needs and environmental issues. The coastline bill that Peterson sponsored in 1971 helped ensure a clean environment. That the law also gave "upstream chemical plants a monopoly over available industrial land and use of the Delaware River for waste dis-posal purposes," (as Phelan and Pozner remark) is probably irrele-vant. The law could not change what already existed. Peterson was in-suring that Delaware's coastline did not come to resemble the blighted wasteland upriver in Marcus Hook, Pennsylvania.

The issue of jobs for blue-collar workers was not easy to sort out in a state that chose to keep heavy industry away. By 1971 the issue was complicated further when Governor Peterson reported to the legis-lature that Delaware had a $30 million deficit, including a $10 mil-lion accounting mistake. (Someone had miscalculated the franchise tax income.) Delaware's decision makers hoped a solution lay in the service industry sector, John's specialty. Delaware's laws were written to attract corporations but not industries. According to the Delaware Chamber of Commerce self-assessment in 1969, "The state has no tax on securities or personal property. There is no stock transfer tax, no state real estate tax, no tax on goods in process, machinery, equip-ment, or raw materials. . . . Compared to the restrictive taxes in many other states, Delaware's tax laws are relaxed and are eminently fair to industry."

By turning away heavy industry it appeared that Delaware's leaders expected to take care of the state's deficit by conjuring money out of thin air. In the eighties, the well advised and prescient Governor Pete du Pont pushed through the Financial Services Act. Liberal credit laws brought big banks into Delaware. An army of lawyers, account-ants and financial consultants swarmed down from New York. The

state took on a newly prosperous appearance a little like Switzer-
land—lacking only mountains and cuckoo clocks.

Dozens of new housing projects were being routinely approved by
a complaisant county council. New construction marched up hill and
down dale. Out along Routes 48 and 7, where du Ponts had once
chased foxes, houses and condos sprouted. Where deer had been
roaming in January, families were moving in by September. Signs advertising these new neighborhoods bore hopeful names like "Brack-
enville Woods," "Chestnut Valley," or "Stirrup Farm." Traffic and traffic lights proliferated. The Concord Pike was widened and stop signs
sprouted like dandelions. Nervous deer crept through the broken
stone walls along Route 92 with greater caution.

John, a man of seventy, was now hiking into the unknown terrain
of retail selling. He faced the combined forces of the absentee JMB
Realty Corporation (owners of the Concord Mall a mile south) and
the Civic Council of the Brandywine Hundred. CCOBH had religiously opposed whatever move John ever made. In a way, the organization had taken up where Henry B. du Pont left off. Their
most ardent spokesperson was Mr. Robert Weiner, a lawyer, enthusiastic barbershop quartet singer, and passionate advocate of the status
quo. To Weiner, John was Mephisto who must be chained by lawyers
and dragged down to that hot hell where devious developers all
belong.

Back in the seventies, William Prickett and CCOBH had lost their
battle to stop Rollins Broadcasting from introducing cable television
to the state. Now Robert Weiner joined battle to stop the mall project, greeting John's plan for new construction as if the devil were pro-
posing to drop the Great Wall of China squarely across the Concord
Pike.

Unfortunately for Weiner's plan to halt the mall's construction, his
CCOBH colleagues worked themselves into such a frenzy of detestation that they overstepped the bounds of simple decency. According
to Ralph Moyed, writing in the *News Journal* of February, 1991, the
CCOBH "infuriated members of the County Council by portraying
them [the councilors] as . . . a bunch of crooks and flunkies."

Moyed had made a habit of attacking John Rollins with savage glee
for years. John's was just about the only human face that journalists
and political activists like Weiner could attach to the steamroller of
development that was turning Delaware's pleasant vales into
overnight neighborhoods. Blaming the anonymous corporations
that owned a hundred other franchised outlets and bulldozed a hun-

dred hills was much less satisfying. The corporate persona somewhat resembles one of those expressionless masks ancient Greek actors used to play gods. John was a living, breathing individual. And John's project was enormous, ninety-seven acres with a projected budget of $125 million.

But in his February article, Moyed performs a surprising pirouette and disapproves strongly of the self-righteous fury animating Weiner's organization. Possibly the support of the unions for John's project, and the opposition of certain reactionary voices turned him around.

"Bob Weiner and other CCOBH spokespersons made it a personal fight against John Rollins," Moyed writes, "invoking his name the way Bible-thumping preachers speak the name of satan. It doesn't wash. Some Delawareans probably view Rollins as a political predator, but people who know him, or have met him, tend to regard him as a man with a sharp, rough-hewn intellect and plenty of down-home charm. People who must cast the votes [in other words, the council members] know the latter John Rollins."

Did Delaware really need another mall? Simply put, John saw shopping as the best solution to his racetrack problem. In an age of mass consumption and the automobile, in a time when most cars contain only one person and parking and the traffic jam have become social issues, the mall appears inevitable—as inevitable as castles in the age of the crusaders. Imbued with the romantic ideals of his southern heritage, John decided he would build the most outstanding mall in Delaware and call it the Brandywine Town Center.

CCOBH saw not a mall but a monster which they would hate and fight as best they could. They argued that this mall would increase the traffic on Concord Pike. That fifteen to twenty-five thousand people had flocked to the race track in the evenings a few years before was not mentioned. The vehement nature of their detestation lent their attack a religious fervor. They challenged every change in subdivision, every record plan, every demolition request, every minor design alteration.

John's practical concerns were fixed on the rapidly evolving world of retail selling, a business bent on entering a virtual reality of its own. Markets have always popped up where people congregate. Set a plank on two boxes to sell tomatoes at a crossroad, and it's a market. Over time the market became a store and the store became a department store, a cultural artifact no less. London's Crystal Palace in 1852 offered an initial blueprint, a modernistic structure of steel and glass.

The Browning and Lehman store built in tiny Charleston, South Carolina, that same year astonished buyers when it opened. Supported by thirty-six Corinthian columns of iron, a seventy-foot gallery rose the full height of the structure. The dome with twelve-foot panes of glass was seventy-eight feet high and the effect beggared anything in the Arabian Nights.

The Charleston *Evening News,* in 1852, speaks of "the spirit and taste which characterize [the store] as a whole" and adds, "The dome is beyond our power of description," concluding that the "whole enterprise . . . has given to our city a noble and highly ornamental specimen of architecture, and commences for her, as it were, a new epoch in the wholesale and retail line, presenting business prospects of the most encouraging and animating character."

Little Charleston had produced something more lovely in its effect than New York's own Crystal Palace of 1853, a conventional construction with columns of cement. Department stores sprouted all over the nation. Siegel-Cooper opened its giant department store in New York City in 1896. Wanamaker's, Macy's, and Marshall Field & Company tried to express the grandeur of commerce. But as Browning and Lehman's store in Charleston demonstrates, New York was not the center of the mercantile universe. J. C. Penney's opened its first store in Kemmerer, Wyoming. Neiman Marcus was founded in Dallas. Woolworth began in Lancaster, Pennsylvania. These enormous stores had orchestras, restaurants with fountains, opera stars warbling in the shrubbery, and gloved clerks trained to please the customer. With the establishment of the first mall at the Northgate Shopping Center outside Seattle around 1950, the age of the heroic department store was drawing to a close. The mall with its conglomeration of stores was less the creation of urban decay than communication technology. The mall is the creature of the franchise, and the franchise is made possible by electronic communication. Only computers can control the information necessary to run several hundred stores with several million items of merchandise.

The grand pretensions of the Gilded Age (borrowed from Victorian England and a decayed French aristocracy) have been erased by electronic wizardry and a new social ideal. And the surprising thing is that John Rollins, well into his seventies, was interested only in putting up a center that would surprise and give pleasure. It's unlikely he'd ever heard of Charleston's Browning and Lehman, but he was born into the same regional tradition, a tradition that values grand civic statements.

What Marshall Field created in Chicago with an elaborate flowery decor, the orchestras, and the overflowing abundance of goods today is replaced by a virtual reality featuring videos, rock, and light shows. America's culture is all about technology and how it can be made to work on the job, with nature, or in sports and entertainment. The merchant's role is to give customers what they are willing to pay for. John liked to do more besides.

With the merger of Rollins Environmental to Laidlaw, John's son Jeff and Frank Minner (a Rollins financial vice president) were freed up to join Michele Rollins, who is president of the Brandywine Town Center project. The immediate future of retail selling is exemplified by the center. The mall is designed in a curve around an artificial lake with two branching arms and a crystal palace entrance lobby leading from the main parking apron to the shops. A raised walkway looks across the water and leads to restaurants with glass domes.

Andy Lubin, a consultant on the original Brandywine team, says this curving connector "carries all the critical architectural features, including 200,000 square feet of specialty stores. They will ultimately create all the synergy at the Brandywine Town Center." The mall has room for about sixty of these specialty stores or "signature" stores.

Set far out on the wingtips of the mall are the giant stores that lead back toward the parking lot, stores designed to make shopping more than just picking up something necessary. Shopping today is a combination of retail and entertainment. Because there are generally two wage earners in a family, they have a limited amount of time. Thus there is a fusion between shopping and entertainment. Consequently the combination of an amusement center and the "big box" signature store with small specialty stores and restaurants sets up "lifestyle shopping."

These big stores with their 600 thousand square feet of shopping space came into their own when Bed Bath & Beyond established its "concept" in the abandoned Siegel-Cooper building in New York. Bed Bath & Beyond is one of the Brandywine Center's attractions along with Lowe's (hardware, lumber, lamps, ladders, you-name-it), Dick's Clothes and Sporting Goods, and Target.

The Brandywine Town Center's northern border parallels the state line. Thus it becomes a magnet, inviting buyers to avoid Pennsylvania's sales tax. Andy Lubin says that saving that "six percent sales tax has such a dynamic impact on retailers that those who are enjoying business today along this corridor are in the top three, four and five percent of all those in their national franchise group." And indeed these corporate entities are lined up along Concord Pike, the fields filling with category killers like Circuit City and Borders Books, housed in structures the size of aircraft hangars, franchise restaurants with bright "don't-miss-me" colors looking like giant versions of the plastic toys sold at Toys Я Us. The mushrooming of these strip malls is so overwhelming near the state line that the CCOBH objections to the Brandywine Town Center sound like cries for help in a hurricane. It's clear that nothing on earth will stop the people in Pennsylvania from taking advantage of that six percent tax break, so the enormous corporate boxes line Concord Pike like whales feeding on krill.

Though it was John's initial idea to bring upscale shopping to little Delaware—the kind of quality stores that New Yorkers and San Franciscans take for granted—he found that department stores like Nordstrom's and Neiman Marcus demanded millions for their presence. They expected small specialty shops to pay for both their own spaces and those of the celebrity stores. Driven by consumer demands and a new electronic technology, the retail market is evolving dramatically. Compared to the old department store that established a rich association with a high culture now defunct—ferns, music, carpets, polite service—the Brandywine Town Center architectural rendering resembles a space port. Target was selected because it's the shopping industry's response to shoppers who are catered to on every hand and become increasingly expert at finding quality for a low cost. Despite some dire predictions, it's unlikely electronic shopping will destroy old-fashioned retailing. Touching and feeling the goods still offer greater satisfaction than staring at a screen and tapping computer keys. For millions of families, going to the mall is a recreational activity. An astounding cornucopia of products is reprised in each of the giant stores at the Brandywine Town Center (which opened for business in 1998). In Dick's Clothing and Sporting Goods, for example, an entire wall devoted to basketballs, another to baseball mitts, another to tennis racquets. Five aisles of fishing rods rise up like a bamboo thicket. Over thirty models of exercise machines are displayed as well as two dozen parka styles, all manufactured overseas in Sri Lanka, Korea, Indonesia, Singapore, Thailand. It's an amazing demonstration of what the term "global culture" means.

Think back to when the century was young and John barely a teenager. For entertainment, he liked to stop off at the local courthouse and watch the lawyers pleading their cases. It was great theater and it made a deep impression on him. The judge, the lawyer, and the man on trial were usually people he knew firsthand. The court-room palaver exposed him to the law and taught him something about the civil society and the dramatic power of language. He saw how words may determine the fate of men.

By century's end, a later generation of young people live in a world changed out of all recognition from that of John's childhood. Teenagers probably take in a hundred movies a year, a thousand com-mercials, and they walk through life with their favorite singers war-bling through the speakers eternally plastered to their ears. In some ways they know a thousand times more than John's generation knew. In some ways, they know far less. It's confounding to imagine a time when a fourteen-year-old farm boy could find courtroom proceed-ings first-class entertainment. It's just as confounding to see that same boy, now grown old, able to connect with the highly evolved and very different teenager of today. True, John has teenage children of his own. But he shrugs off any suggestion that the old poverty was better for kids than the new plethora. Every generation has its own cross to bear. Whatever may be best for children, there never was a society that provided it. Only the family may do that. A perfect grade point tends to make John suspicious. "It may show they've been so busy studying they haven't had time to do anything else."

The suburban subdivisions that ring our cities appear designed to promote isolation. Like most American cities today, Wilmington drops dead around 5 P.M. every weekday. The workers drive away. The streets fall silent. But that's when things begin to pick up at the Brandywine Town Center. Young and old stream into the new Regal entertainment complex. Sixteen cinema screens are advertised. A small merry-go-round designed for tots spins next to the miniature golf course. The vast interior of the Regal building has a weird com-plexity, as if Walt Disney and Pirenesi collaborated on the design. Arches, escalators, and grottos serving fast food dart off in every di-rection. The walls are painted pale pink with white trim. There are party rooms, a "virtual" reality realm, video games, a miniature bowl-ing alley, and a track that snakes through the building where kids drive racing cars at speeds that probably strike them as too sensible. The broad landing below the theaters is lined with six-foot-tall gold Oscar statues, arguably the most famous and least attractive piece of sculpture ever created by human hand. But these golden idols leave no doubt you're going to be entertained.

On an icy February afternoon there are two hundred cars parked in the lot outside. The interior is so immense that it appears almost empty. By evening, however, the parking lot is full and the place is jumping, the movie theaters filling up. The eye is confused by conflicting lines and unconvincing colors. Country-western music delivered over a fuzzy sound system adds to the general uproar.

The kids love the confusion and flock in droves, avidly eyeing each other. The Regal Funscape has provided what's missing in their lonely suburbs—a modern substitute for the Roman forum where crowding together, making friends, and dashing about provides a little genuine excitement. Yes, the setting is hokey and makeshift with its confused architecture, computer creatures knocking each others' heads off and a tiny tots merry-go-round that resembles a stale wedding cake. And yes, the air carries the synthetic smell of popcorn and fast food. But the young need to be crowded together; they long for any excuse to gossip and preen and try out attitudes. The parents are there too, keeping an eye on the smallest children or going up escalators to the film houses. This surreal plastic world has been created with no thought to improving the young, or correcting them, or stuffing their heads with the dry straw that educators too often mistake for learning. The architects of this place only want them to spend their parents' money.

Regal's Funscape is the carnival updated. Love its mad variety or hate its vulgarity, the place reflects what we're becoming—affluent, technically sophisticated, dead to high art. We've somehow combined the peasant, the proletarian, and the plutocratic in a new technological synthesis that works for kids. Life has never been more various for the young and the Funscape is about as far as one can get from the childhood pleasures of the Rollins brothers—a ride on the wagon to the cotton gin, a glass of fruit juice, a story by candlelight.

29
Giving Back

Working at his office one afternoon, Wayne realized that he was suddenly blind in his right eye. He phoned the Emory University Clinic from the couch where he was sitting and described his symptoms to Dr. Charles Hatcher. Dr. Hatcher is the man who'd organized the open-heart clinic at Emory Medical Center. The doctor determined that the carotid artery in Wayne's neck was blocked. After an operation (Wayne insisted both carotid arteries be cleaned up), his sight came back.

The medical history of both the Rollins brothers is long and detailed. Wayne and John were raised on an American farmer's diet—buttered biscuits, pork with plenty of fat, and milk, the creamier the better, a combination not the best for businessmen who endure high anxiety and don't exercise as much as they should.

In the 1980s John underwent open-heart surgery at the Emory Clinic. In 1995, when his heart began dashing like a squirrel in his chest, he went back to Emory. A catheter was run into an artery serving his heart; the specific muscle carrying the wrong message was short-circuited to reroute the heart's electrical system. After the bypass surgery, John began to take long walks, swim regularly, and give up the pork sausages he'd savored since childhood.

Throughout his life, Wayne had to work hard for his health. Tuberculosis came close to killing him as a child. As a young man, he'd coped with the lower back injury that affected him the rest of his life. The struggle to keep his body in order was complicated by ceaseless overwork. In his later life, he would rise before dawn and swim laps in the pool behind his Atlanta house. "When I swim of a morning," he said once, "I go over as many things as I can. I try to keep my mind working. I've always counted a whole lot on my head, one reason you'll never see me with a computer."

On the threshold of old age, the question now facing both brothers was how to deal with the fortunes that would outlive them. John was painfully aware that money's power to create order, or chaos, depends upon the wisdom of the person employing it. The philanthropist is limited by his own perceptions of what is lacking in his society. Thomas Jefferson, looking at the United States around 1800, felt that great emphasis should be placed on basic education and technical training. Jefferson's America had primitive communications, poor roads, and no public education to speak of. Across the Atlantic, the high arts of Europe were at their peak in France and Germany. In that regard, the United States seemed a pale reflection. Yet advances in education grow out of the arts and sciences. The Rollinses' philanthropy starts with this perception. That education begins with the arts, with the realm of the imagination, is all too often an idea not easy for the "practical" American intelligence to grasp.

John has supported a string orchestra in his time, but he personally prefers country music and the theater. His lifelong grants in education have combined with support for the arts. He has made substantial grants to set up programs at both Ursuline and St. Edmond's Academies: Rollins Performing Arts Centers have been established at both schools. In 1999, John and Michele established a grant to restore the Grand Theater in Dover, and gave substantial gifts to the Millsboro and Lewes Libraries.

As we've seen, the Rollins brothers attacked racism as vigorously as John went after hazardous waste. Their radio network supported black radio programming and played directly into the African American struggle that emerged during the fifties. There is John's lifelong habit of granting scholarships to kids from the inner city. As early as 1952, while lieutenant governor of Delaware, he made it a practice to turn over his $3,000 a year salary to the United Negro College Fund. The Horatio Alger Society which he reenergized awards outstanding businessmen recognition, but he reoriented its agenda and made its main work the administration of scholarships to worthy high school graduates who could not afford college without financial aid. At Duke University, John established the Rollins Scholars, a program that helps students working on an MBA degree.

Both brothers have made substantial contributions to the medical infrastructure. Wayne's struggle with poor health made him particularly interested in medical research. He had overcome TB and put up with years of excruciating back pain before he ran into problems with his heart and a pulmonary edema that clogged his right lung. An upsetting shortness of breath plagued him through the last decade of his life. By his own count, he went under anesthesia a dozen times at least, "But I never thought I wouldn't come back."

John has remarked that his brother is "as tight a guy with a quarter as you've ever seen." But Wayne eventually put millions into medicine. He was principally interested in cancer research and Alzheimer's disease because these were afflictions he had seen strike down people in his own family.

Wayne's friendship with Dr. Hatcher was good news for the Emory Medical Center. Among the first American open-heart surgeons, trained by Dr. Christiaan Barnard in the fifties, Dr. Hatcher had brought the new procedure to Georgia. No less important was Dr. Hatcher's talent for connecting Emory to big money in Atlanta. Hailing from a small town in the south of Georgia, the doctor knew how to make himself understood in the boardrooms of big foundations. The men there who made the decisions had backgrounds like his own—though he admits he never was relaxed in their company, knowing too well that the future of Emory medicine depended on what he said.

By the year of his retirement in 1996, the Emory Medical Center's budget had risen fourfold to $125 million annually. Dr. Hatcher remarks that the most generous people inevitably are those who've made their own fortunes. "And some of the tightest people in the world are those that inherit it. They live with a morbid fear of being without it. But anyone who's made money is not that taken with it. They feel they can do it again."

The cultural life of American cities is largely controlled by the big nonprofit foundations that grow in the soil of business. Dr. Hatcher recalls a donation to Emory Medical made years ago that arrived in the form of Coca-Cola stock "worth about $110 thousand. Since then it has ballooned to over $2 billion." To increase his wealth so exponentially, a Caesar or Tamerlaine would have to conquer a nation and slaughter thousands. Coca-Cola achieves its astounding wealth by selling fizzy sugar water, and while astronauts sip Coke in outer space, Emory funds research into the molecular design of viruses.

Dr. Hatcher told Wayne Rollins that with over five hundred doctors and three thousand beds in two separate hospitals, Emory compared with the best. But it lacked research facilities. "We needed labs. And we had no space for them."

Wayne began his contribution to medicine at Emory with a $10 million gift. The building bore the Rollins name, though the total cost for a complete facility would come to $40 million and Hatcher knew that naming a building after a lead donor "immediately knocks out a lot of other big donors." He says he had a feeling "there might be more."

Wayne went on to fund the "Grace Crum Rollins Building of Public Health" on the Emory campus. His friendship with Dr. James Laney at the Candler School of Theology in Atlanta led to a grant of over $1.5 million for a new chapel. Wayne developed and funded practical fieldwork to increase the effectiveness of student ministers. He underwrote a new planetarium at Young-Harris College, awarded over a $1.5 million to Cumberland College in Kentucky (to build a 3,000 seat convention center), and flew President Jimmy Carter out as guest speaker. Besides granting some millions to help Carter set up the Atlanta Project (designed to help teens at risk and to alleviate social decay in Atlanta's ghetto), he helped refurbish Martin Luther King Sr.'s Ebenezer Baptist Church. His $100,000 grant to Berry College was spent over ten years to build new fences, fertilize pastures, and establish a Beef Research Center. In response, Wayne's beneficiaries have showered him with awards that included, among others, a Doctor of Laws degree from Emory.

Wayne seems to have faced his own death without much comment. His son, Randall, says their conversations were never of a very personal nature. Neither man came from a time or place where people went on about their feelings. Emotions were better kept to oneself. Wayne's heart was regulated by a pacemaker during his last years. He had it replaced when he was seventy-nine and died after the operation in October of 1992. Buried at Arlington in Atlanta, he lies near his granddaughter Rita's grave and not too many miles from the hills where he was born. According to John, Wayne's many millions will eventually create foundations that support science, medicine, and religion.

Perhaps the most dramatic among John's philanthropic works was saving the Beebe Hospital in Lewes from collapse. The hospital was founded in 1916 by the Doctors Beebe, two brothers who performed their first operations on a kitchen table. Over the years the hospital tacked on additions to the original, columned house, until the facility resembled a military barracks attached to a set from *Gone with the Wind.*

When Norman Baylis and Gene Bookhammer, members of the Beebe Hospital board, came to John in the seventies asking for a million dollars to save the hospital, John came through with a gift that made it possible for the institution to complete a five-story wing and raise money for a new clinical building. The Rollins addition includes a wraparound portico with tall windows that lends some semblance of architectural unity to the entrance.

Perhaps John's most useful (and controversial) gift to the hospital was his wife, Michele. "I became chairman of the foundation thinking we were going to raise three million dollars for the oncology center," Michele says. "But the hospital decided to do a master plan for what we really needed. . . . Their plan ended up as a twenty-three million dollar development that added in-patient and out-patient surgical facilities, laboratories, and the new clinical building."

When Michele Rollins first joined the board, the board's lawyer addressed her as "little lady" until she reminded him that she, too, was a lawyer. At the time, the hospital was embroiled in a lawsuit with a building contractor. Board members had backed themselves into a legal hassle over the construction of a parking garage that threatened to shut down the entire institution. The board was at cross purposes on how to deal with the contractor who was apparently incompetent, and they grumbled about her insistence that the hospital cut its losses and get rid of the contractor. An official who begs anonymity says gruffly, "Michele has more balls than the whole damned lot of them."

Through the Rollins, Beebe now has an affiliation with Emory. John had suggested medical suites at Emory that made it possible for spouses to stay with the patient during critical recovery periods, and he's made the money available to construct them. They were dedicated May 21, 1996. He now proposed the same for Beebe, as well as a conference center and a preventative care system that made possible physical examinations at almost no cost. He asked the doctors to donate a day each month to this end and suggested a communications satellite system to link Beebe to Emory. The system made possible instant consultations, examinations, and the passing along of expertise. Dr. Bhaskar Palekar, chairman of the board while these changes were occurring, says there's no doubt the Rollins family not only rescued Beebe Hospital from collapse but put it on a new path as well.

30
Old Man of the Sea

Herman Melville, in his mysterious novel *The Confidence Man,* invents a protagonist who may be almost anyone. He appears among the crowd on a riverboat moving down the Mississippi, and while his guises are many, his intentions are never clear. Melville's confidence man is shadowy and mutable, his identity a mask for getting on in a world where the only homegrown tradition that sticks is financial gain. Americans, as the enormous sales of self-help books indicates, often experience difficulty in deciding what they want and who they are. In a society so mutable, how can we put down roots when the houses, the neighborhoods, the entire landscapes of our childhood are continually bulldozed away?

All through the thirty-thousand days of his life, John's ceaseless activity merged with and added to the cataract of change that rushes through our century—a period marked by creation and destruction that beggars the imagination. America has produced a new ethos that turns the entrepreneur into a power figure, a creative source. He has few doubts about his role. He must continually adapt himself to change. His identity emerges from being whatever he must be to prosper.

John began to make himself over from an early age, working to adapt himself to our Alice in Wonderland world where mutability rules. Unlike the English lord or Parisian shopkeeper, he would exist with ceaseless change. The question "Who is John Rollins?" is as old as John's career. As "Uncle John, the working man's friend," flogging the cars on his first lot, he took on the persona of a local character, a "good old boy." He exhibited a gift for easy repartee that obscured his keen intelligence to the less perceptive. Proud of his humble past, he was the least solitary of men. His work kept him in constant communication with others. He wasted little time on passing judgment, or holding grudges. His glance was sharp, but not hard. His ability to work inhuman hours and take terrible chances frightened some, including his first partner.

Powerful family ties, especially to his mother and grandfather John Franklin, established his roots. The value-free contemporary world where he soon established himself could hardly have been more different from the hills where he was raised. Whatever the first impression he made, the rate at which his business grew was undeniably extraordinary. Every time his contemporaries glanced his way, his holdings had somehow doubled in size. John's I-can-do-anything style perplexed a state that had gone to sleep like a village in a fairy tale. He had arrived not to learn his place in Delaware, but to do business.

Over the generations, the state has produced few hardscrabble entrepreneurs like John. Delaware's leaders were more comfortable inviting well-upholstered, safe, and predictable corporations to set up offices around Wilmington. A force like John caught them off guard. The question popped up repeatedly: who does this guy think he is?

He was everywhere, running for political office, offering plans for the city, threatening to take over the airwaves, fiddling with the infrastructure. He was fatally drawn to good works, and to modernization in all its forms. Call it progress or money-making, a powerful force that combined consumer demand with technology appeared inevitable. It has introduced a new god, or perhaps a new demon, into the world. John's response was not to run from the thing but seize it directly by the throat.

In doing so, John appears like the Old Man of the Sea, a protean figure who takes on whatever form he needs to survive in his struggle with the demon of change. Each of the roles he's assumed over his lifetime demanded a new set of skills—farm boy, ditch digger, milkman, athlete, shop foreman, radio personality, ordnance inspector, super salesman, gambler, politician, fund raiser for presidents, tireless litigator, ecologist, architect, developer, entrepreneur, philanthropist. The one part he has not played is victim. His mother nipped all signs of self-pity in the bud.

Most surprising, most instructive, has been John's ability to take jobs most people would have found stultifying and depressing and make them over into a challenge for himself. He was able to infuse the dullest work with new energy, with some personal meaning. He learned early that drudgery is an anchor that can be cut loose to free the imagination. He turned even the worst jobs into lessons, or a challenge for himself. There is in this lifetime of unremitting effort an element of the Zen master's philosophy, the ability to find in the simplest thing a universal energy awaiting release.

Mankind has always dreamed of flying carpets, spirits that appear at the rub of a lamp, slaves that come and go at the speed of light. John has turned the drudgery of his early years into the fantasy of his old age. It doesn't take much imagination to see him at century's end as a latter-day Kubla Khan, erecting pleasure domes on a tropical island and raising temples to our materialism in his vast mall, the Brandywine Town Center. His most successful companies—the hazardous waste disposal facilities, the reconstituted Dover track, the mall, the Ritz-Carlton in Jamaica with a golf course designed to attract the attention of the world to that island—are practical. But an element of the fantastic figures in their conception. Dorothy's Emerald City of Oz with its translucent green towers looms wherever skyscrapers of reflecting glass shoot into the sky.

John believes that a man's fate springs from his will. "Anyone could have done what I've done if they worked as hard as I did," he says. The question lingers—what drives John to such fantastic lengths? Money is the obvious answer, not miser's gold but money transformed into a historical force by the entrepreneur. In an era when commerce achieved its greatest victories and swept every other institution into its camp, John's will merges with the will of his time.

Perhaps only when this age has passed will people allow themselves to see the fantastic figure of the entrepreneur for what he was. John has sailed on the greatest tide of commerce in world history. This doesn't infer that the tide was easy to catch. He's seized his chances in some very rough surf, gambling on a scale that would terrify most men. Yet when people close to him are asked who he really is, they don't say, "He's a gambler." Joe Seymour, his chauffeur for over forty years, says, "What makes him different? His determination. He'll tell you he's pissed away more fortunes than the average man will ever make. And it's true. He'd take a chance in a minute. Sometimes good, sometimes bad." Seymour remembers that many years ago he waited two hours for John who was trying to borrow money from a local bank. When he finally emerged, he dusted off his hands energetically, and laughed, "No looking back, sir! No, sir! No looking back!"

John rode the crest of the wave he helped create into his eighties. Dover Downs Entertainment, the enterprise that exasperated him for decades, is flourishing. The company has bought up NASCAR tracks in Nashville, Memphis, St. Louis, Long Beach's Grand Prix. "NASCAR is the fastest growing televised sport in the United States," John says. "In a decade it will have more viewers than football, baseball, or any other type of athletic competition. NASCAR is advertising now in thirty-eight of the fifty top-rated television markets in the country, and we have plans to be in all of them. You can understand why I'm looking to the future."

The writer, Norman Macrae, has said, "For [the United States], after all, is the society in which the last important stage of man's long economic revolution is succeeding." He lists our most vital institutions, in order of importance, as "the mechanisms of living together" (culture, beliefs, manners), the government, and the business corporations. Exactly how business and government improve, or corrupt, these human "mechanisms" has been studied for years by economists, humanists, political scientists. Having gained control of the arts (and turned them into "intellectual properties"), business has moved directly into the heart and mind of society. It stands in danger of corrupting the sources of its own power. Commerce has seized control of the arts and, by vulgarizing them for mass consumption, has given the young a sort of mental pablum that stunts the intelligence and breeds illiteracy and passivity. Suddenly, the corporation finds it necessary to teach its workers basic skills—writing, math, even reading. The "mechanisms of living together" are being threatened by the enormous success of commerce itself. The institutions that produce educators, artists, and informed citizens are in danger of being submerged in a rising tide of money.

Social questions of this kind are much on John's mind. In a society increasingly decentered, he worries about the future, about education, inner-city decay, the whole range of social ills that afflict contemporary life. For over fifty years, he's made a practice of granting money for projects that shore up the "mechanisms of living together." He's tried to focus some economic power where he believes it may do the most good.

But questions of culture can't be solved with business solutions. Michele Rollins, who sits on half a dozen school boards, objects vehemently to "bottom line" thinking in education. The "bottom line" on graduation day should be students intellectually armed to meet a complex and mysterious world. John, too, is irritated by schools that lack serious arts programs. In fact, the Rollinses moved their own children from a school where they believed the importance of the arts was not understood to one where they were. They gave grants to both schools to strengthen the arts programs.

While John's older children were attracted to business, the youngest are working in the arts. Speaking of his long career in business, John's firstborn, John Rollins Jr., describes his sense of accomplishment this way. "I'm not an artist. I can't paint a picture. I can't invent anything. But I can really make a difference with these companies. The opportunity that I have during my life to create something that I can see makes a contribution to society before I die—that's the most rewarding thing. From the year I began working [in business] to the time I finish, I'll be able to see what I've done."

John's youngest son, Marc, is considering architecture as a profession. Michael, a year ahead of Marc in high school, is drawn to painting. Their older sister, Monique, already majors in Fine Arts at Syracuse University. Michael says his father has not pressured him to go into something more practical. Monique quotes her father saying, "It makes me happy that you can do this. The work I've done means something if I know my kids can be painters and musicians." John remains convinced that success is only possible to the child who follows a natural bent.

While John Sr. was putting together his corporate empire, his reputation in Delaware was a long litany of rumor, innuendo and wild charges. His legal battles appeared under bold headlines; his philanthropy was generally confined to squibs on back pages. The fact that a farm boy from Georgia with only a high school education could achieve so much more than men steeped in privilege may be difficult for some to accept.

Over the years, John has received a number of awards that recognize his philanthropic work. Most of them have come from outside his home state: the American Academy of Achievement's Gold Plate Award (1970), the American Management Association's Executive of Year Award (1980), the Commander of the Cross (Knights of Malta, 1966). More recently, the colleges where his grants to scholars are substantial have awarded him honorary degrees—Goldey Beacom College (Doctor of Business, 1990), Cumberland College in Kentucky (Doctor of Laws, 1991). In his eighty-second year (1998), however, Delaware came through. John received the Wilmington Chamber of Commerce Josiah Marvel Award, the most prestigious commendation for business and social achievement in his home state. Previous winners feature a host of individuals tied to the du Pont power nexus—I. B. Finkelstein, Pierre S. du Pont IV, Edmund N. Carpenter II, and Irving Shapiro. The Delaware establishment's long-standing question about the identity of John Rollins was settled. They were saying, "He's one of us." And a few months later he and his wife received Delaware's Philanthropist of the Year award.

John, who may be described as a very old-fashioned American grafted onto a very up-to-date American, has been a local legend for a generation at least. In his own home, John is a father with foibles, spoken of with affection by his children. His eldest son calls him a "teddy bear." His youngest daughter calls him "a cutie pie." Nineteen-year-old Monique says he gets "sulky" when he feels "his girls are ignoring him." She takes pleasure in his teasing, in "that devilish little smile of his." Daughter Cathy says, "The thing is, he can read right into anybody. I've inherited that from him—part of the reason I'm a good supervisor." Jeffrey, Linda's son, says, "Whenever I've asked him for advice and didn't follow it, I've had to realize that I should have."

John Jr., who has worked closely with his father most of his life, says,

> When I was a kid he used to tell me, "If you need me, talk to me. If you have a problem, if you get in trouble, whether it's wrecking a car, whatever it might be, as long as I hear it from you first and not somebody else, you'll have no problem. If I hear it from somebody else first, you will have a big problem."
>
> I've tested him on several occasions. And he'd say, "Okay." Never a word of reprimand. Not even a critical word. He knows people. Certain things you do in your life, certain things you don't. Never lie. Never.
>
> I've never heard him say to another person, "You're stupid," or "that's dumb!" He has too much respect for the basic value of the human being. He knows how you can destroy people and ruin their self confidence with just a few words.

Tocqueville's classic description of the energetic and enigmatic American of 1830 will serve pretty well as a final glossy snapshot of John Rollins: "His reverses teach him that none has discovered absolute good; his success stimulates him to the never ending pursuit of it. Thus, forever seeking, forever falling to rise again, often disappointed, but not discouraged, he tends unceasingly towards that unmeasured greatness so indistinctly visible at the end of the long track which humanity has yet to tread."

Near Ringgold, in the Smith Chapel graveyard, the tombstones stand in uneven rows. They contain the names of people he loved, now long dead, but still alive in his mind's eye. Grandfather John F. Rollins with his shock of white hair, Emma with water buckets lined up on a shelf in front of her hilltop house, Claudia and the sick husband she nursed for over ten years. They all lie within sight of their church, side by side. Wayne is interred in Atlanta's Arlington Cemetery next to Rita, his granddaughter.

Claudia and Henry's tiny house stands where it stood at the outset of the twentieth century, guarded by an electrified wire that Wayne installed to keep the cattle from pushing through the picket fence. Grace went there not long ago with a visitor who was curious to see the Rollins place of origin. The April day was bright—springtime in Georgia. The cottage hardly resembles the weatherworn shack it was in the depths of the Depression. Then its siding was rough slatboard, fading to nubby gray. Today the tiny house is painted white. Grace drove all the way up from Atlanta, but forgot to provide herself with a key. She was obliged to circle outside the house and peer through the windows of the rooms where she'd lived when she first married Wayne.

Bent with age, hard work and a degree of self-denial unimaginable to a later generation, she stared into the tiny space where she and Wayne had first slept together. The rooms were unfurnished, bare in the morning sunshine. The floors gleamed in the pure blue light. Invisible hands had kept the interior spotless, the windows clean. Wayne was dead three years now, but he'd preserved everything—from the tiny outbuilding with its rough rafters where the pork was smoked to the porch looking out across the green valley.

Grace, peering through the clear windows, was herself encircled by the past, by the images of children grown and grandchildren and great grandchildren born to live in a distant future. Past time and future time were wound about her, as close as the dim interior of the house with its spectral figures—the two small boys pressing against their mother, the sick father raising himself up in bed to listen as Claudia lights the kerosene lamp and sits down in the pale glow, opening the Bible across her knees to read.

Index